Gunz:

Dear sweet man,

I hope you enjoy the little labor of love that I undertook in my more naive days. I still love Kant though. Almost as much as I love you.

♡/ -H.

Global Justice, Kant and the Responsibility to Protect

This book provides an innovative contribution to the study of the Responsibility to Protect and Kantian political theory.

The Responsibility to Protect (R2P) doctrine has been heralded as the new international security norm to ensure the protection of peoples against genocide, ethnic cleansing, war crimes and crimes against humanity. Yet, for all of the discussion, endorsements and reaffirmations of this new norm, R2P continues to come under fire for its failures, particularly, and most recently, in the case of Syria.

This book argues that a duty to protect is best considered a Kantian provisional duty of justice. The international system ought to be considered a state of nature, where legal institutions are either weak or absent, and so duties of justice in such a condition cannot be considered peremptory. This book suggests that by understanding the duty's provisional status, we understand the necessity of creating the requisite executive, legislative and judicial authorities. Furthermore, the book provides three innovative contributions to the literature, study and practice of R2P and Kantian political theory: it provides detailed theoretical analysis of R2P; it addresses the research gap that exists with Kant's account of justice in states of nature; and it presents a more comprehensive understanding of the metaphysics of justice as well as R2P.

This book will be of much interest to students of the Responsibility to Protect, humanitarian intervention, global ethics, international law, security studies and international relations (IR) in general.

Heather M. Roff is Visiting Associate Professor at Josef Korbel School of International Studies at the University of Denver. She is also a Research Associate at the Eisenhower Center for Space and Strategic Studies with the US Air Force Academy.

Global Politics and the Responsibility to Protect

Series Editors:

Alex J. Bellamy
Griffith University

Sara E. Davies
Griffith University

Monica Serrano
The City University of New York

The aim of this book series is to gather the best new thinking about the Responsibility to Protect into a core set of volumes that provides a definitive account of the principle, its implementation, and its role in crises, that reflects a plurality of views and regional perspectives.

Global Politics and the Responsibility to Protect
From words to deeds
Alex J. Bellamy

The Responsibility to Protect
Norms, laws and international politics
Ramesh Thakur

Humanitarian Intervention and the Responsibility to Protect
Security and human rights
Cristina G. Badescu

Sri Lanka and the Responsibility to Protect
Politics, ethnicity, genocide
Damien Kingsbury

International Responsibility and Grave Humanitarian Crises
Collective provision for human security
Hannes Peltonen

Global Justice, Kant and the Responsibility to Protect
A provisional duty
Heather M. Roff

Global Justice, Kant and the Responsibility to Protect

A provisional duty

Heather M. Roff

Routledge
Taylor & Francis Group
LONDON AND NEW YORK

First published 2013
by Routledge
2 Park Square, Milton Park, Abingdon, Oxon OX14 4RN

Simultaneously published in the USA and Canada
by Routledge
711 Third Avenue, New York, NY 10017

Routledge is an imprint of the Taylor & Francis Group, an informa business

British Library Cataloguing in Publication Data
A catalogue record for this book is available from the British Library

Library of Congress Cataloging-in-Publication Data
Roff, Heather, 1980-
Global justice, Kant and the responsibility to protect : a provisional duty / Heather Roff.
pages cm. – (Global politics and the responsibility to protect)
Includes bibliographical references and index.
1. Kant, Immanuel, 1724–1804–Political and social views.
2. Responsibility to protect (International law) 3. Justice. I. Title.
JC181.R56 2013
320.01'1–dc23 2013002614

ISBN: 978-0-415-66081-5 (hbk)
ISBN: 978-0-203-07383-4 (ebk)

Typeset in Times
by Wearset Ltd, Boldon, Tyne and Wear

FSC www.fsc.org MIX Paper from responsible sources FSC® C013056

Printed and bound in Great Britain by
TJ International Ltd, Padstow, Cornwall

Contents

Foreword

Problems and possibilities in institutionalizing the Responsibility to Protect

Students and scholars of humanitarian intervention and the Responsibility to Protect (R2P) have had much to write about during recent decades. While many developments have been promising and suggest that there is hope that mass atrocities can be prevented, such atrocities have continued to occur with alarming regularity, many times with little or no response from the international community.

Like many writers on the subject, my own interest in humanitarian intervention was born out of a strong desire to see the international community take more decisive action to protect innocent people from mass atrocities. My work on the subject thus sought to reconcile the ethical and legal aspects of humanitarian intervention with the much more challenging and frustrating "political" or practical dimension. In short, there seems to be a modest consensus among scholars and analysts on when humanitarian intervention is thought to be morally and legally permissible. Yet there is very little consensus on how to go about convincing powerful actors to intervene in those cases where civilians are in urgent need of protection, yet abstain from doing so in those cases where such intervention would seemingly do more harm than good.

It is in this "political" dimension where the R2P doctrine holds much promise, yet its institutionalization at the 2005 United Nations World Summit sent profoundly mixed messages. On one hand, as originally envisaged in 2001, R2P seeks to institutionalize certain duties—or a "responsibility"—to protect innocent people from mass atrocities. Yet UN member states interpreted this in 2005 as more of an option, or something discretionary, as opposed to a bona fide duty or responsibility. As a result, a vast majority of the extant literature on R2P falls into one of two camps: One suggesting that R2P is a revolutionary new norm of international society that has become internalized by states; and another that sees R2P as simply political rhetoric that permits the continued inconsistent and erratic practice of intervention at the discretion of the world's most powerful states.

Heather Roff's important book, however, moves beyond this impasse, leveraging the tools of International Ethics to understand R2P as a moral and legal duty and theorizing the juridical institutions that are necessary to provide the practical implementation of this duty. Not content with the current state of affairs as they pertain to R2P, and motivated by a desire to make practical, workable prescriptions, Roff's book is one of the few recent treatments of the subject that promises to truly break new ground—something exceedingly difficult to do given the staggering amount of scholarship on R2P and humanitarian intervention published during the past decade.

Utilizing International Ethics to make practical prescriptions is certainly a challenge, yet Roff has succeeded in this by building from the moral and legal philosophy of Immanuel Kant. Anyone even vaguely familiar with the field of International Ethics will recognize the centrality of the work of Kant; and it is truly surprising that, until this book, there have been few, if any, comprehensive Kantian treatments of the vexing ethical and practical issues surrounding R2P and humanitarian intervention. Indeed, a Kantian analysis has much to offer in the broader debate over R2P, given Kant's sophisticated account of the duties of justice and what these duties morally require of capable agents. A fresh analysis of R2P that explicitly draws from Kant is thus long overdue in the literature on R2P and humanitarian intervention. And as one of the most well-read emerging scholars of Kantian ethics, few people are more qualified to write such a book than Professor Roff.

Unfortunately today, "implementing" R2P as a moral and legal duty of states to prevent, react and rebuild has simply meant that they more or less undertake such actions at their discretion. Yet as Roff points out in this book, a Kantian approach sees such a status quo as highly problematic and ultimately untenable. That Kant provides the tools to perceive this, as well as offers suggestions on how to potentially remedy it, renders the Kantian approach all the more urgent and appropriate. Thus, the fact that my own thinking about humanitarian intervention has been influenced mostly by consequentialist considerations, and that I remain highly skeptical of deontological approaches, is a testament to the strength of Roff's execution of this book. In short, the arguments in the pages that follow will be found useful and compelling by *all* scholars and students of R2P and humanitarian intervention, and anyone who seeks to reconcile the ethical and the practical.

Eric A. Heinze
Associate Professor of Political Science and International Studies
University of Oklahoma
Author of Waging Humanitarian War: The Ethics, Law and Politics of Humanitarian Intervention
Norman, Oklahoma
February 9, 2013

Acknowledgments

While writing this project, I had the great fortune to travel to Friedrich-Alexander Universität Nürnberg to work under the direction of B. Sharon Byrd and Joachim Hruschka. Over many afternoons of discussion, cake and coffee, we agreed that Kant's theory of politics is much more nuanced and complex than most current Kant scholars want to admit. We disagreed on several issues, as will become apparent throughout this book, but our primary source of consensus was: The need for supranational juridical institutions is a requirement of Kant's theory of justice, and coercing states into such an institution is not merely permitted, it is necessary. Such agreement is not often found in those studying Kant.

In the course of this project, I have sought the expertise of many Kant scholars, international ethicists, friends and family. Thus a number of people should be mentioned for their patience, efforts and insight. I owe a very large debt to Jason Robles, without whom I would still be banging my head against a wall over Kant's permissive law. Moreover, his keen editorial eye and criticisms have helped me with substantial portions of this project. I owe him a great debt. In addition, I thank Terry Nardin for his gentle coercion to push me to be a better theorist and writer, the "amazingly amazing" Robert Hanna, without whom I would have been quite adrift among many Kantians, Elisabeth Ellis, Aubrey Westfall, Ajume Wingo, Katrin Flikschuh, Gary Banham, Tim Waligore and Garrett Wallace Brown. Of course, I also thank two anonymous readers for Routledge Press who provided helpful suggestions and gentle criticisms.

There are also some individuals who deserve special recognition. Much appreciation also goes to David R. Mapel, who has provided me with years of mentorship and wisdom. His guidance, academic and non-, has made all the difference. It has been a privilege to work with and learn from such an intelligent, creative, caring and (constructively) critical sage. Moreover, I owe much to B. Sharon Byrd and Joachim Hruschka, who opened their home and hearts to me. I especially thank them for their warm hospitality, keen insights, comments and assistance. Their ability to provide criticism in a constructive and supportive manner has been invaluable. I am truly privileged to have these two mentors. I am also greatly indebted to my husband, Chris Perkins. He not only provided moral and emotional support for me, but his careful editorial eye also caught many a (humorous) typo. I would also like to express my gratitude to my parents, especially my mother. She is the voice in my head, the ember of my heart. Finally, this book is ultimately for my daughter, Jane. May she grow up in a world that is constantly progressing towards moral enlightenment and respect for human rights.

Several of the chapters are reproduced elsewhere. Chapter 1, "Kantian Provisional Duties" appears in the *Annual Review for Law and Ethics*, Vol. 18 (2010). Additionally, a shorter version of Chapter 2, "A Provisional Duty of Humanitarian Intervention" also appears in *Global Responsibility to Protect*, Vol 3 (2011). Some ideas from Chapter 2 also appear in "Response to Pattison: Whose Responsibility to Protect" in the *Journal of Military Ethics*, Vol. 8 (2009).

Abbreviations

LoE	*Lectures on Ethics* (1762–1793)
CrP	*The Critique of Pure Reason* (1781)
UH	"Idea for a Universal History with a Cosmopolitan Intent" (1784)
WE	"An Answer to the Question: What is Enlightenment" (1784)
G	*The Grounding for the Metaphysics of Morals* (1785)
CPrR	*The Critique of Practical Reason* (1788)
R	*Religion within the Bounds of Mere Reason* (1793)
TP	"On the Proverb: That May Be True in Theory, But is of No Practical Use" (1793)
TPP	"Towards Perpetual Peace: A Philosophical Sketch" (1795)
DR	*The Doctrine of Right* (1797)
DV	*The Doctrine of Virtue* (1797)
MM	*The Metaphysics of Morals* (1797)
VMdS	"Vorarbeiten zu die Metaphysik der Sitten" ("Preliminary Work of The Metaphysics of Morals") (1797)
CF	*Conflict of the Faculties* (1798)
OQ	"An Old Question Raised Again: Is the Human Race Constantly Progressing?" (1798)
OE	*On Education* (1803)

dSME	Domestic supreme moral emergency
HI	Humanitarian intervention
iSME	International supreme moral emergency
R2P	Responsibility to protect
R2PI	Responsibility to protect institution
SME	Supreme moral emergency
UPR	Universal principle of right

Introduction

Kant, global justice and Responsibility to Protect

> In matters of truth and justice, there is no difference between large and small problems, for issues concerning the treatment of people are all the same.
>
> Albert Einstein

This book attempts to delineate the theoretical underpinnings and juridical requirements of a duty to protect, grounded in the legal and moral philosophy of Immanuel Kant. In practical terms, it endeavors to provide broad answers to the questions of what a duty to protect entails; what its features are; how assignment takes place; when we know it is fulfilled; and, most importantly, what we can do when an agent fails to perform its duty to protect. These two functions are inherently related, as we cannot answer these questions without first framing them within a theory of justice. The Responsibility to Protect (R2P) must first and foremost be understood as a moral and legal duty, and once we grant it this status we can begin the processes of building the requisite juridical institutions to provide the particulars the duty.

The Responsibility to Protect is not, and never will be, a duty of virtue. That many view R2P this way is due to a misunderstanding of the universal nature and requirements of justice. We live in a world populated with self-interested individuals, who form—either by consent or coercion—self-interested states. These states, for the most part, view their duties as one-way: to their own people. Saving strangers is not a foreign policy priority, and if a state decides to undertake such an action, it is typically with mixed motives of prudence and benevolence, but more often than not it is due to purely prudential reasons.

Yet if we grant that justice is universal, and many of the international treaties and norms regarding the protection of human rights espouse this position, then the state system with its unidirectional focus is incomplete and will only perpetuate problems of justice. Kant's political theory foresaw this problem, and this is why he viewed its solution as encompassing three interrelated levels of juridical interaction: the individual, the state and the cosmopolitan. Without creating the necessary authorities within and between each level, then justice can remain only provisional.

What a provisional duty of R2P means for us in the here and now is that assigning a duty to prevent, react or rebuild will mean nothing more than states or coalitions of states voluntarily undertaking such actions. Even if the United Nations Security Council (SC) charges a particular state or regional security organization, such as the North Atlantic Treaty Organization (NATO), to carry out an R2P mandate, there is no recourse should that state or organization refuse or fail to do so. Compliance is purely voluntary. It could also mean the possibility of states self-assigning their duty to protect without SC authorization. Those capable have a duty to protect, and there is little to dissuade any possible duty bearer from acting without such authorization. For Kant, this situation is untenable. It is untenable because it perpetuates the problems of "who shall judge"; it perpetuates a state of nature.

What is more, a provisional duty of R2P means that the scope of the duty is left to the private judgment of the state fulfilling it. Plainly, it means that questions about rules of engagement and operational mandates are not answered by any international public legislative authority, for no such authority exists to demarcate and lay down these rules. Since the scope of a duty of R2P is open, it is incredibly difficult to ascertain when or whether the duty is fulfilled. Traditionally, wide duties are so because the agent must use her practical reason to set the limits of a duty, and once she has done so, she also takes the necessary steps to fulfill it. It is this procedure of settings ends and matching means to ends that ultimately cultivates virtue and practical reason. However, for duties of justice, we are not concerned with an agent's virtuous disposition and character; we are concerned with actions. We see, therefore, the tension that erupts when we grant that a duty is one of justice but the actions to fulfill it are not specified *in advance* by a public legislative authority. Being a judge in one's own cause in this situation threatens not only the establishment of a universal system of justice, but determining whether justice has been achieved in any particular case.

Public justice requires "a system of laws for a people, that is, a multitude of human beings, *or for a multitude of peoples*, which, because they affect one another, need a rightful condition under a will uniting them" so that these people or peoples can enjoy their rights.[1] Such a system requires all the three authorities of legislative, executive and judicial, backed by a public coercive mechanism to ensure compliance. Until that time, right is merely provisional: justice is in a sense meted out happenstance.

Present challenges to the Responsibility to Protect

With recent events in Libya (2011) and Syria (2011 to the present), the Responsibility to Protect doctrine has come under intense scrutiny. Indeed, at the beginning of the Arab Spring, many lauded R2P as the new normative and political framework of the twenty-first century. Then again, six months later, that tune began to change. Cracks in the R2P doctrine started to emerge—particularly when the world stood by to watch Syria's President, Bashar al-Assad, bombing civilian centers in Homs, Idlib, Damascus, and other northern towns. The doctrine's vulnerabilities became clearer when Western powers refused to discuss military intervention in Syria, and Russia and China exercised their vetoes in a 2012 United Nations Security Council draft resolution to condemn the Assad regime. As I write, there is still no certainty as to what will happen to the Syrian regime or to its people.

Much of the discussion and criticism about R2P is not, however, new. The practice of military humanitarian intervention over the past forty-odd years received many of the same accusations: case selectivity, a ruse for power politics, or a disguise for imperialism. In this sense, R2P is no different. Since the beginning of the Arab Spring to the present, R2P has also been charged with selectivity and a guise for regime change and the machinations of the West. These charges are not unfair; they are a factual assessment of the practice of states. What is unfair, however, is to claim that these practices can never be changed and they are brute facts about international politics. Moreover, we must also make the careful distinction that R2P is broader than the mere practice of humanitarian intervention. It encompasses not only the possibility of coercive military response, but also the categories of prevention and post-conflict rebuilding. Therefore, capacity building and development are also crucial aspects of this new doctrine.

While prevention and rebuilding are very important elements of R2P, the primary concern of this work will tend to focus on the second element of R2P: reaction. The "Third Pillar" of R2P is essentially the most contentious bone of the bunch, and when prevention fails, as we see happening more often than not, the international community's responsibility to protect is triggered. It is at this juncture that many seek answers to what that responsibility looks like. I contend that all of the current questions about R2P, and in particular the coercive side of military intervention (who ought to intervene, when, to what extent and when they should leave), are associated with the doctrine's status as a duty of justice in what amounts to a "state of nature."

The current practice of states ought to be expected because the international system lacks the requisite executive, judicial and legislative authorities to properly call it a *civil* society. A civil society is one where the rule of law and juridical institutions regulate and thwart actors' criminal behavior. Without such a civil condition, agents find themselves in a situation that is a "society compatible with rights" but not a rightful society, in Kant's terms.[2] In other words, the present international society does not enable a condition "under which alone everyone is able to enjoy his rights," where such enjoyment consists in the equal recognition and protection of such rights and freedoms.[3] I argue that if we are to solve some of the problems facing R2P, we must first understand the nature and requirements of justice in international society. This in turn requires us to understand whether, in a state of nature, there are duties of justice (such as a duty to militarily intervene under the umbrella of R2P), and if so, how we might categorize and assign them to delineate what is required for their fulfillment. Our first task, then, in determining what ought to be done is to understand the scope and limits of international justice. Only when we have cleared the conceptual underbrush can we begin to make normative and practical prescriptions about fulfilling our Responsibility to Protect.

As Kant reminds us:

> [T]he canon of reason is related to practice in such a way that the value of the practice depends entirely upon its appropriateness to the theory it is based on; all is lost if the empirical (hence contingent) conditions governing the execution of the law are made into conditions of the law itself, so that a practice calculated to produce a result which previous experience makes probable is given the right to dominate a theory which is in fact self-sufficient.[4]

Thus the academic, "who works for them all, for their own good, on matters of theory," is not "a pedant" whose work is of little practical value.[5] We must first have a theoretical understanding of justice and then apply it to the case.

My strategy throughout is to balance theoretical and practical considerations. On the one hand, I begin from Kant's theory of justice and examine its fundamental underpinnings. On the other hand, I apply this theory (or at times an updated version of it) to the case of R2P. Kant's theory of justice is universal in form, and that means that it requires what Garrett Wallace Brown terms "a tripartite system of jurisprudence."[6] In other words, because justice is ultimately concerned with regulating the external actions of moral agents, a system of jurisprudence that regulates actions between individuals, between states, and between states and peoples, is required. Justice demands systems of domestic, international and cosmopolitan law. Without each of these systems in place, individual and state rights are merely provisional.[7] Yet, up until now, no other scholar has attempted to pull apart and examine the moral requirements of agents in the interim periods, or transitional stages, of Kant's theory of justice. No scholar has as closely considered Kant's account of duties of justice in states of nature, and no other scholar has then applied such theory to a timely and important case, such as R2P.

Instead, most scholars influenced by Kant who debate about a duty of intervention argue over what kind of duty it is. They attempt to categorize it as either imperfect or perfect.[8] No one appears to realize that a duty to intervene does not fit neatly within either category; instead, the attempt to push the proverbial square peg into a round hole is simply repeated. Once familiar with this debate, it became clear to me that what is required is an examination of the very nature of duties in Kant's framework, and duties of justice in particular, before we can determine what Kant's theory implies for R2P. Questions about the categorization of a duty of protection are secondary to understanding what is required of agents when civil society is absent.

The Rubik's Cube: contemporary thinking on Kant and international politics

At this point, the reader may ask: Why Kant? I am not positing that Kant's theories are the only way to understand or to practice international justice. I admit there may be other productive ways of addressing these issues.[9] Yet Kant also provides a fruitful approach. His highly organized and analytic framework allows us to examine thoroughly the structure of his arguments about justice in a methodical way and then attempt to apply them to current problems of international justice. Of course, there is still debate about how Kant's moral and political theory should be applied to the international and cosmopolitan levels. Moreover, there is ongoing disagreement about whether state sovereignty is sacrosanct, about the legitimacy of states' territorial interventions, and about the issue of coercing states into a supranational juridical state.

Some scholars, such as Howard Williams, Fernando Tesón, Georg Cavallar, Hauke Brunkorst and Alyssa Bernstein, argue that Kant's theory of justice emphasizes the legitimacy of domestic state institutions, but that "state sovereignty is relative in the sense that it is dependent upon popular sovereignty."[10] Popular sovereignty, these scholars argue, can be separated from formal state sovereignty. They allow that when a government's expressed will and actions are opposed to the will of the people (i.e., popular sovereignty), formal sovereignty may be infringed for the sake of protecting the rights of the people.[11] Thus, these scholars argue that Kant "defends state sovereignty with his principle of nonintervention," while concurrently providing "arguments in favour of qualified humanitarian intervention in failed or despotic states."[12]

Interestingly, though, such scholars also maintain that "Kant claims that in international relations, no country is entitled to end the state of nature by means of force."[13] Coercion of states into anything resembling a world state, or even "a federation (like that of the American states) based on a constitution," is impermissible.[14] Intervention, which is by its very nature a coercive activity, is only justified when either the will of the people in the target state is not affected or the state has dissolved to a point where there is no state to coerce. Coercion is not, and indeed cannot be, justified to put an end to the international state of nature (which seems to be one of the roots of the problems associated with a duty to protect).

Another group of scholars in this debate, represented primarily by B. Sharon Byrd and Joachim Hruschka, argues that sovereignty, whether popular or formal, is not the central issue. They do not particularly address the issue of humanitarian intervention, but instead, the issue of justified coercion into what they term a state of nation states.[15] In other words, Byrd and Hruschka are concerned with the practical and theoretical requirements of Kant's complete theory of justice. They attempt to show that Kant's tripartite system of domestic, international and cosmopolitan law requires a formal institutionalized public right that regulates the behavior of all agents capable of affecting the rights of another. Until public law, arbitrated by a neutral judge, and enforced by a legitimate and authoritative coercive mechanism, can secure the rights of persons and states, they argue, justice is merely provisional. Byrd and Hruschka claim, then, that coercion of states into a state of states is legitimate. For them, the question of intervention is peripheral; though, because they endorse coercion of states into a state of nation states, they may too endorse a qualified right of intervention to push states down the juridical path.

A third group of scholars in this debate about Kant's theory of justice takes the notion of sovereignty and public international justice as maintainable, though only through the voluntary acceptance of international laws to regulate the international community. They stress Kant's assertion that the domestic state has "outgrown" the need for coercion, and so "in principle, there could be no justification whatsoever for the forcible interference by one state in the constitution and government in another state."[16] What is required is the voluntary coming together of all states into a federation of free states where they "express their will and agreement to be bound by the law that the federation was to base."[17] In effect, scholars such as Thomas Pogge and Charles Beitz, and to some extent Charles Covell, argue that "states jointly practicing self-restraint" apply to themselves "the principles [they have] co-legislated with all others."[18] To this end, states "view themselves as co-legislators" and "acknowledge their membership in the community of states."[19] The question of intervention, then, can be resolved if states agree to intervention when they fail to abide by the communally established rules.[20]

Katrin Flikschuh makes a fourth argument about the nature of Kantian international justice. She frames the problem in terms of a dilemma between the requirements for absolute sovereignty in the domestic state and the achievement of universal (and thus international and cosmopolitan) right. Instead of arguing that domestic right ought to be applied by analogy to international relations, she argues that Kant's theory of right should be viewed as "systemic," meaning domestic, international and cosmopolitan right are interdependent. Arguing by analogy produces the "sovereignty dilemma" where, on the one hand, right requires the establishment of a fully sovereign domestic state, and, on the other, this fully sovereign state is supposed to be then coerced into a fully sovereign state of states. She maintains this is conceptually incoherent. Her solution is to view Kant's theory of right as a system where "domestic rights relations are not fully just unless embedded in just relations between states," and that "international right is not complete without cosmopolitan right."[21] For her, the domestic state cannot be coerced into a state of states, and the internal affairs of a state are not open to coercive interference by other states. In other words, Flikschuh does not endorse a principle of humanitarian intervention, and she claims that only in exceptional cases would intervention be permitted (via Kant's permissive law).[22]

Each of these interpretations addresses what might be thought of as a Rubik's Cube of Kant's theory of justice, which requires us to align correctly sovereignty, coercion, rights, law, freedom and juridical institutions. When one starts with sovereignty, the problem of intervention raises its head. When one starts with freedom, the problem of coercion comes to the fore. Or, like Flikschuh, when one attempts to examine the problem from a systemic vantage point, Kant's own worry arises that justice, and the goal of perpetual peace, will prove an "empty chimera."

Looking at the possibility that there is a duty to protect allows us to see that the aforementioned elements of Kant's theory are connected. One cannot privilege right at the expense of freedom, and one cannot forsake international juridical institutions for the sake of sovereignty. The international community's (or individual state's) acknowledgment that it possesses a responsibility to protect (and to intervene when prevention fails) highlights the tensions inherent in an incomplete system of justice. Acknowledging that one has a juridical duty to do X, while simultaneously refusing to create a juridical condition to do X, undermines the very notion of having a juridical duty.

Kant vs. Kantian

One may approach Kant's work through strict exegesis or reconstruction. Ultimately, this project demands the latter, as obviously Kant did not address the question of a responsibility to protect or humanitarian intervention. I look to his writings to find exegetical support for my arguments about R2P, and in particular the "reaction" phase of R2P, but I cannot simply point to one passage and claim that Kant is an adamant interventionist, nor can I point to a passage and claim that he is a strict noninterventionist. His theory is too complex to make such easy judgments. Thus, I attempt to extend or to supplement Kant's moral framework when it does not directly address an issue or is particularly ambiguous or contradictory. Whenever possible, I try to make these arguments on the basis of careful exegesis of the texts we have, but because they are my own, they are therefore Kant*ian*. However, since I try to remain as close to Kant's texts and to the general spirit of his writing, much of the analysis is relevant for Kant scholars as well.

I am also unafraid of using Kant's *Lectures on Ethics*. This text is an amalgamation of student notes from his courses on ethics, which it is said he taught over 30 times. The lecture notes are not Kant's mature published thought, such as the *Metaphysics of Morals*, but they do offer valuable insight into his thinking about political and ethical problems. As the notes span such a large time period, we can see how they reaffirm earlier thinking and develop more fully later. Moreover, they provide us with insight into how such difficult concepts can be relayed to students—i.e., beginners. By using examples from history and clearer everyday language, we can supplement Kant's more mature and published work with that of his students' lecture notes to gain further clarity.

Many critics of reconstruction complain that political theorists take too much license with Kant's works, and that these theorists make interpretive choices that are clearly unsupported by many of Kant's theories.[23] However, scholars who choose to do narrow exegesis will find themselves unable to address many contemporary political and moral problems because Kant did not explicitly address them. It is necessary to walk a difficult line between exegesis, interpretation and reconstruction. Following Höffe, I believe "one can still make use of Kant in order to go beyond Kant,"[24] but I am of course also wary of "slapping the morally reassuring label 'Kantian'" on an argument to provide it with legitimacy.[25] One can remain true to Kant's texts and still find a place for critical evaluation and reconstruction. This project engages both Kant and Kantians, and attempts to provide a particular account of Kant's theory of justice as applied to the case of R2P. For the most part, I am engaged in exegetical reconstruction to support my prescriptions. However, when some of Kant's more specific arguments about political theory cannot be applied clearly to the current state of international affairs,[26] I attempt to provide support for my views by returning to more foundational Kantian commitments. I cannot claim that my arguments are all Kant's, but I try not to be too hermeneutically generous.

Summary of chapters

The book is organized into six chapters, each beginning with some theoretical considerations and then moving toward more practical problems. Chapter 1, "Kantian provisional duties," argues that Kant's traditional dichotomized framework of perfect and imperfect duties is not complete. Duties of justice in a state of nature ought to be considered provisional, as they are correlates of provisional right. Such duties require that institutions of justice be established; that is, provisional duties must transcend their provisional status and become perfect.

Chapter 2 applies the theoretical framework of provisional duties to the case of R2P, particularly its military intervention, or "Third Pillar" component. I argue that repeated attempts to categorize a duty of intervention as either perfect or imperfect misrepresent the nature of this duty. We must first understand the categorization as one of right (justice) not benevolence (ethics), and only then can we understand the need for the duty to be institutionalized. Institutionalization is not merely a route to the best consequences; but it is necessary because of the logic of justice.

Chapter 3 explores Kant's permissive law as apparently the most appropriate principle for authorizing the coercion of states into a formal R2P institution. Such an institution is necessary to make a provisional duty of R2P peremptory (or "perfect"). I argue that Kant's permissive law applies in what I term "Supreme Moral Emergencies," or conditions where following the dictates of reason as if one were in the ideal world would threaten to undermine the ends of reason in the nonideal world. For the sake of reason, the permissive law allows agents to do something they otherwise are prohibited from doing.

Chapter 4 then applies Kant's permissive law to the current international system. I argue that the international system is currently in a supreme moral emergency due to two factors: a majority of states consistently violating the rights of their peoples; and the lack of effective juridical institutions at the supranational level. I argue that Kant's assumption that the domestic state will adequately secure and protect the rights of its people is empirically false. Using data from the Failed State Index, I show that well over half of the worlds' states violate the rights of their peoples. Moreover, I also argue that Kant's second assumption that the greatest threat to Right will come from outside the domestic state is also false. Civil wars account for a loss of life and property five times greater than the destruction visited by interstate wars.[27] Since Kant's assumptions do not hold, I argue that the blanket prohibition on international coercion cannot be sustained. The domestic state cannot be held inviolable.

Chapter 5 proceeds with an argument for the institutionalization of R2P. I argue that the institution should promulgate public rules to govern the practice of R2P, thereby solving the problem of indeterminacy. This institution should have the ability to monitor human rights violations (in all countries) that have the potential to trigger a humanitarian crisis, and should provide a centralized information network to the United Nations (UN) and society of states. However, it must be an autonomous institution from the UN. At the international level, it ought to mirror the independent status of National Human Rights Institutions (NHRI) at a domestic level. The UN should execute the institution's rules, and, when individuals or states do not comply with those rules, a strengthened International Criminal Court or International Court of Justice should adjudicate controversies about noncompliance. Moreover, I suggest that to execute effectively the rules of the R2P institution, the UN ought to have a rapid reaction volunteer military force. I also argue that the UN ought to be the agent that coerces states into institutionalization via its Chapter VII powers. I conclude with an explanation of how reforms to the international system can satisfy Kant's requirements of protective, commutative and distributive justice, thereby rendering a provisional duty of R2P peremptory. We must have public rules governing the practice of R2P, as the requirements of justice are institutional: R2P is not just a moral problem; it is a legal one too.

Chapter 6 concludes with an examination of the R2P cases of Libya and Syria. I analyze both cases in light of my arguments about provisional protection and show how the R2P doctrine, as the UN is currently practicing it, will continue to yield unsatisfying results. States will continue to choose when to intervene selectively, and power politics and political machinations will be the order of the day. This is an effect of the juridical vacuum in the international system, and not a fact about states themselves. I argue that Kant gives us the theoretical tools to perceive this, and he also provides us with the advice on how to remedy it.

As Kant was a cautious optimist, so am I. We should remember that moral progress in international society is achievable, though not easily won. As the Professor from Königsberg reminds us, states are capable of regulating their behavior in accordance with laws of right, and it is not a "pedantically childish academic idea" to think that they cannot.[28] There will undoubtedly be many "unsuccessful" attempts at bringing states' behavior under the rule of law, but it is not an impossible task. This work is thus an attempt to provide the conceptual background for the current status of a duty to protect, and what is required to make that duty peremptory. Progress may not be immediate, but if we are to understand what we must ultimately do, then we must grant that these prescriptions are difficult to achieve. Their difficulty is not a sign of their uselessness, but a sign of what is so important about the requirements of justice. Plato's Republic is not something easily achieved, nor is Rousseau's ideal community, but that is not to say that either philosopher's prescriptions and requirements have no practicality. We can continue to evolve international practices and to reform international institutions with the ideal in sight.

1 Kantian provisional duties

Before we can assess why the Responsibility to Protect (R2P) doctrine is open to such charges as selectivity, lack of political will and a guise for power politics, we ought to ask ourselves what a *responsibility* to protect means. More specifically, what kind of duty or obligation is this responsibility? The answers to such questions will provide us with valuable theoretical and practical insight as to what can be expected, by whom, when, and what might happen if one fails to uphold these obligations.

Typically, when one speaks of a responsibility, one is discussing not a right or a permission, but an obligation or duty of some sort. Rights, in the Hofehldian sense, can be thought of as a cluster of differing ideas, such as: claims, powers, liberties or immunities.[1] For example, I can have a claim right to, say, freedom of speech. It is everyone else's duty, all things considered, to forbear from infringing upon my right to free speech. When a right as a power is concerned, we think of this as a positive right to do something, say to act as an agent for another person. This type of right confers certain "powers" on its holder, such as a capacity to change someone else's rights. Rights as liberties are seen freedoms; that is, they are not obligatory. We might say that I have a liberty-right to drive my car, but it is not obligatory that I do so. Finally, immunity rights are those rights that protect against something, say having one's rights arbitrarily transgressed or changed. When we discuss a responsibility, we are not discussing a right. We are, instead, looking to one or more of a right's jural opposites or correlatives, typically either a duty or a liability.

Whether R2P is considered a duty or a liability is open to dispute, but I would suggest that the notion of duty best suits the notion of responsibility attributed to R2P. If we thought that a leader had some sort of protection, freedom or enhanced capacity to violate her citizens' rights, then we might claim that the leader is liable for her action. However, this is not the common-sense way of thinking about R2P. Instead, when we discuss R2P, we are concerned with manifest failures of states or leaders to uphold their citizens' rights (as claim rights). It is the basic fact of the violation of particular human rights, notably genocide, ethnic cleansing, war crimes and crimes against humanity, that compels or triggers the international community's responsibility to protect.[2] Thus, since the correlative of a claim right is a duty, we should think of R2P as a duty, and not a liability.

Once we begin to think about a duty to protect, the next question becomes: What kind of duty is it? To understand the differing types of duties, let us turn to one of the most prominent thinkers to consider these categories and to formalize them: Immanuel Kant. Certainly some might object to using Kant's deontic system, citing it as "inconsistent or incomplete,"[3] but there is no overwhelming consensus that such a charge is true. For instance, Nelson Potter and Otfried Höffe find no problem with Kant's overall moral and political system, and therefore find no problems with the duties derived from it.[4]

Yet such disagreement over Kant's deontic taxonomy points to a tension in our thinking about duties, and duties of justice in particular. This tension raises questions pertaining to moral guidance in situations where we know what duty requires, and we may be physically capable of acting, but remain highly doubtful, or even certain that our actions will fail to bring about their goal. The result is that acting to fulfill our duty may end up violating a tenet of the moral law: respecting humanity in oneself and others. This is, of course, exactly the case with R2P. Do states that have a capacity *to do something*, but not a capacity to fully alleviate the suffering or stop genocidal killings, have a duty to intervene, militarily or otherwise? Do states have a duty to intervene if they know their actions will fail or make the situation worse?

At first glance, Kant's deontic framework does not seem to explicitly address these questions, and any answers it does provide lead to puzzlement. This puzzlement arises from the fact that Kant seems to place moral duties in various crosscutting categories (right or virtue), which permit or require different sorts of things. Moreover, these categories seem to yield different conclusions with respect to the kind of problem I have just described, where we can act, but where our action seems bound to fail or worse. What is required, then, is to understand the relationship between Kant's first-order distinction of justice and virtue, and then proceed through his second-order classifications of "perfect" and "imperfect." Once this is accomplished, we can see that interpreters have missed a third kind of duty in Kant's system, which I call provisional duty. Provisional duty resolves the suspected tension between right and virtue, and it helps us determine what is required in these especially problematic situations, particularly, in the case of R2P.

Kant's taxonomy of duties

Right and virtue

Kant's first-order category is a division between the concepts of *Recht* (translated in different contexts as "right," "justice" and "law"[5]) and *Tugend* (virtue). *Recht* pertains to all actions having to do with the right of another person. For Kant, only one "innate" right exists: a right to freedom.[6] *Tugend*, or virtue, on the other hand, pertains to acts having to do with moral perfection. He insists that virtue is "the strength of a human being's maxims in fulfilling his duty,[7] and such actions express a person's internal freedom."[8]

Recht and *Tugend* are different mainly in terms of lawgiving. In other words, if an action is self-imposed, then that action is for the sake of one's inner freedom. If an action is externally imposed, say through positive law, then it is for the sake of her external freedom.[9] A person is internally free, and autonomous, when she has given herself a law to follow without any influence from outside forces (i.e., inclinations, desires, fears). A person is externally free when she can go about her life, by making projects and plans, unrestrained from the unjust physical hindrances of others. This rule-governed external freedom allows agents to coordinate their actions with a high degree of certainty because there is a system of law that dictates what actions are licit and illicit, a neutral judicial institution to adjudicate rights disputes, and a system of punishment to enforce these laws. External freedom must be limited to allow for the full exercise of internal freedom, as a person's internal freedom is affected by her physical security and ability to self-legislate. In other words, *Recht* paves the way for *Tugend.*[10]

However, the distinction between *Recht* and *Tugend* cannot be wholly reduced to forms of lawgiving, and Kant employs other ways of explaining the *Recht/Tugend* distinction. A second, and related, way of understanding the difference between the two is by incentive.[11] Namely, one's motivating reason plays a deciding role in how one's action is categorized. If an agent takes her motivating reason to be the moral law, for the sake of the moral law, then her act is virtuous. If, on the other hand, an agent takes fear of punishment as her motivating reason, then her action is merely just or legal. If, however, an act is in accordance with the dictates of *Recht* and is done from the motive of duty, then it is deemed "moral."[12] Actions are judged as "moral" if an agent freely, that is autonomously, acts; however, if one acts in conformity with a moral or legal rule (say not stealing) but does so from some external cause (like the fear of being caught and punished), then it is not a "free" action (in Kant's terms it is "heteronomous"). Virtuous actions are all moral actions by definition. It is, perhaps, easier to think of right and virtue as subsets of morality, where all legal duties can be externally motivated or coerced and are the subject of juridical legislation. All ethical or virtuous duties are, by virtue of their lawgiving, "moral."

A third way to distinguish right and virtue is through the doctrine of obligatory ends. Here, Kant argues that the moral law prescribes actions such that

> one can think of the relation of end to duty in two ways: one can begin with the end and seek out the maxim of actions in conformity with duty or, on the other hand, one can begin with the maxim of actions in conformity with duty and seek out the end that is also a duty.[13]

Acting in accordance with the moral law requires, Kant thinks, that all men adopt certain ends. If one takes the concept of duty to be the primary incentive for all action, then one "will have to establish maxims with respect to ends we ought to set ourselves," and these ends are our moral perfection and the happiness of others.[14] The moral law requires that we treat "humanity in ourselves and others always as an end and never as a means," and if we truly hold this conviction, then we must seek to perfect our own humanity and to help others perfect theirs. Examples of virtuous actions are giving to charity, not being insulting, and showing courage in trying times.

Actions in accordance with *Recht*, though, do not necessarily set particular ends for an agent. *Recht* permits an agent to "set [ends] for himself and in accordance with them prescribe the maxims he is to adopt...."[15] These juridical maxims are also adopted "on empirical grounds" and are based in "self-seeking" motives.[16] Thus, I can set an end for myself, such as buying a house. I might think that buying a house will be a good investment, will enrich my life in non-material ways, or will merely provide me with suitable shelter. Once I adopt this end, set my maxims of actions and go about acquiring a house, any agent that interferes with my actions does me wrong. That is, of course, on the assumption that I am not interfering with anyone else's freedom of action while pursuing my plans for home ownership.

Finally, *Recht* and *Tugend* can be differentiated on the basis of coercion. Kant claims:

> To every duty there corresponds *a* right in the sense of an *authorization* to do something (*facultas moralis generatim*); but it is not the case that to every duty there correspond *rights* of another to coerce someone (*facultas iuridica*). Instead, such duties are called, specifically, *duties of right*.... What essentially distinguishes a duty of virtue from a duty of right is that external constraint to the latter kind of duty is morally possible, whereas the former is based on free self-constraint.[17]

This type of differentiation is linked to his discussion of lawgiving, as an external lawgiver has an authorization to employ coercion. Such coercion, though, must be seen as "reciprocal." Any act an agent performs that hinders another agent's external freedom is wrong, and any act that is opposed to this wrong is right. This is why Kant claims,

> if a certain use of freedom is itself a hindrance to freedom in accordance with universal laws (i.e., wrong), coercion that is opposed to this (as a *hindering of a hindrance to freedom*) is consistent with freedom ... it is right.[18]

But an agent's decision to adopt an end for herself cannot be coerced. One cannot force another to adopt an end or a maxim of action, as this is an exercise of someone's internal, as opposed to external, freedom. Thus *right* can coerce actions, but it cannot coerce maxims of actions (i.e., it cannot coerce virtue).

As we can see the differences between *Recht* and *Tugend* are mainly concerned with law, lawgiving, incentives for following law, and coercion. All of these distinctions are important to note because all of these meanings are bound up in the definition of *Recht*, and Kant seems to employ most, if not all, of these same meanings throughout his works. His is a specifically legal understanding, where justice and law are codependent. Virtue, though, is concerned with the realm of action that is freely chosen by an agent. Freely, here, means a rational exercise of choice, where an agent is not determined by any "pathological" determinant (inclination, desire, fear). Virtue is the realm where one, in theory, has no need of claims, titles and guarantees because an agent is always capable of acting freely if she is rational (and thus recognizes the moral law) and employs her will (*Wille*).

However, this is not to say that all people are virtuous or that virtuous action does not require empirical factors. Quite the contrary: because human beings possess rational capacity, we can *become* virtuous, but we must also accept that we are subject to and affected by the empirical world and "pathological forces." Kant's later views on virtue are more tempered than his famous, earlier, view that moral action can only be judged by a "good will" that "like a jewel, still shine[s] by its own light."[19] As David Heyd notes, "virtue is an intermediary concept between the rational motive and psychological set up of action in the world. Its inculcation is partly the outcome of moral reasoning, but partly the product of exercise, habit, education, or *Bildung*."[20] The "purely good will" of the *Grounding* is a "*holy*, or absolutely good will," something that human beings cannot actually achieve, but only approximate through its status as a regulative ideal.[21] Heyd argues that this is why Kant, in his later work, the *Metaphysics of Morals*, does not focus on the necessary presence of an absolutely good will for virtuous action.[22] In the later work,

> such constraint [the categorical imperative], therefore, does not apply to rational beings as such (there could also be *holy* ones) but rather to *human beings*, rational *natural* beings, who are unholy enough that pleasure can induce them to break the moral law, even though they recognize its authority.[23]

Human beings require character formation and education, and these things require law, society, teaching, parenting, norms and various opportunities for virtuous action. Virtue, then, requires a protected sphere of action for it to emerge and to flourish.

The relationship between right and virtue, then, is symbiotic. *Recht* supplies external protection necessary for *all* agents to exercise their rational capacities in relative freedom. It provides the formal public framework of laws that ensures agents' actions "can coexist with the freedom of everyone."[24] Virtue provides agents with opportunities to become moral beings, where "[h]uman morality in its highest stage can still be nothing more than virtue, even if it be entirely pure (quite free from the influence of any incentive other than that of duty)," because human beings are not "finite *holy* beings (who could never be tempted to violate duty)."[25] Human beings lie "between the animal and the holy: purely animal operation is not agency, and purely holy action is not human."[26] Thus to make up for our tendencies towards unholiness, or rational egoism, we must provide external guarantees for our freedom; we must provide law.

Recht and *Tugend* are both ruled by the moral law. *Recht* must follow the moral imperative in form, while *Tugend* must provide the moral imperative with content. Each are necessary for the other, for as Kant famously states, "[l]ike the wooden head in Phaedrus's fable, a merely empirical doctrine of right is a head that may be beautiful but unfortunately it has no brain."[27] Right must be ruled by morality, and virtue is morality employed in the empirical world.

Perfect and imperfect duties

Kant's second-order classification is between perfect and imperfect duties. He distinguishes these kinds of duties in an expansive and at times somewhat bewildering variety of ways. According to his system, perfect duties are: coercible; subject to external legislation; juridical; directly contradictory to the categorical imperative; concerned solely with actions (as opposed to motives); they pass the "contradiction in conception" formulation of the categorical imperative; identify a specific agent; have a specified content for fulfillment; fully dischargeable; and are demanded by right. In contrast, imperfect duties are: uncoercible; subject to internal legislation; ethical; solely concerned with "ends;" judged by an agent's internal motivations; unable to produce a "contradiction in willing;" they specify no particular agent; they specify no particular content; they are not fully dischargeable; and they are not demanded by *Recht*.[28]

Duties can also be characterized as positive or negative. Positive duties require a specific action, while negative duties require an agent to refrain from acting. Kant's thinking on *Recht* indicates that he views duties of right as mainly negative: to forbear from interfering with the freedom of another person. Examples of negative duties include: not wronging another person and refraining from actions that disrespect another person, say by mocking or "exalting oneself" above another. Duties of virtue are typically positive, in that they require an agent to do something for someone else or for oneself. Examples of positive duties include giving to charity, coming to the aid of someone in distress, establishing institutions or mechanisms that allow agents to live a moral life. However, there are negative duties of virtue, and, contrary to some of Kant's more explicit assertions, positive duties of right. Two of the most basic positive duties of right include the duty to exit the state of nature and form civil society, and the duty of sovereigns to reform their constitutions in accordance with "republican principles."[29] There are also other positive duties of right at work in Kant's system, such as the state's duty to provide a basic minimum welfare system, where wealthy citizens are taxed and the monies received are distributed to attend to the basic needs of the poor.[30]

At some points in Kant's work, he also suggests that perfect duties are "strict" and "narrow," while imperfect duties are "wide."[31] These last two distinctions are meant to highlight how much leeway an agent has in fulfilling her duty. Perfect duties provide "narrow" leeway, in that agent, recipient and scope are identified (and possible coercion if a contract is involved). For example, I borrow five dollars from Jane, and in borrowing the money I agree to repay it to her within a week. I am the agent; Jane is the recipient; and repaying five dollars in a week is the scope. An imperfect duty of charity, say, will only stipulate that agents ought to be charitable and to take others' happiness as their own. Imperfect duties identify agents (all people), but identifying recipients is left to the discretion of the duty bearers. Furthermore, the leeway is considered "wide" because the agent determines the scope of the duty. Whether I donate time or money to charity, or how much of either, is left up to my discretion. Coercion is also impermissible, and the duty is never in a sense fully or "once and for all" discharged, as I have a duty of charity my entire life.

For the most part, Kant takes all duties of right to be perfect duties and all duties of virtue to be imperfect duties.[32] Duties of right, since they concern only external actions, are therefore directed towards others. Duties of virtue, contrarily, concern ends and can apply to oneself and to others. Unfortunately, Kant's discussion of these distinctions is not always consistent. This is because he also argues that human beings have perfect duties of virtue—to themselves and others. Perfect duties of virtue to oneself fall under the precept: "respect the end of humanity in our own person."[33] These actions include: abstaining from suicide,[34] defiling oneself by lust,[35] stupefying oneself with food or drink,[36] lying to others,[37] avarice[38] and servility.[39] A perfect duty of virtue to others includes the duty of respect. Here, Kant does not use the term "perfect" duty, but only "narrow," because the action owed permits no leeway for an agent, and is, "strictly speaking, only a negative one (of not exalting oneself above others)."[40] Acts of respect include: recognizing the dignity in others,[41] forbearing from contemptuous action,[42] refraining from scandal,[43] abstaining from arrogance,[44] forgoing from defamation,[45] and refraining from ridiculing others.[46] Thus there is not an easily reducible one-to-one ratio (*Recht*: perfect duties and *Tugend*: imperfect duties).

Giving rise to the confusion regarding Kant's first- and second-order classifications is the table he provides in the *Doctrine of Right*.[47] This table is quite unhelpful, as it does not take into account any of the perfect duties of virtue, and, due to such ambiguities, it opens him up to Willaschek's charge that his "system of moral duties is neither consistent nor complete. [And that] there are moral duties which are neither duties of right nor duties of virtue."[48] While Willaschek does not give us any hint as to what these other duties may be, or why they do not fit into the imperfect/perfect and right/virtue distinctions, he has identified (albeit from a different and in my opinion incorrect perspective) a serious problem in Kant's theory: the need for an expansion of Kant's taxonomy of duties.[49]

Public and private right

Ultimately, the tension in Kant's system is due to his particularly legal understanding of *Recht*. This conceptualization forces Kant to require the establishment of a civil condition to guarantee universal justice because only public law can guarantee the rights and freedoms of everyone, regardless of their physical capacities. Individuals in a state of nature, where law is not public and not backed by an authoritative coercive force, can only secure their rights by their own strength. Absent a state, or a condition of what Kant calls "public right," his taxonomy of duties is problematic at best.

Thus one of the most important aspects of Kant's deontic system is the presence or absence of a civil society. His reasoning is that if we begin from the assumptions that there is only one natural right,[50] the right to freedom, and there are natural (moral) laws, then people must secure property to actualize their freedom. This is because I realize my freedom through acting and pursuing projects. Whatever those projects might be, they require things, and at bare minimum they require a location in space for me to reside. However, in a state of nature there is no guaranteed way to secure property (i.e., things) beyond what one can physically possess because there is no neutral judge to adjudicate disputes and no public and agreed-upon laws backed by a coercive force to protect rights. In a state of nature, each person is judge in his own cause and "might makes right." Property and *Recht*, he claims, can only be deemed "provisional." Yet the moral law requires us to (i) maintain our freedom and (ii) establish a condition to secure further, or "acquired", rights to property. The only way to do both of these is by grounding the principles to determine rights (against genocide, ethnic cleansing and crimes against humanity, and ruled by law, arbitrated by a neutral judge and backed by a coercive force to enforce laws and punish offenders.)[51]

The *Doctrine of Right* reflects these arguments in the set-up of its two parts: private right and public right. Private right is the condition of right in a state of nature, where only natural and private law rule. Natural law for Kant is roughly "law determined by reason which concerns the interrelation of persons in so far as one person's exercise of freedom can have an influence on the possible exercise of freedom of some or all others."[52] Private law regulates relationships outside of civil society (like the family), and includes one's innate right, including the authorization to acquire provisional property, and the right to compel others into a civil condition. In this condition:

> [T]here are no public law courts … no public means of enforcing decisions made by law courts, … [and] natural assumptions about a person's intentions are based on what is not explicit and certain. As a result there can be irresolvable disagreement concerning what a person truly had in mind when he/she made an agreement or performed a certain action.[53]

Here, one can have justice, but it is subjective (one's interpretation of the natural law) and limited to only those who can secure it through their strength.[54]

Public right, contrarily, is the condition of civil society, where laws are promulgated publically and rights are rendered peremptory. As Leslie Arthur Mulholland notes, Kant employs three different kinds of justice to explain public justice (or public right): commutative, distributive and protective. "Commutative justice only provides rights against a determinate person," while "distributive justice …

[requires] a judicial decision ... because only a court of law by whose judgments everyone is bound can provide the peremptory resolution of claims to property and thereby bind an entire society."[55] Further, he writes that "protective justice is the enforcement of a judicial distribution of rights through coercion, including punishment," and "protective justice makes rights possible."[56]

Public right, and thus civil society, must have legal procedures, courts, judges and coercive mechanisms for enforcement and punishment. These procedures must be public, and courts must render decisions through "legally determined principles of judgment."[57] Furthermore, there must be rules for determining and identifying who has "the requisite features as empowered to exercise authority within a court."[58] Since the role of judgment in the state of nature (private law) is a major source of contention, public judgment (and judges) must resolve this tension by rendering certain, final and impartial judgments.[59]

Kant's public law solution seems to tidy up many problems witnessed in a condition of private right, but it does not resolve problems of justice completely. We are still left with a nagging question in Kant's theory: If there is no state to secure justice for all, then what happens to duties of justice outside of a civil condition? Willaschek's charge that Kant's system of duties is incomplete begins to have more and more of a footing, especially when we consider duties of justice at the international level, in failed or collapsed states, during times of civil war, or in almost every instance of an R2P crisis. Moreover, Kant's answer in Chapter II of the *Doctrine of Right* that states ought to form

> A league of nations ... not in order to meddle in one another's internal dimensions but to protect against attacks from without. [And] [t]his alliance need not, however, involve a sovereign authority (as in a civil constitution), but only an association (federation); the alliance can be renounced at any time and so must be renewed from time to time[60]

is rather unhelpful. Problems of justice will remain even with a league of nations, and it does not answer questions about duties of justice in failed states, collapsed states, civil wars, or in states witnessing mass atrocities due to war, civil war, genocide or crimes against humanity.

Kantian provisional duties

The necessity of civil society

A perfunctory reading of Kant yields the conclusion that justice only exists in the realm of *Recht*, and that *Recht*, or a condition of right, only exists in a civil society. This is because "right" is determined in accordance with external laws, and these laws determine what is "just." Consequently, one's judgment of what is just or unjust can only be made when an external law is transgressed.[61] However, a closer reading of the *DR* yields a subtler conclusion: justice is, at least partially, everywhere because in every condition a form of *Recht* inheres.[62]

This is so because a form of *Recht* subsists either outside of civil society or where "there are cases in which a right is in question but for which no judge can be appointed to render a decision,"[63] and for this reason there are problematic cases excluded from the *DR*.

These problematic cases arise in situations outside of civil society (private right) and in instances of uncertainty (situations of what Kant calls "ambiguous right"). In a condition of private right, the existence of *Recht* for an agent is guaranteed only by physical capability. Kant claims that in this condition, objects of one's choice (property, security, life) "[are] that which I have the *physical capacity* to use as I please, whose use lies within my power (*potentia*)."[64] Though anything "external as one's own[,] in a state of nature[,] is physical possession which has in its favor the rightful *presumption* that it will be made into rightful possession [in civil society]."[65] Thus even though Kant only argues that a presumption, or a rule that one assumes, is valid until a time when evidence disproves it, it is still a rule of *rightful* presumption, and so it has a modicum of *Recht.* Furthermore, ambiguous right is "right in a wider sense (*ius latium*), in which there is no law by which an authorization to use coercion can be determined."[66] Here, Kant acknowledges areas of life (what he calls cases of equity and necessity) where agents have "such true or alleged rights," but the lack of institutional mechanisms of civil society relegate agents' claims to "the court of conscience."[67]

If we follow the line of reasoning that right, and thus rights, is provisional, then in conditions of private and ambiguous right, duties of justice should also be considered provisional. Duties are the jural correlatives of claim rights, and rights to external objects of one's choice are claim rights. Provisional rights exist when there is no system of law to guarantee noninterference, no common judge to adjudicate disputes, and one's security depends on one's own strength. One's right is considered provisional and not "conclusive" or peremptory because agents do not have the ability to make *legitimate* claims on others.[68] Only a civil society is capable of legitimizing these claims and establishing full (or conclusive) *Recht*. Kant notes:

> It [civil society] is the final end of all public right, the only condition in which each can be assigned *conclusively* what is his; on the other hand, so long as those other forms of state are supposed to represent literally just so many different moral persons invested with supreme authority, no *absolutely rightful condition* of civil society can be acknowledged, but only *provisional* right within it.[69]

There is a potentially large problem for Kant's system, though, if we grant the argument for provisional duties. This is so because the notions of duty and provisionality appear to be at loggerheads. Famously, Kant declares that all duties are *ipso facto* necessitations to act, but what if I have a "conditional" duty due to certain empirical conditions? Under this usage, it would be incoherent to claim that one can have a merely conditional or contingent necessitation. That is not what I am claiming here. Instead, "conditional" or "provisional" duties are duties that are *conditioned by* structural features, i.e., they have *enabling* conditions. As long as people are enabled, then they are under a strict necessitation to act. But if some people are disabled or disempowered, then there is (or at least might be) no duty for those agents. If an agent has a duty, then that duty still stands as a strict necessitation to act. Thus *provisional here means limited by some special nullifying hindrance of a temporary nature*, e.g., the hindrances of a state of nature, civil war, civil breakdown during a natural disaster, or anything *which makes some incapable of fulfilling duties of justice.* In the absence of an authoritative neutral judge and the rule of law backed by a coercive force, duties of justice are provisional. Some examples might be helpful here. Looking solely at Kant's works, four provisional duties are easily identifiable: initial acquisition of property, initial institution of civil society, autocrats governing in accordance with republican principles, and sovereigns delaying the institution of preliminary articles 2, 3, and 4 of "Perpetual Peace."[70]

A provisional duty, then, is a duty that *permits an exception on the basis of capacity.* In the *Grounding*, Kant asserts in a footnote that "I understand here by a perfect duty one which permits no exception in the interest of inclination."[71] Yet he does not give what one would think is the logical converse, that imperfect duties permit exception on the basis of inclination. Duties, as I have noted, cannot make room for inclination in the sense that if one does not feel like fulfilling a duty, then one does not have a duty. I take Kant to mean, instead, that perfect duties "permit no exception in the interest of inclination" *on how or when to fulfill them.* Perfect duties stipulate who, when, what, where and how. Imperfect duties, on the other hand, allow for an agent's inclination—on how, when and to whom—to fulfill them. But one still has to fulfill one's perfect duties, and the inclination to shirk one's duty cannot be a legitimating reason to do so. Therefore, if Kant's puzzling footnote about perfect duties permitting no exception for inclination is to actually work, then we have to add a clause that reflects Kant's later use of the terms "wide" and "narrow."[72]

Provisional duties, on the other hand, are similar in terms of inclination to imperfect duties. Here, we have a duty that is based first and foremost on the *ability or capacity* to act. If one has the ability to act in a condition outside of civil society or highly degenerated civil society, one has an unconditional "provisional" duty of justice. Not all agents have duties of justice in these conditions; only those that have the ability to fulfill them do. But for the agents that do have a provisional duty of justice, the scope of the duty is left up to them to determine. Because there is some structural hindrance nullifying public right, then the actions an agent must undertake to fulfill a duty are left up to him to determine. There is no public legislature or court to rule otherwise. Thus the exact content of a provisional duty remains dependent on an actor's private judgment and exercise of power. This means that everyone is not subject to exactly the same rules and in exactly the same way.

Some might object here that if we grant that a provisional duty is a duty that permits exception on the basis of ability, then we run into a familiar objection:

"ought implies can," so what? From an exegetical standpoint, Kant is certainly aware of the "ought implies can" distinction, but his understanding of it is more about rational capacities and not a question of physical and material means. What's more, no matter how we might like to dispute that empirical and contingent material factors play no role in Kant's theory of morality, we cannot because:

i Morality must be universal in scope,
ii Justice is a part of morality, so
iii Justice must be universal.
iv If justice is to be universal, then human beings must have a universalizing and equalizing mechanism that protects their rights equally (i.e., civil society), but
v Absent civil society duties of justice apply only to those people that have the physical capacity to fulfill them.

Capacity and material considerations

To gain a clearer understanding of how capacity plays a role in Kant's deontic system, we can turn to his discussion of the differing types of duties in the *Grounding*.[73] There, he constructs four examples to highlight the different kinds of duties: perfect duties to oneself, perfect duties to others, imperfect duties to oneself and imperfect duties to others. While the relevant section in the *Grounding* is concerned solely with duties of virtue, it is still a helpful guide to aid us. Especially considering that there is nothing precluding the existence of provisional duties of virtue, as well as provisional duties of justice, in Kant's system.

Kant's four cases are: *Suicide*, *Borrower*, *Loafer* and *Miser*. *Suicide* is about a man so "reduced to despair" that he desires to exit this world and relieve his sufferings by committing suicide; *Borrower* desires to obtain a loan he knows he cannot repay; *Loafer* wants to wallow in laziness and gluttony and neglect perfecting his talents; *Miser* desires to hoard his money and refuse to help those in need. In the cases of *Suicide* and *Borrower* Kant assumes the empirical condition of one having rationality. Both men are capable of recognizing the moral law, and they do not suffer from any sort of physical or pathological hindrance. In the cases of *Loafer* and *Miser*, Kant assumes the same empirical fact but adds material capabilities (time and money) to the equation. The point here is that in each example Kant assumes the agent's *ability* to act. From *Suicide* to *Miser*, each person has the means (rational and material) to will his maxim and undertake action. The man contemplating suicide can rise above his sufferings and abstain. The borrower, while in need, is able to understand the ramifications of his decisions and to choose not to undertake a debt he cannot repay. The loafer, while completely content to indulge in his hedonistic lifestyle, understands that as a human being he possesses certain faculties that ought to be developed, and so employs his material wealth to do so. The miser recognizes that the world may be able to go on consistently with his maxim of stinginess, but he could not will his stingy maxim universally. He may, in his own time of need, want others to help him, so he too must use his material wealth to help those less fortunate.

The *Grounding* is, of course, Kant's first attempt to ground a universal system of morality on the basis of rationality and humanity. Rationality, or the ability that allows us to know the moral law, is a human (and thus universal) trait. If human beings are to have morality, Kant argues, then they must be free. Free in the psychological (or in Kant's terms "noumenal") sense. We are not determined beings, like animals that cannot choose different courses of action.[74] While humans are *influenced* by their surroundings, they are also simultaneously aware that this influence does not wholly determine their actions. Human beings can choose to be moral or debased beings, even if they have difficultly doing so.[75]

Kant's arguments in the *Grounding* and the *Metaphysics of Morals* posit that it is the pursuit of projects and ends that produces moral awareness. The four examples highlight this fact. One must act or do something with and around others to become aware of others' influence on us, and it is the awareness of others' influence that gives rise to a deeper self-awareness, which in turn forces us to recognize the worth of others and their projects. This self-realization and self-love drives humans to exercise our reason to ensure our freedom; it drives us to understand morality.[76] Kant's entire system, then, is first built upon the rational capacity to know the moral law and to recognize one's (and thus others') moral worth, but implicitly his system also relies on empirical, contingent factors (such as strength, wealth or intelligence) that enable human beings to fulfill all of the dictates of morality. For without the material factors, we cannot actually do anything.

It is no surprise, then, that Kant's four examples show the nobleness in rising above inclination and that the moral law applies to us all because we have the ability to know it. His attempt is to get away from conditioning morality on anything contingent. Yet the fact that he makes his entire discussion about virtue, and ignores the question of justice, leaves us with a problem: determining whether we have, and how to fulfill, our duties of justice when the enabling conditions of civil society are absent. This may not seem an important observation, as again obviously "ought implies can." However, it begins to assume greater importance when we reflect that there is nothing in his discussion about what to do *if one does not have the means* to fulfill a duty, and the means here are not rational but *material*. Justice requires a civil condition, and without it we are uncertain about what our duties of justice are, or if we have any. Thus, Kant, at least in this work, ignores one of the most important questions of practical life.[77] (Or at least he does not come to consider material capacities more explicitly until his later political writings where they come to the fore.)

One may object here that my concern about the practical and empirical underpinnings of some Kantian duties is overstated. He does, after all, devote a small book to moral education, where he discusses issues ranging from swaddling to sex. However, this work is not addressed to agents with limited material capacities.[78] All of the action guiding principles in this work are directed towards moral educators, people who possess full rational *and* material capacities for educating children. Furthermore, this work is concerned with the moral education of children *in a civil society*. For Kant, one can only follow the dictates of morality through proper education, and proper education requires "discipline and culture."[79] Culture is found only in society, but he goes even further:

> It is difficult to conceive a [moral] development from a state of rudeness (hence it is so difficult to understand what the first man was like), and we see that in a development of such a condition man has invariably fallen back again into that condition, and raised himself out of it. In the earliest records of even very civilized nations we still find a distinct taint of barbarism, and yet how much culture is presupposed for mere writing to be possible! So much so that, *with regard to civilized people, the beginning of the art of writing might be called the beginning of the world.*[80]

Kant was aware that writing began in civilized (i.e., ruled by law) society, and whether he is referring to the Sumerians or the Egyptians is irrelevant.[81] His educators and their pupils have sufficient degrees of protection and reciprocity via a legal system,[82] even if that system is run by an autocrat. He is not concerned with man's moral development in states of nature, civil wars, or any circumstances that undermine agents' capacities to fulfill their duties.

Of course he speculates about man's moral development in later essays, such as "Idea for a Universal History with a Cosmopolitan Intent," "What is Enlightenment," "Theory and Practice" and "Perpetual Peace." However, each of these essays postulates, implicitly or explicitly, two things: the influence of nature and the inevitability of civil society. Nature, he claims, has implanted the seed of man's "unsocial sociability."[83] This character trait gives man, through his trials and tribulations, the impetus to enter into civil society and then into foreign relations and eventually into pacific international federations.[84] While man's progress is noted in each of these essays, the driving force is not practical guidance about what men ought to do, or how to do it; rather, nature is the only actor responsible for man's progress. Man is left not with an understanding of his duties of justice, but only with the advice that "nature should thus be thanked for fostering social incompatibility, enviously competitive vanity, and insatiable desires for possession or even power. [For] without these desires, all man's excellent natural capacities would never be roused to develop."[85] Human beings have no agency in fostering the conditions for their progress or enlightenment; nature is the driving force.

Unfortunately, this line of reasoning is disappointing because states of nature, such as civil wars, or any circumstances that undermine agents' capacities to fulfill positive duties of justice, are all too familiar in the real world. Civil wars still occur, breakdowns in civil society still plague many states across the globe, and, as Kant declares, the international system is a state of nature. Indeed, the entire doctrine of R2P presupposes that there is sufficient negligence or wrongdoing on the part of the state that other states are obligated to act. We cannot be content to just let nature watch humans' progress "be interrupted" with such conditions, and hope that we will emerge from such "interruptions" wiser and more just than before. We must discover a way for an agent in a state of nature to understand when or if she has a duty of justice.

Might makes right?

If we follow Kant in thinking that man's highest goal is to become a fully autonomous agent, then we must also posit that complete autonomy requires undiminished freedom. In other words, an agent must be both internally and externally free. External freedom is freedom from nonreciprocal physical compulsion. Internal freedom is an agent rising above his inclinations and choosing to act according to the moral law, i.e., acting autonomously. Internal freedom stems from the capacity to act in accordance with the moral law. What is at issue here is that if one's external freedom is limited, say by imprisonment, then the positive expression of one's internal freedom might also be limited. For example, I might have the capacity to will a maxim, but due to, say, my imprisonment, my capacity for actually exercising my will is diminished. Thus, because my external freedom is limited, my ability to fulfill some of my moral duties is also limited. I cannot fulfill many duties of justice, especially positive ones, if I am in solitary confinement my entire life. I can, of course, be considered a moral agent, insofar as I have the capacity to choose (*Willkür*), but my ability to fulfill duties of justice or live, in a sense, a "complete" life is hindered. *Complete* freedom requires the exercise of both external and internal freedom.

Absent civil society, those without the capacity to fulfill their duties of justice are hindered. They lack the capacity or material means to follow some of reason's commands. Under Kant's system, justice must be universal; so all agents must enter into a condition of public right where everyone's freedom is secured. Civil society enables man's moral progress. Might, for Kant, does not equal Right, but it paradoxically helps to make it.

Civil society enacts equal laws for all people, equally protects all people, and equally holds all people accountable for their actions. The state provides a degree of protection and reciprocity necessary for people to perform not merely their negative but their positive duties as well. The state provides law, a "rightful form of association" where "everyone is able to enjoy his rights, and the formal condition under which it is possible in accordance with the idea of a will giving laws for everyone … [it is a place of] public justice."[86] The state, therefore, allows the *possibility* for *all* to follow the dictates of morality. In a civil society, all are now equally protected and can act because their external freedom is secure. Moreover, the meaning of "justice" is defined in the same way and by the same authority, and therefore the specificity problem is also remedied. If one is wronged in a civil condition, then the necessary legal frameworks are present to adjudicate disputes and restore rights. In one sense, then, the state's monopoly on the use of force (might) makes *Recht* possible for everyone.

Recht requires a priori a civil condition. As Kant claims:

> The first thing [he] has to resolve upon is the principle that it [he] must leave the state of nature, in which each follows its [his] own judgment, unite [himself] with all others (with which it cannot avoid interacting), subject [himself] to a public lawful external coercion, and so enter into a condition in which what is to be recognized as belonging to [him] is determined by law and is allotted to [him] by adequate power (not [his] own but an external power); that is, [he] ought above all else enter into a civil condition.[87]

However, who ought to institute this society and how is not immediately clear. Kant's student Vigilantius explains that "Professor Kant remarks in passing that the tales of King Romulus and King Numa are probably not historical truths, but fictions. In idea there was a progress from Romulus (signifying power) as the natural condition, to one of legal order under Numa, who symbolizes law."[88] What is clear is that, in another sense, might makes right because if we require a Romulus to establish a civil condition, then we require a force strong enough to coerce others into the rule of law.

Provisional to peremptory

Important to note for the concept of provisionality, and especially for provisional duties, is Kant's employment of the term *vorläufig*, which implies temporariness. Provisional, again, means: *limited by some special nullifying hindrances of a temporary nature.* If justice requires the institutionalization of the state, then provisional duties require the institutionalization of whatever mechanisms (a state, institution, agency, procedure, etc.) are necessary to transition them from provisional to peremptory or "conclusive." One has conclusive rights in a civil condition, and *Recht* loses its provisional status because individual subjective judgment and the private use of force are removed. In an analogous shift, then, provisional duties of justice become peremptory duties of justice in a civil condition because the state dictates who, what, when, where and how to fulfill them, and there is no room for "inclination" or subjective judgment. Arbitrary and subjective characteristics that allow agents in a state of nature to fulfill duties of justice are supplanted with purposive and objective standards of law and order. Moreover, the requisite authorities in a civil society remove the "wide" aspect of provisional duties. Once a duty of justice is peremptory, the scope becomes narrow.

By including provisional duties in Kant's framework the tension in the original deontic framework is diminished. That is not to say that provisional duties provide all the answers to some of our questions—far from it. What we can say is that there exist duties of justice in systems of private and ambiguous right, and that if an agent has the capacity to fulfill her duty, she must. How she fulfills it, though, is up to her. Moreover, we might also claim that *when* she fulfills it is also up to her. To see this more clearly, we can turn to the few discussions Kant makes about duty and provisionality.

First, recall that Kant notes that one can have "possessions" in conditions of private right, but they are not much more than mere "holding," and thus ownership of objects is only temporary or tentative until formal mechanisms make such ownership "conclusive."[89] Kant writes, "But in the former condition, that is, before the establishment of the civil condition but with a view to it, that is, *provisionally*, it is a *duty* to proceed in accordance with the principle of external acquisition."[90] While my arguments for the inclusion of a provisional duty in Kant's deontic taxonomy are reconstructive, it does, at least in this passage, seem that he acknowledges, at least implicitly, a provisional duty of property acquisition. Unfortunately for us, he does little to explain it. Nevertheless, if my interpretation and construction is correct, provisional duties are like provisional right in that both concepts require the institutionalization of legislation, judgment and enforcement to realize justice, and that in a condition of provisional (or private) right, the agent proceeds according to her own subjective will.

Second, in the *Conflict of the Faculties*, Kant provides us with a clue as to not only the temporality of his notion of "provisional" but also as to how empirical factors play a key role in determining when and how to fulfill one's duty. It is worth quoting Kant in full here:

> Consequently, it is a duty to enter into such a system of government, but it is *provisionally the duty* of the monarchs, if they rule as autocrats, to govern in a republican (not democratic) way, that is to treat the people according to principles which are commensurate with the spirit of libertarian laws...[91]

This passage is important because it shows that Kant believed that certain duties were tentative and required: (i) certain structural features to be present for duties of justice to be fully conclusive; and (ii) an agent's ability to fulfill a duty. In the first instance, monarchs have a provisional duty because they are limited by international structural hindrances to the realization of *Recht*, namely, that the international system does not have all the necessary requirements for a civil society. In the second instance, only domestic rulers—not the people or outside rulers—have this duty. It is only the domestic monarch who has the ability to rule according to republican ideals, and even then it is up to her discretion as to when she deems it fit for such reforms to take place.

This of course is a tenuous point. One could say that foreign rulers have the capacity to force domestic sovereigns to rule according to republican principles, say by overthrowing the government or instituting a puppet regime, or that the people could revolt and force the institutionalization of a republican government. However, both of these positions undermine the idea and function of the state. The state's function is to insure *Recht* by providing positive political goods and increasing its citizens' freedom, but for a foreign ruler to interfere or force change undercuts *Recht*. Moreover, a domestic insurrection or revolution would abolish the state itself and thus undermine *Recht* entirely.[92]

Kant's concept of provisionality is the key to understanding how right and virtue fit together in his moral system. Unfortunately, this concept has seen little attention in the literature, except by Elisabeth Ellis. Ellis argues that all of Kant's political works have a "provisional" feature to them, and that a regulative ideal is always explicit or implicit in his political works. Ellis's focus on Kant's idea of provisional acquisition of property allows her to build a Kantian theory of "provisional right," where one's maxim is: "act in such a way that one does not render the eventual realization of the ideal state impossible."[93]

She argues that Kant's entire political theory is "provisional" where justice is always in a state of "becoming," and all societies are in a continual condition of provisional right. Each state attempts to achieve the ideal of *Recht* (a republican constitution with enlightened citizens), but because it is only a regulative ideal a state can only approximate it, and thus it remains in a provisional condition. Progress towards the ideal of *Recht*, she argues, can only happen when states' justness is judged in the public sphere by a "judging public." She writes that:

> What is at stake here is nothing less than the causality of freedom. If the ideals expressed by the judging public have the power to promote concrete progress in human affairs, then freedom is not merely an internal experience but a force in the world.... [T]he free interplay of ideas in the public sphere leads to gradual enlightenment; that is, the principles of political reason, such as the necessity of republican rule, the evils of war, and the sanctity of human rights.[94]

Though I disagree with Ellis's assertion that *all* societies are in a condition of provisional right, especially as most states satisfy the Kantian requirements of separation of powers and rights of free speech, her interpretation of Kantian provisionality compliments my discussion of provisional duties and vice versa.[95] Provisional duties are temporary (*vorläufig*),[96] and they require one to act in such a manner that "does not render the ideal ... impossible."[97] More specifically, at a minimum *Recht* requires one to abide by negative morality, but for those with the ability, it requires the establishment of a condition in which all people can begin to fulfill positive duties of justice. Nevertheless, when a civil condition is absent, and there still exists a "provisionally rightful condition," duties of justice can only be considered provisional. Ellis's contribution is certainly noteworthy, but her attention is geared towards Kant's overall political theory. She does not look to the role of provisionality in Kant's deontic taxonomy. Thus the argument here provides Ellis's argument for a maxim of provisional right with a stronger and clearer deontic framework.

An additional benefit of my Kantian reconstruction is that it also makes sense of the areas where Kant explicitly refers to "conditional" duties.[98] Recall that "conditional" here means "requiring further enabling features" rather than "contingent upon having an inclination to act." Provisional duties are not *contingent upon* the structural hindrances of a state of nature, civil war or civil/social breakdown; rather they are unconditional duties an agent has *if* the agent possesses the ability to fulfill the duty while residing in a hindered condition. A duty is still a necessitation to act, and a person who has the ability to act must do so.

The imperatives that dictate action here are not hypothetical; for example if I want justice then I set up this institution. Imperatives here are moral, i.e., categorical; one must do what the moral law requires: institute a state in which justice can be realized.[99]

Objections

The critic may object to the argument for provisional duties on two fronts. First, she may claim that material capacities should play no role in Kant's moral framework. This is a perversion of Hegel's famous "empty formalism" objection. In other words, I am admitting too much in way of empiricism. However, as Robert Louden persuasively argues, Kant's ethics must admit of empirical and contingent facts about agents, otherwise there is no practical applicability.[100] Louden's argument for including what he terms "the second part" of Kant's ethics applies to the case of provisional duties as well. As Kant's system is constituted by both justice and virtue (ethics), and justice requires legal, judicial and coercive institutions, so too does Kant's ethical project because "by nature man is not a moral being at all,"[101] and he requires institutions for his eventual moralization. Whether on the path of justice or virtue, material and empirical factors play a decisive role for Kant.

The critic may offer the rejoinder, material considerations notwithstanding, that Kant holds that all human beings, as rational beings, are bound by morality, and all human beings have a set of moral duties—regardless of their ability to fulfill them—and must, therefore, at least attempt to fulfill them. This objection is a variant of the *fiat justitia ruat caelum* belief, and has become, for better or worse, synonymous with Kant. Indeed, she might cite as evidence for her point the second *Critique*:

> *It is always in everyone's power to satisfy the categorical command of morality*; whereas it is but seldom possible, and by no means so to everyone, to satisfy the empirically conditioned precept of happiness … [for] in the latter case there is a question also of one's *capacity and physical power* to realize a desired object.[102]

Two items must be noted here. First, the categorical command for morality, or the categorical imperative, has several formulations, but foremost among them is the formula of the universal law. One must will her maxim as if it were a universal law; if her maxim remains consistent, then she moves on to the next one. Kant's point here is that anyone *with the ability to reason* can do this. The human faculty of reason allows us to know the moral law[103] and to understand which acts accord with it. So, yes, all agents are capable of knowing morality, and insofar as we can know the moral law, all agents with rational capacity can satisfy the categorical imperative. Yet Kant's point in the above-quoted passage is to argue against using a principle of obtaining happiness as a *determining ground* for moral action. His ultimate purpose is to show that happiness, or any attempted outcome which maximizes a nonmoral good,

> bases morality upon incentives that undermine it rather than establish it and that totally destroy its sublimity, inasmuch as motives to virtue are put in the same class as motives to vice and inasmuch as incentives merely to teach one to become better at calculation ...[104]

The critic must concede that just because I am aware of the moral law does not necessarily mean that I am obligated to fulfill every possible duty that can be derived from it. Moreover, I may know how to satisfy its imperatives, like instituting a civil society, but I might not be like a powerful Romulus to actually do so.

Second, Kant claims "people are always preaching about what ought to be done, and nobody thinks about whether *it can be done*."[105] The context of this statement is in regards to Kant's work on moral anthropology, but it has direct bearing here. Kant understands that human beings exist between two worlds (i.e., the noumenal and phenomenal), and that they are simultaneously subject to both nature and freedom. The study of morality must take this into consideration. Moreover, if we again follow Louden's conclusions, then "can" here is not just about rational capacity. The "can" is concerned with so many more material and institutional factors, and these factors (including rational, institutional, and even physical capacities) are crucial components of Kant's system.

To fully convince our critic, though, let us turn to Kant's discussion about "willing" versus "wishing." "Willing" is special, and one cannot "will" any maxim. One must have the means (and thus the *ability*) to carry out her maxim for the agent to actually "will" anything. For example, I might try "willing" to fly. I could even go up to the roof of my house and jump off while screaming, "I will to fly; it is my maxim to fly!" Unfortunately, this does not pass Kant's test. The only "will" I have here is the fact that I will find myself sorely disappointed. As I plummet to the earth, I realize I do not have the ability to fly—unless I am on board an airplane. "Willing" in such a manner is not, for Kant, even considered willing; it is wishing. Wishing occurs when "one's consciousness of [his] *ability* to bring about [his desired] object by [his] action" is not present,[106] or when one does not *possess* a faculty that is necessary for the idea of "choice."[107] Choice, therefore, directly relates to action,[108] and one cannot will a maxim one does not have the *ability* to fulfill. Birds have the ability to fly; human beings do not.

The critic may still go back to the "ought implies can" distinction. There are only two ways to meet this objection. First, by claiming that the "can" here is dependent upon something contingent; it is dependent upon physical attributes that are, ultimately, morally arbitrary. It is a matter of moral luck who is born strong and who is not. This conclusion is something most Kantians would be reluctant to endorse; however, it is not at all at odds with Kant's writings and moral system. Because man is simultaneously a free and a determined being, and as the natural world presents him with situations that potentially limit his capacity for moral progress, we should explore what this entails instead of assuming it away. Provisional duties allow us to do this because they exist at the intersection of freedom and nature, and they make a necessary allowance so that freedom does not undermine its own purpose. Ought does imply can, but this is really at a meta-level.

One can think of it like this: all agents have a duty, call it Δ, but in order for all agents to fullfill Δ, rules, procedures, judges and enforcement mechanisms must be put in place, call these Ω. Absent Ω, all agents cannot Δ, even though reason requires it. We can then say, $-\Omega$, all agents have a provisional duty to Δ, call it $\varphi\Delta$. However, not all agents can $\varphi\Delta$ due to a lack of ability, so these agents are exempted, temporarily; they are $-\varphi\Delta$. Those agents that can, must, and they remain bound to $\varphi\Delta$. The necessary feature to make this determination, though, is an agent's physical ability, and one of the agent's first duties is to institute Ω.

The second response to the "so what" objection is really rather simple: there is debate among Kantians about whether "ought" really does imply "can." For instance, Louden adamantly believes that the agent's abilities are extremely important to Kant's writings. Others too, such as Jens Timmerman, also believe that "can" is important for Kantian obligation, but the "can" involved is a necessary and not sufficient condition for one to actually be obligated.[109] On the other hand, scholars such as Wayne Martin argue that one may have an obligation where one has no ability, in other words, an "ought when one cannot."[110] The point is not to settle the debate, but to at least open up a space for the notion of provisionality. If ability as a ground of obligation is open to dispute, then there is at least theoretical room for provisional duties.

Conclusion

Provisional duties are a necessary feature of Kant's moral system. While he does not explicitly include them in his taxonomy or his rather unhelpful two-by-two table in the *Doctrine of Right*, this should not necessarily worry us. Kant's purpose in the *DR* was to set up "the sum of those laws for which an external lawgiving is possible" according to "reason alone."[111] In other words, he was concerned with laying out the requisite features for the emergence of the rule of Right, and the principal feature for this to happen is the creation of civil society. His project is geared toward setting up why civil society is necessary, and once created, how such a society should be organized. We might forgive his failure to discuss the intricacies of an incomplete system, as these were not his primary purpose.

He does, however, make several fleeting remarks about the notion of provisionality and duty, providing us with textual evidence that he believes the two concepts are linked. From these few passages, I have attempted to reconstruct what a provisional duty entails, and how it fits into his overall deontic framework. This is an important first step, for we must first understand all the possible categories of duty before we can start to classify particular duties, such as a duty of R2P. This is necessary, for any discussion of one's duty must proceed in a sequential manner from first-order to second-order classifications. We first determine whether a particular duty is one of *Recht* or of *Tugend.* Once this is accomplished, we can then move on to determining whether the duty is perfect, imperfect or provisional. We must ask ourselves whether we find ourselves in a situation of public or private right and whether rights are involved. If we are in a condition of private right, and our duty is one of justice, then it is by definition provisional.

The concept of provisionality is key to many of Kant's writings, and it brings with it a focus on capacity and the empirical world. While many Kant scholars abhor the notion of the empirical, citing only the importance of the ideal, this is a disservice to Kant. While his central concerns are with understanding metaphysics, ethics and epistemology, he is not unaware of the pragmatic concerns regarding human beings. These concerns, whether one likes it or not, filter into his metaphysics and his writings on morality.

We cannot shy away from the empirical world, and we certainly cannot ignore that there are times when civil society is either weak or absent. During these periods, morality and right do not vanish, but their dynamic does change. How it changes and for whom become prominent elements. Material capacities to fulfill one's duty come to the fore, and the temporariness of the situation forces us to acknowledge the additional steps that must be taken to ensure the instantiation of universal justice.

By identifying and analyzing the concept of a provisional duty, we can move discussions of moral responsibility forward, especially for pressing problems of international justice, like R2P. If agents, individuals or states, find themselves in a condition that does not meet the Kantian requirements for public right, we have a mechanism to identify duty bearers and to assign to them the duty. The challenges ahead, though, are many and not easy. If one claims that an agent provisionally has a duty, then one must also provide a measurement of ability and an analysis of what will count as enabling or disabling in that context. For assigning a duty to an agent is dependent upon that agent meeting some sort of capacity threshold. This will be the task in the following chapters. For now, we must turn our attention back to the case at hand, R2P, and defend an account of why a duty to protect is not a "perfect" or an "imperfect" duty, as some suggest, but instead a Kantian provisional duty.

2 Provisional protection

The Responsibility to Protect as a provisional duty

> I believe that we must embrace the responsibility to protect, and, when necessary, we must act on it. This responsibility lies, first and foremost, with each individual State, whose primary *raison d'être* and duty is to protect its population. But if national authorities are unable or unwilling to protect their citizens, then the responsibility shifts to the international community to use diplomatic, humanitarian and other methods to help protect the human rights and well-being of civilian populations. When such methods appear insufficient, the Security Council may out of necessity decide to take action under the Charter of the United Nations, including enforcement action, if so required.
>
> Secretary General Kofi Annan, from "In Larger Freedom"

The Responsibility to Protect doctrine emerged from a series of reports, dialogues and UN resolutions. As the doctrine is a body of principles, it is still undergoing change and adaptation. However, its core lies with the paramount conviction that all peoples have a right to be free from genocide, ethnic cleansing, war crimes and crimes against humanity, and that it is the responsibility of domestic states, the international community and the UN to protect this right. How this responsibility is fulfilled, however, is a different question, and what this obligation entails is not entirely clear. Much ambiguity exists over how to best discharge a duty to protect, and this could be due to R2P's broad mandate or to the politicking that has inevitably occurred for its adoption. While both of these are fair assessments, I believe the primary reason for the ambiguity lies elsewhere: the duty's provisional juridical status.

To gain a better appreciation of how R2P evolved and why it is beyond humanitarian intervention, let us briefly canvass the history of both. Awareness of R2P's historical predecessors allows us to highlight the strengths and weaknesses of the current doctrine. Moreover, in doing so, we can also more fully understand why prior attempts to categorize a duty of humanitarian intervention (HI) as either a perfect or an imperfect duty are misguided. While it is certainly true that R2P is not tantamount to HI, we should not overlook these previous attempts, for they provide us with a body of scholarship; R2P is a relatively new norm and scholarship is still developing, while HI has received more attention. In addition, HI is still an element of R2P's framework (prevention, reaction and rebuilding), and it is unarguably the most contentious part. Coercive responses to R2P crimes, including but not limited to military intervention, threaten one of the hallmarks of the current international order: sovereignty. Finally, if we are to fully apprehend what a duty of R2P requires, we must shift the debate over second-order classifications and determine its first-order status as a duty of justice or virtue (ethics). Establishing the first-order classification will guide us in how a duty of R2P ought to be fulfilled, who has this duty, and how we might begin to assess when it is discharged.

History of the debate

Historically, HI was argued to be a "right" of a state.[1] Grotius, for example, claimed that states possessed a discretionary right to intervene "on account of injuries committed against themselves or their subjects, but also on account of injuries which do not directly affect them but excessively violate the law of nature or of nations in regard of any person whatsoever."[2] Since Grotius, however, scholars have stepped back from this more permissive notion of intervention and debated when a state could legitimately override the more contemporary norm of nonintervention to violate another state's sovereignty.[3] At issue in the early modern debates was a moral right to intervene, where now the issue is primarily one of legality.[4] This move, from morality to legality, and the subsequent legal arguments for and against intervention, has undergone three shifts.

The first shift came with the establishment of the United Nations in 1945. The UN's Charter explicitly forbids the violation of state sovereignty except in extreme circumstances where a state acts in self-defense or the UN takes collective action against a transgression that poses a threat to international peace.[5] Even in cases of self-defense, a state is expected to seek UN authorization, if possible, before taking coercive measures against the belligerent party. The first phase is marked, therefore, by a policy of strict nonintervention codified in the UN Charter.

While interventions during the 1970s occurred, they were justified, not on humanitarian grounds, but for reasons of international security and self-defense (India in Pakistan, 1971; Vietnam in Cambodia, 1979; Tanzania in Uganda, 1979).[6] As Nicolas Wheeler explains, states did not try to find new grounds or create new norms for state behavior. Rather, they attempted to justify human protection exercises within the existing legal framework. Humanitarian concerns may have been noted, but they were not *primary* reasons for intervention.

The second shift came with the end of the Cold War. States' public justifications changed, as they were no longer concerned with maintaining a strict balance of power between the former Soviet Union and the United States. Reasons beyond security came to the fore, and states began to once again openly employ the language of a right of HI. The intervention that sparked this shift was the 1991 Iraq intervention. A window opened when France, Belgium, the United Kingdom and the United States submitted a draft resolution to the Security Council (Resolution 688) to end the human rights violations of the Iraqi Kurds and Shiites.[7] Though the resolution "demanded an improvement in the human rights situation of a member state [Iraq] as a contribution to the promotion of *international security*", this was not the sole justification for action.[8] The United States-led coalition ultimately overextended Resolution 688's mandate in creating safe havens and no-fly zones, and normally such mission creep tends to garner derision from the international community. However, in this case, the coalition's actions were met with "acquiescence … rather than tacit legitimation," and this appeared to be due to the coalition's public justification in "humanitarian concerns".[9] Indeed, British Foreign Secretary, Douglas Hurd, explicitly claimed that "recent international law recognizes the *right* to intervene in the affairs of another state in cases of extreme humanitarian need."[10,11]

The third shift occurred after the international community's failure to intervene in the 1994 Rwandan genocide. Though debates over the legality of HI persisted, scholars, lawyers and diplomats began to entertain the idea that HI is (or ought to be) more than merely a permissive right exercised at the discretion of willing and able states. Some scholars went so far as to suggest that HI ought to be considered a *duty*, and that state actions to stop genocide, mass human rights violations and crimes against humanity are *obligatory*, not discretionary.[12]

The major turning point, however, came in 2000 when the Canadian government supported a move to reconcile human rights protection and state sovereignty.[13] To do this, it formed the International Commission on Intervention and State Sovereignty (ICISS). The ICISS report, *The Responsibility to Protect*, concluded that states shoulder a dual responsibility: "externally—to respect the sovereignty of other states, and internally, to respect the dignity and basic rights of all the people within the state."[14] Sovereignty, the basis of the international system since 1648, was redefined in terms of "responsibility," rather than "control."[15]

While the ICISS certainly sought to be inclusive by consulting prominent international leaders, nongovernmental organizations (NGOs), academics and international lawyers from all areas of the globe, the ideas behind the doctrine were not entirely new. Shifting away from sovereignty as control within one's borders to "responsibility" for one's people followed Francis Deng's work on the Kampala Process in the early 1990s, and Secretary General Kofi Annan's adoption of Deng's work in a 1999 *Economist* article.[16] Annan's piece is worth quoting at length:

> State sovereignty, in its most basic sense, is being redefined—not least by the forces of globalization and international cooperation. States are now widely understood to be instruments at the service of their peoples, and not vice versa. At the same time individual sovereignty—by which I mean the fundamental freedom of each individual, enshrined in the Charter of the UN and subsequent international treaties—has been enhanced by a renewed and spreading consciousness of individual rights. When we read the Charter today, we are more than ever conscious that its aim is to protect individual human beings, not to protect those who abuse them.[17]

Gone were the days when the UN upheld state sovereignty in the face of mass atrocities, such as the "shameful episode of the 1980s, when the United Nations ... allowed the Khmer Rouge to continue to occupy the Cambodian seat in the General Assembly for more than a decade."[18]

The ICISS report sought to move away from the language of HI and to reformulate the discussion. This was a crucial move, for the international community in 2000 was still reeling from the 1999 North Atlantic Treaty Organization (NATO) intervention in Kosovo. In the Kosovo intervention, the UN again found itself mired in political mud and unable to come to consensus about peacekeeping and civilian protection in the face of mass atrocities. Acting without UN authorization, NATO undertook tactical bombing to stop Milošević's genocidal campaign against Kosovar Albanians. Shortly after, the Independent International Commission on Kosovo found that NATO's actions were "illegal" in that they were advanced without UN mandate, but "legitimate" in a moral sense.[19] The UN Security Council (SC) was trapped by the institutional strictures of the Permanent Five (P-5) veto, but that was not reason to let thousands of people die. The ICISS's report, therefore, was a timely endeavor to extricate states and the UN from the problems associated with unauthorized intervention, and to do this, the Commission sought to change the debate's language and provide a set of foundational principles to guide states' and the international community's responsibilities in the face of such crimes.

By changing the language of the debate, R2P's framers sought to sidestep certain moral and political problems.[20] One such problem is the use of the term "humanitarian" to describe military action, which relief and aid workers feel is not "humanitarian" in any way. Another is the belief that labeling interventions in such a manner "prejudge[s] the very question in issue—that is, whether the intervention is in fact defensible."[21] Moreover, labeling armed interventions as "humanitarian" can easily be construed as an attempt to mask moral and political imperialism.[22] Thus, the ICISS invoked a new term—one it hoped was less corrupt—the "responsibility to protect."

The ICISS's other task is to provide a set of principles to guide the international community's response to mass atrocities in the twenty-first century and beyond. These principles (prevention, reaction and rebuilding) are broad themes to guide the various aspects of a duty to protect.[23] Within the framework of R2P, then, the principles provide a subset of flexible policy options to specific R2P crises, and note that each R2P situation ought to be evaluated on its own merits and not according to a strict bureaucratic response. Responses can include coercive measures short of military intervention, such as: economic sanctions, arms embargoes, travel bans, asset freezes, or membership suspensions or expulsions from international, regional and subregional organizations, as well as full military intervention should the situation warrant it.[24]

Prevention, however, is always the best medicine, and the international community agrees with this viewpoint. States were quick to affirm this position, and capacity building and the "prevention" portion of R2P is certainly important. However, if states cannot prevent an R2P crisis, and the domestic state has failed or is unwilling or unable to protect its citizens, the responsibility to protect falls to the international community.[25] The international community, in turn, must look to the UN Security Council to determine what action (if any) is necessary to maintain peace and security and restore human rights.[26]

The most controversial aspect under the "reaction" heading is one where military responses are involved. The ICISS report claims that when all other measures fail, and the proper channels authorize such a response, military action is a valid option. To determine when military actions are permissible, the report provides a further set of sub-criteria: just cause, right authority, right intention, last resort, proportional means and reasonable prospect of success.[27] These principles are not new; they are the cornerstones of just war theory.[28]

The novelty from the ICISS's perspective is taking the old just war principles and adapting them to the purposes of R2P. For instance, the notion of just cause is only satisfied by two criteria: actual or apprehended large-scale loss of life due to a state's deliberate action, negligence or collapse; or actual or apprehended large-scale ethnic cleansing manifested through killing, expulsion, terror or rape.[29] Only in these situations is the "threshold" met. Now, what exactly "large-scale" entails is open to dispute. Right intention is satisfied by a mission's aim to "halt or avert human suffering," and not for any other reasons such as regime change. The proportional means requirement entails that any military action undertaken to protect populations from large-scale loss of life or ethnic cleansing does not exacerbate the situation. In other words, the scope, intensity and duration of the activity should be minimal and the overall suffering should be minimized. Last resort and the reasonable prospect for success follow traditional and common-sense views of just war theory, and do not change with R2P's adoption. States must try all avenues first before employing military force, and their military endeavor cannot be doomed from the start.

Thus the ICISS's report simultaneously extends traditional notions about the use of force and initiates a sea change about the notion of state sovereignty. On the one hand, it continues the ideas and practice of just war theory, while on the other it conditions sovereignty on the protection of human rights and places the authority to determine when sovereignty can be violated outside the state. To be sure, the procedure of looking to the Security Council for guidance or approval is not new,[30] but reforming the long-held absolutist nature of state sovereignty certainly is. As Gareth Evans recently quipped, "R2P … is not and never has been old 'humanitarian intervention' wine in a new bottle."[31] Military intervention, from the R2P perspective, is only one tool in a box of many, and R2P is broader in scope than its predecessors.

Politics and problems: R2P and the outcome document

2005–present: the role of the United Nations and R2P

The ICISS report underwent significant changes between its publication in 2001 and its formal adoption by the UN in 2005. The 2005 World Summit Outcome

Document (OD) at once broadened and narrowed the scope and application of the 2001 recommendations. The Summit's OD expressly declared:

> *Each individual State has the responsibility to protect its populations from genocide, war crimes, ethnic cleansing, and crimes against humanity.* This responsibility entails the prevention of such crimes, including their incitement, through appropriate and necessary means. *We accept responsibility and will act in accordance with it.* The international community should, as appropriate, encourage and help States to exercise this responsibility and support the United Nations in establishing an early warning capability.
>
> The international community, through the United Nations, also has the responsibility to use appropriate diplomatic, humanitarian, and other peaceful means, in accordance with Chapters VI and VIII of the Charter, to help protect populations from genocide, war crimes, ethnic cleansing, and crimes against humanity. *In this context, we are prepared to take collective actions, in a timely and decisive manner, through the Security Council, in accordance with the Charter, including Chapter VII, on a case-by-case basis and in cooperation with relevant regional organizations as appropriate, should peaceful means be inadequate and national authorities are manifestly failing to protect their populations from genocide, war crimes, ethnic cleansing, and crimes against humanity.*[32]

From here we see that the UN accepted only some of the ICISS's recommendations, thereby limiting its possible execution while simultaneously broadening the possible situations that qualify as R2P crises. The OD firmly places all authority for coercive action under the authority of the SC, and makes no mention of alternative avenues if the Council finds itself ensnared in gridlock. Furthermore, the potential roles of the UN Secretary General and the General Assembly are not even considered here. Yet the OD does include other types of human rights violations, particularly war crimes and crimes against humanity, that were not part of the original ICISS report. By including these acts, the OD allows for a further entrenchment of international law norms and reifies existing international humanitarian law treaties.

Since 2005, however, implementing any of the UN's mandates relating to R2P has been met with weak support. Weiss notes that the initial lack of public support for a more open policy on intervention and R2P was due to the Bush and Blair administrations' attempts to justify their 2003 invasion of Iraq on humanitarian grounds.[33] He attributes the "stalling" of formal institutionalization of intervention and R2P guidelines to the "poisonous atmosphere" in the General Assembly since the Iraq invasion.[34] Others, such as Alex Bellamy, argue that establishing criteria for the use of force associated with R2P is not merely due to the 2003 Iraq invasion, but is perennially contentious. In fact, three of the P-5 members oppose institutionalizing criteria, for reasons that range from limiting states' freedom of action to the probability of abuse of such criteria.[35] Other nonpermanent members, such as India, Brazil and South

Africa, are also typically hesitant to endorse any policy that threatens traditional notions of state sovereignty.[36]

This is not to say that work on implementing R2P is not forthcoming. Secretary General Ban Ki-Moon attempts to explain and to garner support for R2P's institutionalization in three reports. The first of these, "Implementing the Responsibility to Protect," seeks to demarcate and explain the "Three Pillars" of R2P.

The Three Pillars were not original to the 2001 ICISS report. Rather, they arose from Annan's 1999 piece "In Larger Freedom." While the 2001 document looks to the three principles of prevention, reaction and rebuilding, subsequent UN adoptions speak of R2Ps three "Pillars" of responsibility. Pillar One places the primary responsibility to protect populations with the domestic state; Pillar Two notes that other states and the international community have a responsibility to assist states to meet their duty via capacity building; Pillar Three stipulates that the international community, as represented by the United Nations and, in particular, the Security Council, has a duty to respond in a timely and decisive manner when a domestic state fails to protect its populations from the crimes listed in the OD. The Three Pillars of R2P do not map onto the prevention, reaction and rebuilding principles; instead, the Pillars attempt to explain the various obligations that states, the international community and the UN have. Unfortunately, the scope of such obligations is not explained, and even the idea that each Pillar ought to sequentially follow the next is open to debate.[37]

Ban's other two reports, a 2010 piece on early warning and assessment abilities and a more recent 2011 report on the role of regional and subregional organizations, attempt to clarify how other UN bodies and international organizations can help to realize R2P. Unfortunately, Ban's reports seem to point only to problems with R2P's implementation and do little to give concrete guidance on how to actually address them. For instance, with reference to early warning and assessment, Ban points to "communication gaps" and a lack of information sharing within and between differing UN bodies. But the only concrete solution offered is Ban's statement that the two offices of the Special Adviser on the Prevention of Genocide and the Special Adviser on the Responsibility to Protect should join forces and consider ways to "save resources, eliminate redundancy and maximize synergies and effectiveness."[38] Unfortunately, the position of the Special Adviser on the Responsibility to Protect is currently vacant, and has little prospect of being refilled. Nevertheless, if the Secretary General can appoint another Special Adviser on R2P, such acts by both Special Advisers are still subject to the General Assembly's approval, and any information that the Advisers deem appropriate to an R2P situation must be mediated through the Secretary General to "the Security Council and other relevant intergovernmental organs."[39] It is unclear, therefore, whether such reforms will actually address the communication gaps or exacerbate them.

Ban's other report on the role of regional and subregional organizations suffers from similar problems. While it is indeed true that regional and subregional organizations do much of the heavy lifting in peacekeeping and protection of civilians operations, and indeed in providing information to other UN bodies, such as the Security Council, their legal status in relation to the UN is murky. As Ban notes, Chapter VIII of the UN Charter places authority with member states to resolve disputes through "regional arrangements" *before* referring situations to the Security Council. Any actions, though, seem to authorize only mediation efforts, while any "enforcement" actions are impermissible without prior Council approval. Guidance from the UN might appear relatively clear on this matter; however, in fact this is not the case. Some regional organizations, such as the African Union, have their own charters that authorize the organization to undertake coercive "enforcement" measures without seeking prior Security Council approval. Thus the claim of a member state of both the UN and a regional organization is open to dispute.

Ban's 2011 report does well to highlight the universal nature of R2P, and that any successful implementation of it must be supported by states, intergovernmental organizations, nongovernmental organizations and even individuals.[40] What undermines his approach, though, is his insistence that "each region will operationalize this principle at its own pace and in its own way."[41] In practice this might seem like the correct way of doing things: different regions have different cultures and are at different levels of development and stability, and so we should allow them to work within their capacities. However, such an approach is actually anathema to implementing R2P—if we are to grant that R2P is a universal principle. Universality necessarily implies that the principle is the same everywhere at all times. Yet allowing the implementation of it in differing ways particularizes it, and so makes it subject to charges of relativism. For example, R2P states that actions that "terrorize" a population are potential triggers for collective enforcement action, but what would count as "terrorizing" in one region may not count as it in another. Perhaps female genital mutilation would be seen as requisite to one culture, and so widespread practice of it is viewed as legitimate, whereas other cultures might view it as a coerced choice and an act of terror against women to subordinate them within the culture (much like how rape is used as a tool to do this). Or perhaps state-sanctioned violence and legal discrimination against lesbians, gays, bisexuals and transgender people would count as acts of terror against a particular group. The notion of "terrorizing" as part of ethnic cleansing is thus open to differing interpretations for certain cultural practices if we deem the principle of R2P to be relative.[42] Indubitably Ban's 2011 report is a positive step towards implementing R2P, and discussing the complexity of the international system and the plurality of international actors is key to understanding how we are to discharge a duty of R2P. However, the discussion, for at this point it amounts to only discussion, is ad hoc and results in inconsistent theoretical and practical solutions.

Legal prestidigitation and the problems with the R2P doctrine

Despite Secretary General Ban's attempts at institutionalizing R2P within the UN bureaucracy, we are left with three fundamental problems with discharging a duty to protect. First is the failure of the ICISS's concept of R2P and the "Outcome Document" to identify an appropriate agent as a duty bearer: the "international community" is not (and cannot be) an "agent" proper, for it lacks a *will* and *capacity* to act. More precisely, as the international community lacks the necessary criteria for moral agency, we cannot properly speak of it in terms of responsibility, much less duty. Of course, both documents seem to solve this problem by suggesting that the UN, particularly the Security Council, might be something of an agent *in loco*. However, the problem of inaction remains unsolved: the institutional strait jacket of the P-5 veto hinders the Security Council.

I am not alone in identifying this problem: both the World Federalist Movement and the Institute for Global Policy have also noted their concerns about "what should happen if the Security Council failed to act."[43] It is no surprise then that scholars continue to debate about who should intervene, as the UN has not undergone substantial reform, and no specified unit, organization or institution other than the "international community" is charged with a duty to intervene.[44] The success of R2P in changing the terms of the debate from a right to a duty is ultimately undermined because assigning a duty to protect to a vague "international community" amounts to nothing more than a semantic sleight of hand.

Moreover, disagreement persists over whether the Security Council even has a duty to intervene. Paraphrasing John R. Bolton, the former US Representative to the UN, Bellamy writes:

> He argued that the Security Council was not *legally* obliged to protect endangered civilians, whereas host states were. Bolton also argued that the Security Council must have the freedom to decide upon the most appropriate course of action on a case-by-case basis and that the language of obligation [in the "Outcome Document"] should be toned down accordingly.[45]

This position clearly compounds the problem: if the "language of obligation" is placed on the chopping block and the Security Council's agency is called into question, then the debate is likely to regress back into the terms of a state's discretionary right to intervene.

In addition to the problem of inaction by UN, there is a second, and related, problem of the role of regional organizations. As previously noted, regional organizations have the capacity to play helpful roles in discharging a duty to protect, but they also present serious difficulties. Some scholars insist that, when the Security Council is unwilling or unable to act, others should take its place.[46] However, it is not clear whether this "should" is a moral or a legal prescription. For Bellamy points out there may be instances where regional organizations carry out interventions on their own mandates because they "need not defer to the UN Security Council in humanitarian emergencies."[47] He clearly notes that the African Union's (AU) Constitutive Act grants its members a right of (collective) intervention, and thus "strongly implies that the AU, not the UN Security Council, may assume primary responsibility in the face of humanitarian emergencies."[48] Among other problems, this position is inconsistent with the OD's claims that the Security Council's approval is required (as a legal matter). The tension between regional organizations and the UN is yet another instance of "dueling sovereignty" and "dueling responsibility" that further muddies the water. If we are to take seriously the problems of dueling sovereignty and dueling responsibility, we could extrapolate from the AU example and envision the possibility that all 12 of the regional organizations currently in existence might find themselves in similar situations of conflicting responsibility.[49] It is possible, indeed highly probable, that conflict could result in an intervention deemed illegal by UN standards but legal by the terms of the regional treaty or constitution.

Finally, the R2P doctrine, and the "Outcome Document" in particular, are nothing more than international legal prestidigitation. If institutionalized procedures to act in humanitarian crises were to be embodied in international law, then the problems of identifying a duty bearer (i.e., agent problem) and determining what actions are required to stop R2P crimes (i.e., the scope problem) would disappear. However, as Gareth Evans notes in his recent book:

> The immediate objective must be to get to the point where, when the next conscience-shocking case of large-scale killing, or ethnic cleansing, or other war crimes, or crimes against humanity comes along—as is all too unhappily likely—the immediate reflex response of the whole international community will not be to ask *whether* action is necessary but rather *what* action is required, by whom, when and where.[50]

Evans gives the game away here, for if R2P were such a success it is hard to understand why, seven years after its adoption by the UN, the debate persists. Further examination reveals that the UN's adoption of R2P through the OD and subsequent resolutions is nothing more than legal lip service. On the one hand, the UN claims responsibility to "protect [states'] populations from genocide, war crimes, ethnic cleansing and crimes against humanity."[51] On the other hand, between the caveats of "as necessary and appropriate" and "on a case-by-case basis," the UN does nothing more than "pledge support" for reform of its constituent bodies; there are absolutely no immediate, tangible, or clear plans to consistently fulfill a duty of R2P.

It seems, then, that a duty to protect, as outlined in the ICISS report, the OD and the nonbinding reports issued by Ban is, at best, only vaguely defined. In the event of the Security Council's failure to act, the responsibilities of states and regional organizations remain ambiguous, as there may be conflicting requirements between states and regional organizations. These contradictory requirements may also give rise to incompatible claims as to who violates international law if a state or regional organization undertakes an intervention.

The main difficulty with R2P is, however, conceptual. Whether we want to harken back to labeling actions as a "responsibility to prevent, react or rebuild," or to discuss which Pillar obligates a particular (or in many cases nonparticular) agent to act, the fundamental questions raised by terming R2P a *duty* are left unanswered. If intervening in another state, for capacity building, post-conflict building or militarily to save human life is indeed a duty, then we must understand what type of duty it is. Such a clarification is necessary to determine who possesses the duty, what is required to fulfill it, and whether coercion of the duty bearer is justifiable.

Theory and practice: theoretical limits of R2P

> For it is a scandal to philosophy that we frequently hear advanced the view that what may be true regarding the concept of duty is in fact useless in practice. Indeed, this is said in a lofty, disdainful tone of voice, full of the arrogant desire to use experience to reform reason in that very area in which reason finds its highest honor. And this benighted wisdom believes it can penetrate further and more clearly with its mole-like eyes fixed on experience than with eyes belonging to a being created to stand erect and gaze at the heavens.... [T]he worth of practice rests entirely on its appropriateness to its underlying theory.[52]

> Here, indeed, we are referring to *laesio* dolosa;[53] in this case there is an injury to humanity in our own person; it would be affronted, and the respect owed to it would be lost sight of, if we were willing to let the rights of our humanity be toyed with. We must therefore possess a desire for justice, in order to demand satisfaction from the other for injury deliberately inflicted.[54]

While many scholars and practitioners take great pains to demarcate R2P from humanitarian intervention (HI), we cannot divorce the two concepts completely. For HI remains a potential response to an R2P crisis; indeed, it is the most contentious response. Furthermore, since R2P is a relatively new norm, much of the scholarship on military response for the sake of saving human life is directed toward discussions and justifications of HI. Thus we too should look to the debates about HI to gain a clearer understanding of the more controversial aspects of R2P. In particular, because R2P is a duty, we ought to engage with those scholars who have attempted to understand and classify a duty of HI.

Of this group, Kantian scholars who attempt to categorize a duty of HI as either *perfect* or *imperfect* wrestle with the same problems we witnessed on the practical front, namely identifying an appropriate agent and scope. The Kantian debate over whether HI is a perfect or imperfect duty seems to revolve around these very issues, but the locus of the debate is misplaced and, thus, largely misguided. That the debate misses the point is ultimately the result of two things: one, a misapplication of Kant's taxonomy of duties; and two, a misunderstanding of (or, perhaps, a taking for granted of) Kant's first-order distinction between justice and virtue. Kok-Chor Tan and Carla Bagnoli are the prime movers in this debate and thus are the principal foci of our inquiry.

HI as an imperfect duty: Tan

Kok-Chor Tan argues that HI, *as it stands now*, is an imperfect duty. He claims that this duty is imperfect because "no one has been assigned the duty, and it is not specified what anyone is to do."[55] Tan claims that because the current international system has no institutionalized mechanism for assigning a duty of HI to any particular state (or group of states), compulsory performance of the duty is impossible. Moreover, even if there existed an institution capable of assigning a duty to intervene, the scope of the duty would remain unclear in the absence of well-defined institutional rules and procedures. That is to say, agents (interveners) would be uncertain as to whether their duty would require them merely to stop violence or also to engage in reconstruction and reconciliation. Tan believes that these problems are solved if we simply identify an appropriate agent and delineate for that agent the scope of its duty. In other words, the solution is to turn an imperfect duty of HI into a perfect one. This is accomplished in two arguments: one identifies agents and the other institutionalizes rules and procedures.

His argument for identifying agents takes place in two parts. The first claims that states that "stand in a special relationship to a people needing protecting by virtue of their shared historical ties" ought to be the specific agent to intervene.[56] Here Tan alludes to the responsibility of former colonial powers or states that have some sort of "shared culture ... common history ... [or] other common ties that are unrelated to past injustices," that put them into a closer relationship.[57] The second asserts that if a state has "special capabilities," it ought to intervene.[58] These capabilities may involve military capacity, economic ties or special units trained for peacekeeping missions. The capability requirement designates the "best candidate, compared to others, for doing the protecting."[59]

These solutions, however, are suboptimal, and Tan believes that a better response to the agency problem is to institutionalize the duty to protect.[60] Institutionalizing this duty, he supposes, will allow "all states *in a position to do something* to coordinate their efforts so as to effectively discharge the protection of the duty."[61] By placing an organization, such as the UN, in the position of assignor, the agency and scope conditions can be satisfied. The imperfect duty therefore becomes a perfect duty.

I take Tan to be working within a Kantian deontic framework. For he claims that the "distinction between perfect and imperfect duties is central to Kant's ethics" and then proceeds to define such duties via Kant's *Grounding*.[62] While Tan's prescriptions are not far off the mark, the way in which he arrives at them is problematic. Indeed, the notion that we can turn an imperfect duty into a perfect one does not fit with the Kantian notions of perfect and imperfect duties. This might seem an unimportant observation, for who cares what we call the duty, as long as the take-home message is similar or the same? But this viewpoint is misguided, for it is only by correctly classifying a duty that we can judge whether the normative prescriptions for the duty's fulfillment are correct.

Tan's application of Kant's framework, though, is problematic, for he knowingly reverses a principal distinction in Kant's deontic system: the priority of agent over claimant. He notes:

> It might not be quite accurate to say that a duty to intervene is an imperfect one, for in this case, it is clear to whom the duty is owed—it is owed to the people whose basic rights are being seriously violated by their own state. Still, I think that treating a duty as imperfect on the grounds that no agent has been specified, as Walzer and O'Neill do, is not inconsistent with the spirit of the Kantian distinction.[63]

On the one hand, Tan's classification of HI as an imperfect duty is reminiscent of Nardin's understanding: a duty is imperfect because it "grants the recipient a substantive benefit that is indeterminate in form or quantity. [And it] is imperfect because what needs to be done cannot be precisely specified."[64] On the other hand, where Nardin correctly follows Kant in stating that imperfect duties do not specify content, Tan fails to appreciate Kant's prioritization of agent over claimant. This is important for two reasons. First, for Kant, *all* agents have imperfect duties, such as benevolence or charity, and all imperfect duties are duties of virtue. Kant's reason for leaving claimants of imperfect duties unidentified is precisely to allow *agents* to exercise their practical judgment and thereby further moral perfection.[65] The priority here is on an agent's ability to have leeway as to when and where to fulfill that duty. The prioritization is not on the claimant. Reversing agent and claimant undermines Kant's and Kantian ethics, as both require moral perfection via an agent's exercise of her practical reason. Second, on Kant's (and Kantian) understanding, imperfect duties of virtue take the "ends" of others and not their "rights" as primary. Where one has a legitimate right, either acquired or innate, then there is an identifiable claimant, and the duty is one of justice not virtue.

This can be seen more readily when one presses Tan's use of O'Neill as support for his agent/claimant reversal. Tan's use of O'Neill's argument is suspect because her argument is directed elsewhere. She is arguing that providing food to the poor must be considered a matter of justice, not ethics. Furthermore, her use of scare-quotes around the word "right" seems to indicate that *if* a right to provide food is truly a "right" it is a weak one at that,[66] and "the point of difference is that they [universal economic, social and cultural rights] must be institutionalized: if they are not there is no right."[67] If Tan is insinuating that all human rights are "manifesto rights," which appears to be the case due to his invocation of O'Neill, then a violation of them will "provide meager pickings" for redress. This conclusion points not so much to a duty of HI's status as imperfect or perfect, but to a fundamental problem of international justice. As O'Neill rightly understands, "if it is not in principle clear where claims should be lodged, appeals to supposed universal rights to goods and services, including welfare, are mainly rhetoric."[68] These appeals are rhetoric because justice requires certain institutional features for its instantiation. Tan's reversal of the agent/claimant distinction to support his reading of a duty of HI makes little sense because the original distinction gives meaning to the division of justice and virtue, not perfect and imperfect.

Moreover, Tan's claim that once an imperfect duty of HI is institutionalized it "becomes" a perfect duty is even more dubious on Kantian grounds. Kant does not believe that imperfect duties can "become" perfect duties; *they are different in kind.* Imperfect duties of virtue take the *end* of humanity (i.e., happiness) as the content of the duty. Perfect duties are, for the most part, concerned with the *right* of humanity. Perfect duties may take one of two forms: either they pertain to *internal freedom* (and are thus duties of respect)[69] or they pertain to *external freedom* (and are thus duties of right). Imperfect duties provide an agent with latitude (*Speilraum*) in how she decides to fulfill them; they are "wide" in scope. Perfect duties are considered "narrow" because they prescribe acts or omissions. Imperfect duties to others, namely benevolence, deal with "satisfaction in the happiness (well-being) of others," and the maxim from which the agent acts is concerned with beneficence ("making [the] happiness [of others] one's [own] end").[70] Because an agent must take another's end as her own and will a maxim in accordance with the moral law, an imperfect duty cannot be coerced. The moral worth of the duty derives its importance from the end and the maxim, not the action, and so coercion can play no part. Perfect duties of justice, on the other hand, can be coerced because they all pertain to the rights of others. Motives for performing perfect duties of justice do not matter, only that an agent performs or forbears from a particular action. This is why when an agent fails to perform her imperfect duty she cannot be held culpable for it; rather her character can only be said to have a moral defect.[71] Thus an imperfect duty cannot become a perfect duty; their contents and objects are wholly separate.

What's more, Tan's arguments for turning an imperfect duty of HI into a perfect duty of HI fail to address the issue of coercion, and in so doing leave a deeper question unanswered. That is, why does making a duty determinate with respect to agent and scope also make it coercible? He states that massive human rights violations, which would be the main determinant to a state forfeiting its sovereignty and thus rendering an intervention permissible, trigger a "need to protect human rights, which compels outsiders to intervene."[72] But identifying an agent and defining the scope of a duty does not generate a right to coerce. Something additional is needed. Tan's initial use of Kantian categories could provide him with the resources to address the question of coercion, but in order to do so he would have to categorize the duty as one of justice. The closest Tan comes to acknowledging that HI is a duty of justice is in his claim that "some duties are just too important to be left imperfect."[73] This does little to explain why perfect duties are "more important" than imperfect duties, though. Nor does it help to explain why justice is more important than virtue. Perfect or imperfect, a duty is a duty; fulfillment is not discretionary, it is obligatory, and for all intents and purposes, one kind of duty does not carry more "weight" than the other.[74]

HI as a perfect duty: Bagnoli

Carla Bagnoli represents the other side of the Kantian debate over a duty of HI. She argues that HI is not an imperfect duty at all; its content categorizes it as a perfect duty of justice. She claims that, because part of the categorical imperative (CI) is to respect the humanity within oneself and others (the humanity formula, hereafter CI_2), to violate it is to wrong someone. Humanity, for Bagnoli, is the "capacity to decide what is valuable and what is not ... [it] is the very capacity for rationally setting ends of one's own."[75] She explains that CI_2 demands that we recognize the humanity, and thus the dignity, of others. Once we recognize that "somebody is a person [that recognition] makes a claim on us: it demands that we respect such a person as an autonomous source of value."[76]

To respect others' humanity, she contends, gives rise to a duty to intervene in instances of mass human rights violations because human rights violations are nothing more than treating humanity as a mere means (a violation of CI_2). Moreover, she maintains that, under a Kantian framework, to interfere with a person's setting of ends without adequate justification is a violation of *Recht*, and the violator of *Recht* is subject to coercion. She also counters the objection that, under present circumstances, a duty of HI is "unassignable" and is thus relegated to an imperfect status. Respect for humanity is a duty of justice or right; as such, it "applies to all rational agents."[77] Yet she also claims that assigning a duty of HI (to states) is a political problem rather than a "problem of allocation" because every person has the duty.[78]

Bagnoli maintains that, even though everyone has a perfect duty of HI, fulfilling it requires answering the question of "proper authority." She argues that we must separate the normative force of the duty from questions of fulfilling or discharging it, as some individual duties "ought to be discharged collectively."[79] Morality demands that all rational beings have this duty; law merely deals with the specifics of assigning proper authority and delegation/allocation.[80] Thus, for Bagnoli, the duty of HI is perfect and institutionalizing it is merely a "political" task.

While Bagnoli's conclusions are on a firmer footing than Tan's, ultimately her argument is flawed on three accounts, all of which are ultimately interrelated. First, while she notes that "a lawful state is one in which this conception of right is instantiated through appropriate institutions, and informs personal relationships," she does not seem aware that her categorization of HI as a perfect duty requires such an institution *before* the duty can be categorized as "perfect." If Bagnoli is trying to remain true to Kant's texts, which, given her discussion and method, is highly likely, her argument overlooks the fact that a civil society must be present for perfect duties of justice to even exist.

She correctly claims that perfect duties of justice have, as one of their hallmark features, the ability to use external coercion to ensure compliance. In Kant's *Lectures on Ethics*, Vigilantius notes: "*Obligatio perfecta* [is] an obligation where the agent can be necessitated to an act of duty by the choice of another." However, for this to be "rightful" coercion, that "lawful state," or something that satisfies the institutional requirements of it, must be present. Bagnoli does not claim this. Rather she states that "Kant defends the permission to coerce as a *juridical permission*, according to which one person may force another person to act rightly, that is we may obstruct wrong actions."[81] She seems to be stating, as the reader is left to infer, that any "rational agent"[82] can coerce a state to stop its rights violations.[83]

However, this understanding of *Recht* and the "permission" to coerce is problematic for three reasons. First, for Kant, rightful coercion can only take place in a civil society. The "universal principle of right" claims that "any action is right if it can coexist with everyone's freedom in accordance with a universal law,"[84] and "everyone's freedom" can really only be guaranteed when "a will putting everyone under obligation, … a collective general (common) and powerful will can provide this assurance."[85] Thus "the whole of individuals in a rightful condition, in relation to its own members is called a state (*civitas*)."[86] Absent such a condition, "coercion" is not rightful. Coercion outside of a civil condition is not "coercion" in the Kantian sense; it is, rather, "violence."[87] States in the international system are not in a *civitas*, they are in a *status naturali*. Therefore, Bagnoli's claim that any rational agent can "rightly" coerce the target state to stop violating its citizens' rights is not quite correct.

Second, Bagnoli's claims about the legitimacy of using coercion against target states actually misses the point of about the correlative nature of coercion and perfect juridical duties. In other words, by focusing on the legitimacy of overriding the territorial integrity and sovereignty of the target state and not on coercing the duty bearer, Bagnoli misappropriates the object of coercion (i.e., the duty bearer). For Kant, *agents* with perfect duties can be coerced to fulfill them; we do not coerce the objects of the duty. Now, if Bagnoli wants to argue that states have a perfect duty to their citizens to uphold their citizens' rights, then yes, coercion may apply to them (depending upon many factors and Kantian interpretation), but that is not what she is arguing. She is stating instead that states that violate their citizens' rights are subject to intervention; they have forfeited their right of nonintervention. Yet we are not concerned with the target state; we are concerned with all the other states in the international system. Indeed, she claims that "all rational agents … [meaning] everybody, that is, the entire international community, is bound by the obligation to protect the victims of human rights abuse." If all other states have a perfect duty to intervene, then by Kant's account *those agents* can be coerced to fulfill their obligation.

This gives rise to the third problem: Bagnoli's discussion of "proper authority." In other words, if "everybody" bears a perfect duty of intervention, why is there a question of proper authority? Even more problematic is that "all rational agents" implies not only states (if she agrees with Kant's insistence that states are "moral persons") but people and international organizations (assuming the "moral personhood" of corporations) as well. While she may not want to state this, she in fact does, for all of those entities are "rational agents" that have the possibility of bearing a duty of HI. Which is why it is odd that she then claims that even though "everybody" bears a perfect duty of HI, they do not have the "proper authority" to fulfill it. She says that "although the violation of human rights calls for action, it is not obvious that any particular state has the authority to respond, especially in cases where the state in which the violation occurs is not aggressive and does not pose any immediate threat [to other states]."[88] While it is not immediately apparent why aggression or perceived threats should bear any moral weight on one's perfect duty of intervention, it is even more opaque to claim that an agent that has a duty does not have the "authority" to execute it. Indeed, there might be "easier" ways to execute duties, say by institutionalizing them, but that does not mean that an agent only gains "authority" once the institution is established. In fact, this seems to be quite backwards. Institutions gain authority because the agents bestow it upon the institution, and not vice versa. A state's "moral standing" is said to derive from that of its citizens, and international institutions' authority from that of its member states.[89]

All of these problems stem not from categorizing HI as a perfect duty as such but from the fact that HI is a duty of justice in a state of nature. This gives rise to the second major problem with Bagnoli's argument: a duty of HI cannot really apply to "everybody." Absent a civil society, one that acts as a power-equalizing mechanism, "everybody" cannot fulfill a duty of HI. Thus the debate over institutionalization comes back into the picture: a duty of justice requires legal, juridical and coercive institutions to assign, adjudicate and enforce duties, while simultaneously protecting all agents' external freedom so that they can fulfill such duties. Without these protections, many agents cannot fulfill their duties, and then it would seem that Bagnoli is prescribing an "ought" where one "cannot." Despite Bagnoli's claims that a duty of HI does not face a problem of allocation, it in fact does. The duty falls to those agents that are capable of fulfilling it, but deciding which agents are capable requires a metric for such allocation. Moreover, the insistence on institutionalization is not, in this instance, a "political problem"; it is a logical requirement for Kantian justice.

Ultimately, these problems are the result of how Bagnoli grounds a duty of HI: respect for humanity. Her first move is to say that "human rights are ways to express our humanity," and that humanity "consists in the capacity to decide what is valuable and what is not."[90] Further she claims that "a person is a special *locus* of value, in that it is also the origin of value."[91] She couples all of this with CI_2, to support her argument for a perfect duty of HI. But this reading of Kant is problematic.

It is problematic, first, because the concept of "respect" does not immediately ground a positive duty to intervene in humanitarian crises. As Bonnie Honig argues, Kant employs three types of "respect" in his works: reverence-respect, teleological respect and liberal respect. Reverence-respect "is respect for the moral law as it is manifested in the actions and self-legislation of others."[92] With reverence-respect, "the object of respect is not really persons but the law of laws [the moral law]".[93] Reverence-respect is not "owed" to people; it is a moral feeling that is immediately elicited from us when we witness an example of the moral law via someone else's actions.[94] Since it is not owed to persons as such, only some people awaken this feeling in us; but again, our "respect" is directed at the moral law. This type of respect, then, cannot be the ground for a duty of HI because Bagnoli claims that "persons," not the moral law, "are the locus of value."

The second classification, teleological respect, is respect for "humanity in our persons."[95] Teleological respect has "two facets: one is negative and forbids certain actions, the other is positive and involves an attitude toward others."[96] This kind of respect can be withdrawn when a person's "actions subvert or abase his humanity."[97] Again, it seems that this kind of Kantian respect also cannot ground a juridical duty of HI because this kind of respect requires i) forbearing from actions (negative) or ii) a moral feeling or attitude that can be revoked. Bagnoli's attention is on actions, not feelings, and those actions are positive (coming to aid).

The third classification is Bagnoli's best hope: liberal respect. "Liberal respect is the acknowledgment we give to the distance between individuals. It involves taking others into account when willing maxims and acknowledging their existence as a constraint on our choice of which maxims to will."[98] Persons, as such, deserve this respect, and this respect cannot be withdrawn either. Honig notes: "It requires that men relate to each other from a distance, as equals, and as bearers of rights."[99] The account of liberal respect is drawn from CI_2's insistence that a rational agent never be treated as a mere means. Kant's civil condition is one where "juridical enforcement of liberal respect for persons (respect for rights) disallows actions that interfere with the ability of others to will maxims and act in their own right as free, equal, and rational beings."[100] Moreover, "[p]ositive law ensures that relationships between person in civil society are conducted in accordance with juridical duties whether or not the citizens will morally that it be so."[101]

While liberal respect is the best option for interpreting Bagnoli's arguments, this reading of respect puts us back into the vicious circle of the requirements for *Recht*. Honig notes that the state, that is civil society, is required not only for liberal respect, but for "all three strands of respect" to "reinforce the 'veneer of morality'."[102] Liberal respect may be concerned with people's rights, but its object is one that does not lend itself well to Bagnoli's arguments. First, liberal respect is like "negative liberty" in that it forces agents to *forbear* from doing harm. This in turn does little to help ground a positive duty of HI. Second, civil society is liberal respect's domain. The international society does not have the requisite institutional features to maintain liberal respect. Ultimately, something more than "respect" is required to ground a duty of HI. This something ought not to be contingent on civil society, solely negative, directed exclusively at the moral law, and can be withdrawn. It is not respect that can do this, but rather Kant's concept of the innate right to freedom.

Justice not virtue

The most important classification for a duty of R2P (and implicitly a duty of HI) concerns the Kantian first-order distinction between justice and virtue. The imperfect/perfect distinction discussed above is primarily helpful as a second-order classification to understand what is required of an agent. While it canvasses a large breadth of actions concerning the welfare of others, R2P is primarily concerned with ending mass rights violations, and so is best thought of as a duty of justice not virtue. Certainly the preventive aspects of R2P, such as capacity building, are long term and potentially wide in scope, but the doctrine as a whole is still concerned with stopping or averting particular rights violations.

Yet it is no surprise that many scholars attempt to categorize a duty of R2P (and HI) as an imperfect duty of virtue because intuition and even common law tend to view helping others in need as a matter of benevolence. For Kant, the duty to be beneficent is justified on the premise that "since our self-love cannot be separated from our need to be loved (*helped in the case of need*) by others as well, we therefore make ourselves an end for others; and the only way this maxim can be binding is through its qualification as a universal law, hence through our will to make others our ends as well."[103] Kant is quite explicit that, where others are in need, one "ought to sacrifice a part of [his] welfare to others without hope of return … [and that] it is impossible to assign determinate limits to the extent of this sacrifice [because] how far it should extend depends, in large part, on what each person's true needs are in view of his sensibilities, and it must be left to each to decide this for himself.[104] Thus scholars such as Williams, Walzer, Tan and O'Neill argue that a duty to aid or protect is imperfect because of these very features.[105]

An agent's motives are also a primary concern when it comes to acts of virtue. To be virtuous, one must act for duty's sake, so in the case of R2P one's motives must be humanitarian. Humanitarian motives were strongly emphasized during the debate over a right of intervention; however, with the shift from a right to a duty, scholars (including Tesón and Wheeler) no longer argue that a potential intervener's motives are of primary importance because placing too much weight on them detracts from the suffering and the rights violations of the victims. If we grant, then, that motives are not important, then a duty of R2P looks increasingly like a duty of justice, and Kantian duties of justice are always concerned with rectification and redress, whether to victims, society or right itself.

We find further support for this line of argument when we identify the triggers for R2P crises: gross human rights violations. Following the Rome Statutes and the Outcome Document, a duty to react to an R2P situation is triggered when a state[106] commits genocide, war crimes, ethnic cleansing and/or crimes against humanity against its own people, and each of these crimes *primarily* involves fundamental violations of one's innate right to external freedom. External freedom, according to Ripstein, is "a matter of being able to set and pursue your own ends" without being "subject to the choice of another person."[107] This type of freedom, it should be added, is of a physical nature. It is freedom from the physical compulsion of another. As Ripstein argues, "depriving you of the means you use in pursuit of those [freely chosen] ends, or making you pursue ends you do not share, or using your means to pursue those [forced] ends" results in one being unfree.[108]

The right to one's person is a right of external freedom because one must have one's person to set or pursue ends. To see this clearly we can look to Ripstein's discussion of Kant's concept of "willing." Ripstein claims:

> In order to set an end for myself, that is, to take it up as an end that I pursue, I must have the power to achieve it. There are two ways in which I can have such powers: first, I have my own personal powers, which I have innately, that is my right to them does not depend upon any act that I, or anyone else, has performed.... Second, I might have powers that are external to me; that is, I might have means at my disposal.[109]

One's person is, therefore, the principal means one has to pursue projects. One is entitled to one's person because it is part of one's capacity to set and pursue ends.[110] Viewed this way, if my person is violated in some way, then I am "deprived of means I could have used in pursuit of ends that I have not set for myself," and "I am *wronged* because I am deprived of my ability to be the one who determines how the thing will be used."[111] The right to one's person necessarily entails one's innate right to freedom.

The role of justice in Kant's framework is to limit reciprocally agents' external freedom while they pursue their own projects so that no one unilaterally dominates (makes unfree) another. This is why Kant claims that "any action is *right* (*Recht*) if it can coexist with everyone's freedom in accordance with a universal law."[112] This reciprocal limitation takes the form of reciprocal coercion. Kant claims "right is connected with an authorization to use coercion,"[113] where coercion is the means to furthering agents' freedom by "*hindering a hindrance to freedom*."[114] In other words, B's hindrance of A's external freedom at time T_1 is incompatible with the freedom of all and is unjust (*Unrecht*). However, any subsequent action at time T_2 that *hinders* B's *hindrance* of A at T_1 is just (*Recht*). Moreover, "for the limits [on freedom] to be reciprocal, they must bind all in the same way; that is to say, they must be in 'accordance with a universal law'."[115] This is Kant's distinction between a unilateral, a bilateral and an omnilateral will.[116] Only those actions that conform to an omnilateral (and thus universal and general) will can be considered just.

Referring back to the actions that trigger R2P crises, it is immediately apparent that each of these crimes affects a person's physical ability to set and pursue his or her own ends by unjustly limiting one's physical person. Killing, *physical* destruction, *forcible* transfer of population, imprisonment or other *severe deprivation of physical liberty* in violation of the fundamental rules of international law, rape (*non*consensual or *forced* sex), sexual *slavery*, *enforced* prostitution, *forced* pregnancy, and *forced* sterilization—all of these acts involve the violation of one's right to control their person.[117] Each crime involves illegitimate coercion and the subsequent interference with one's capacity to act.

Crimes against humanity are fundamental violations of *Recht*, for they are the ultimate expressions of Kantian injustice: violating a person's external freedom by depriving her of her powers and means or using her powers and means without her consent. This is why scholars, such as Carla Bagnoli, argue that HI is a perfect duty: HI deals with ending mass violations of human rights, and perfect duties concern stopping or rectifying violations of the innate right to freedom. The content of the duty is squarely within the realm of justice, not virtue, and intervention to stop or redress such a violation is perfectly legitimate because intervention is a "hindrance" at time T_2. Questions of well-being and welfare arise only *after* an agent's external freedom is secure.

One might object here that acts that warrant intervention are concerned with both external and internal freedom, and that these acts actually accord primacy to welfare rather than freedom. While it is true that genocide and crimes against humanity do affect both a person's freedom and welfare, *under a Kantian framework* these acts are "wrong" because they violate a person's external freedom, thereby hindering or removing her capacity to act. As Sharon Byrd notes:

> External freedom is freedom from someone else's necessitating choice. If you are necessitated to do something, it can be either with irresistible or resistible force (brute force or threats of force). If your movement is necessitated by irresistible physical force, one cannot say you acted; for Kant "action" (*Handlung*) is broad in meaning, and when he means a voluntary action he speaks of a free action. Accordingly any physical impact on your person would be necessitation with irresistible force (not a free action) and thus a violation of your right to external freedom.[118]

If one were to embrace a different moral theory, say consequentialism, then one could argue that a person's welfare could be seen as the priority. However, under Kant's moral theory, acts that violate a person's external freedom fall under the category of *Recht* and therefore are issues of justice.

One might also object that acts that deprive a person of his means or powers are acts that occur frequently within states, and that this simply shows that most states are subject to intervention. This objection, however, is mistaken. First, civil society is supposed to act as a way of universalizing protection and rights for all citizens. When a state is systematically violating the rights of its citizens there is no way for those citizens to seek redress. The "normal" channels for justice are absent. The state may either be collapsed and anarchic (as in the case of Rwanda), failed (as perhaps in the case of Cambodia), or considered an "unjust enemy" towards other states because of its treatment of a portion of its population (as in the case of Darfur or Syria).[119] When a state's mechanisms for justice are present, then the citizens may use the law and courts to seek redress for rights violations. Most states, therefore, do not fall into the category that warrant intervention, but there are several that do.[120]

A provisional duty of R2P

We are now in a position to see why a duty of R2P is not a perfect or an imperfect duty, but rather a provisional duty of justice. Absent civil society, *Recht* is provisional, and agents do not have *perfect* duties of justice because there is no civil society. Rather, they have *provisional* duties of justice, and provisional duties are duties that some agents have outside civil society and in some instances of uncertainty (conditions of ambiguous right). Provisional duties of justice correlate with provisional rights, and permit exceptions on the basis of ability. Agents who can fulfill a provisional duty of justice must, while those that do not have the physical capacity are exempted.

If we follow the argument that a duty of R2P is one of justice, and it is a duty of justice present in the international state of nature, then it must be a provisional duty of justice. We can trace this conclusion to the logic of Kant's argument in the *Doctrine of Right*. First, he claims that individuals join a civil society in order to protect their freedom (and thus their persons) and enjoy their rights. Once in civil society, these individuals become "citizens," and each is granted certain rights (lawful freedom, civil equality, civil independence).[121] These acquired rights, listed above, stem from one's rights that existed provisionally in the state of nature, and they now transfer over to the civil society and become "conclusive," or peremptory, through the protection of law. Rights in the state of nature are still a matter of justice, and this is why they remain a matter of justice inside the civil society.

Second, the juridical state is, as previously noted, a priori necessary for the protection of rights and freedom. A juridical state, for Kant, is "the relation of human beings to one another which contains the conditions solely under which each can in fact *enjoy* his rights,"[122] where enjoyment means "free from external coercion."[123] In a state of nature agents cannot fully enjoy their rights without the constant threat of violence, and so agents enter a condition (civil society) to protect those rights. If someone violates a right in a civil condition, then that person is subject to the dictates of law.

Third, and perhaps more contentiously for some, if we adhere to Kant's framework, then rules of justice at the domestic level ought to analogously hold for the international level as well. In other words, if we have a command to leave the state of nature as an individual to protect and enjoy our rights, and the international system is a state of nature, then we must also leave it to do the same. He writes that "a state of nature among nations, like a state of nature among individual human beings, is a condition that one ought to leave in order to enter a lawful condition . . . ."[124]

The domestic civil condition regulates the actions between citizens. It enables all within the bounds of law to seek redress for wrongs done, and it provides protective mechanisms through its juridical institutions and police force. Crimes, such as rape, terror, torture, enslavement and killing, are adjudicated and redressed by these institutions. The state has a duty to intervene to stop these crimes and administer punishment. This situation ought to be no different, theoretically, for the international system. Unfortunately, there is in fact a difference. While states have a duty of justice to refrain from committing these acts, there is no functioning "state of states" or an international civil society to fulfill a duty of protection.[125] Yet this does not mean that a duty does not exist.

Following Kant's command for individuals to leave the state of nature to ensure the establishment of justice and the protection of rights, this command ought to have a parallel at the international level as well.[126] Since agents institute the state to protect rights, the state assumes a duty to intervene to stop crimes and becomes the "most capable" agent (through law and the legitimate monopoly on coercive force). Absent the juridical condition, the right to freedom and the duty to "hinder a hindrance to freedom" do not, however, change. The parallel stays the same, and so the duty falls, in exactly the same manner, to capable agents.

That a duty of R2P is a provisional follows logically from three facts about the metaphysics of Kantian justice. First, the international realm is a state of nature, and all duties of justice in a state of nature are "provisional." Second, intervening to stop atrocity and war crimes is the same in content as a domestic state's to intervene in crimes such as rape, torture, and murder in the domestic realm. Both acts of protection are duties of justice because their contents concern the innate right to freedom (and thus by extension one's person). However, in the international system, no civil condition exists, and so the R2P can only be deemed provisional. Third, the same moral impetus works on the domestic and international levels: exit the state of nature at all costs to secure and protect one's rights. Thus we come to the conclusion that R2P is a provisional duty of justice because it takes place in a state of nature, is concerned with one's innate right to freedom, and correlates to provisional right.

Now, one might object here that Kant clearly prohibits any type of coercive intervention, for he explicitly claims in Article 5 of "Perpetual Peace" that "no state shall forcibly interfere with the constitution and government of another state,"[127] and so the domestic analogy cannot hold. I address this issue at length later; for now I offer two brief rejoinders. First, intervention does not necessarily imply interfering or changing the constitution or government of another state. Moreover, if done with a state's consent, the objection is a non sequitur. The harder case is when state consent is not forthcoming. Such intervention (and in this instance it would most likely be military) can amount to a violation of territorial integrity, but there is no direct link between intervention and the creation of a new state or regime change. Second, considering Kant's cosmopolitan juridical and ethical writings, we might agree with Otfried Höffe that "[i]n view of systematic genocide, unknown to Kant in his day, it is likely that he would approve of humanitarian intervention, albeit only subject to … strict criteria."[128]

The critic might still object here that the international system is not necessarily an absolute state of nature, as there are courts and law and there exists some semblance of civil society. This is the objection Gregory Kavka makes to Hobbes: the choice Hobbes offers between the state of nature, on the one hand, and submission to an absolute sovereign, on the other, are not the only alternatives.[129] The prospect of lasting, meaningful cooperation—a middle ground between the state of nature and absolute sovereignty—is a viable third option. I concede that there is a wider range of alternatives, but this is because the Kantian framework provides a middle ground.[130]

Such a middle ground is the condition of private right. Private right is still a Kantian condition of right. It follows from the natural law and contains within it a "rightful presumption."[131] Thus there are duties of justice and rights and ways in which agents can attempt to resolve conflict. However, the threat of breakdown and injustice always looms large because there is no "absolutely rightful condition" (as there would be in a civil society).[132] The existence of treaty and customary law, and institutions like the International Criminal Court, International Court of Justice and UN, does not transform the international society from a state of nature to a civil society; it merely moves from an extreme version of a state of nature to a slightly more cooperative condition of private right and thus towards public right.[133] The international state of nature is like living in Wyatt Earp's Tombstone: private enforcement at the OK Corral is always a viable option.

The critic might still be unsatisfied and claim that Kant's system provides no support for a juridical duty of intervention; at most it provides only a command to abstain from hindering the "implementation of law throughout the world."[134] This is Williams's position, where he notes that there are only two duties here: first a negative one not to hinder the progress of justice and second a state's duty towards its own people to not commit such crimes in the first place.[135] However, such a position is at odds with all of Kant's writings about a tripartite system of justice, where a violation of right in one part of the world is felt everywhere.[136] Moreover, Kant's rejection of wars of extermination or subjugation on the premise that "this extreme measure a state might use to achieve a condition of peace would in itself contradict the right of a state" lends support to a reading where Kant would abhor allowing a state to subjugate or exterminate a portion of its population for reasons less lofty than perpetual peace.[137] The critic's rejoinder that Kant's only discussion of cosmopolitan legal duties is of those associated with the "universal right of hospitality" or the "legal obligation not to treat foreign nationals with hostility when they are visitors" in another territory glosses over many of the finer distinctions in Kant's system.[138] To be sure, in the preface to the *Metaphysics*, Kant claims:

> Toward the end of the book I have worked less thoroughly over certain sections than might be expected in comparison with the earlier ones, partly because it seems to me that they can be easily inferred from the earlier ones and partly, too, because the later sections (dealing with public right) are currently the subject to so much discussion, and still so important, that they can well justify postponing a decisive judgment for some time.[139]

Clearly, then, assuming that Kant's final and only stance on legal duties in a cosmopolitan order are tantamount to a right of universal hospitality is problematic at best. For his previous sections, especially the lengthy discussions of private and provisional right, apply to the later sections on public right. Complicating matters more, if the critic grants that a legal duty exists to not treat foreign nationals with violence, this raises an important question: who is enforcing this duty? As all legal duties require, for their very nature, legislative, executive and judicial authorities backed by a public coercive force. Whitewashing these finer points only compounds the problems of international justice.

A provisional duty of R2P applies to all states that have the capacity to intervene; those that do not have the capacity are exempted from it. Categorizing a duty to protect in this way does two important things: it relieves us from looking to the motives of the intervener and it requires us to assess capacity. Motives become irrelevant, while physical capacity and action become important. This conclusion follows and adds further support to the current arguments in the R2P and HI debates, but for different reasons. It follows arguments, made by Wheeler and others, against including an agent's motives in the moral calculus.[140]

Second, this conclusion follows the current progression of the HI debate by positing that physical capacities are a necessary factor in identifying those states that have a duty of HI. Two scholars who argue for the importance of capacities are Kok-Chor Tan and James Pattison. While I have noted at several points my disagreements with Tan, he is on to something. He posits that only those agents capable of intervening ought to be assigned a duty, but this is because of the nature of Kantian justice. For Kant, justice requires an outward conformity with *Recht*, and so we must have the ability to do or forbear from doing whatever *Recht* requires.

While an imperfect duty cannot turn into a perfect duty because the two are categorically different, a provisional duty of justice *can* become a perfect (or peremptory) duty. Provisional duties are necessitations to act and are, therefore, always unconditional for the agents who have them. However, they are provisional because the requirements for full, or conclusive, justice are generally lacking in some circumstances. Provisional duties are of a *temporary* or *transient* nature and require institutionalization of something—namely civil society—to transcend their provisional status. Thus, while Tan's arguments are inconsistent with Kant's (and a Kantian) framework, the idea of a duty turning into another kind upon institutionalization is something that can be explained using different categories that are more consistent with Kant's thought.

Some may object that my treatment of Tan's arguments is unfair and mere semantics. However, I think this is misplaced. Tan claims that:

> At any rate, what is of significance for my discussion is not whether the duty to intervene is imperfect in the technical Kantian sense but, rather, the substantive moral claim, following Walzer, that in the absence of a clear specification of which country is to intervene, it is not clear if any can be morally bound to do so.[141]

Granted, Tan does not seem to be too bothered by his (mis)treatment of the framework from which he draws his discussion. However, if his real concern is whether the moral imperative to intervene *exists* absent an identification mechanism, then comprehending Kant's taxonomy of duties is of crucial importance because it not only provides such a mechanism, but gives a resounding answer as to whether such a duty exists. States have a provisional duty to intervene, and that means that capable states—any state that is capable—has a duty to do so. Agents are specified by virtue of their capacities. We do not need to look solely to historical "special ties," nor we do need to limit ourselves to "the most capable" agent.[142]

Additionally, James Pattison follows Tan's conclusions to identify possible interveners. His "general duty approach" argues that all states have a general duty to alleviate suffering, but that in particular cases the "most effective" state should be assigned a duty of HI.[143] Pattison claims "effectiveness" should be evaluated according to five criteria: (1) sufficient military resources; (2) sufficient nonmilitary resources; (3) a suitable strategy for using both (1) and (2); (4) rapid response and deployment capability; and (5) perception of legitimacy by the people subject to intervention.[144] He also acknowledges that circumstances play a vital role in the calculation of "expected-effectiveness," noting specifically that probabilities of success can be affected by interstate relationships, and that if greater rights violations are occurring, then there is "more scope for an intervener to achieve extremely beneficial consequences."[145] Pattison's measurement for sufficient military resources includes:

> (1) a high number of armed, motivated, and trained—and, ideally, experienced—military personnel; (2) military equipment such as helicopters, armoured personnel carriers, and communications equipment; (3) strategic lift capacity (in both air and sea forms) to be able to move personnel and equipment to wherever the humanitarian crisis is in the world; (4) logistical support to sustain this force abroad (without its resorting to looting, etc.)[146]

Pattison argues from a consequentialist ground to justify his list of five criteria to identify a possible intervener, and then based on these principles assigns a duty of HI to a particular agent. His is an account based on the expected utility of beneficent actions of the identified agent. While I have argued at length against Pattison's consequentialist rationale elsewhere, his list of criteria is a starting point to identify agents with a provisional duty of HI.[147] We should also add to his list other nonmilitary resources and ample support from relevant practitioners and academics, as they also play a crucial role in the likelihood of success. Understanding a country's overall history, politics, conflicts and ethnography, and making efforts to take these factors into consideration in a sympathetic and nonpaternalistic way, will help to facilitate a lasting peace, while reducing fears of "humanitarian imperialism." This last nonmilitary requirement will also help to reify the fifth requirement of perceived legitimacy (for the target state's population and for the international community).

Ultimately, many of the problems associated with terming R2P (and HI) a duty stem from the interaction between the nature of a duty (a necessitation to act) and the requirements for a duty of justice. If an agent has a duty of justice, then many of the questions about agent, recipient and scope are already answered by the juridical system; however, if one has a duty of justice and this system is lacking, then we may know what has to happen and when, but we may be uncertain as to who should do it and how to make them do it.

Some may still object that describing a duty to protect as "provisional" makes no practical difference in international affairs and little, if only semantic, difference theoretically. Practically speaking, this label does little to answer the question of when unauthorized unilateral intervention is permissible. In terms of legality, we must acknowledge the tension between what justice requires and the weak framework of international "law" presently in existence. As provisional duties are merely temporary (*vorläufig*) and require, by their very nature, the creation of permanent institutional structures that will turn them into perfect/peremptory duties, we will see how this tension will persist absent such reforms.

Some might counter still that the current international system, headed by the UN, and regulated by custom and treaty, has the requisite institutions to act on duties of R2P. All that need happen is a streamlining of current institutions. This response is flawed, however. The international system, as it stands now, lacks the requisite institutional features to move from a provisional duty of R2P to a perfect one. These requirements include the rule of law, a neutral judge, a legitimate coercive mechanism *and* the separation of powers. Kant stresses that only "republics" accord with *Recht*, and republics are distinguished by "that political principle whereby executive power (the government) is separated from the legislative power."[148] In other words, even if we assume that the international system has a functioning system of law, the international system's courts do not have jurisdiction over all states, and the UN, while consisting of a separate General Assembly and Security Council, does not have a federated system. It acts more like a unitary system where the executive, in this case the Security Council, reigns supreme and the General Assembly and the Secretary General have little if no power.

Practically, then, we must refocus the debate about institutionalization. If we follow Tan and claim that a duty to intervene must be "institutionalized," and we also fall into many a scholar's prescriptions of identifying the UN Security Council as the requisite authority, then we run the danger of repeating this vicious circle. In the spirit of Kant and also the authors of the *Federalist Papers*, real institutionalization requires understanding the necessity of a federated separation of powers and finding a better system of international checks and balances. While the ICISS report gained new ground in identifying and helping codify a duty of R2P, it did little to move the debate beyond the stock answer look to the Security Council.

Conclusion

A duty of R2P is a provisional duty of justice because it exists in a condition of private right. The international state of nature lacks the requisite juridical features to categorize a duty of R2P as "perfect" or peremptory. That the society of states recognizes a duty to protect victims of mass human rights violations is a positive first step; however, it is not sufficient to merely recognize an ambiguously termed "responsibility" attributable to a nebulous "international community." Instead we must correctly classify the type of duty R2P is, and then we must fulfill the requirements of justice.

That the society of states has moved so quickly on its stance over humanitarian concerns is not something to depreciate. To date, the progress on R2P has been hard won. However, the practical problems identified by scholars and practitioners are the effects of recognizing that one has a duty of justice in a juridical vacuum. Communication gaps in large bureaucracies, executive paralysis in the SC, and ambiguity or contradiction over jurisdiction and authority over obligations to intervene all stem from the simple fact that the international system has no clear process for identifying the proper agents or scope of a duty of R2P. Moreover, the UN's continual approach of skirting the issue of implementation by putting off debates to another time or by consistently invoking the right to respond solely on a "case by case" basis perpetuates the problem. Thus R2P will continue to be plagued by charges of selectivity, of being a ruse for power politics, and nothing more than "mere words" due to its status as a provisional duty of justice in an international state of nature. States and the UN can determine for themselves what they ought to do and when, and there is no public enforcement mechanism to make them do otherwise.

The conceptual arguments over a duty of HI help to illuminate this problem. Thus scholars like Tan and Bagnoli help us to sharpen our understandings about the requirements for cosmopolitan justice. While Tan is incorrect that a duty of HI is merely imperfect and can be changed into a perfect one, he is on to something when he stresses the importance of material capacities and abilities of potential interveners. His intuition appears to guide him to the right conclusion, but conceptually his arguments cannot provide him with the means to get there. Imperfect and perfect duties are different in kind, and they are so because they serve different purposes in a theory of morality.

Bagnoli's arguments, too, help us to see that a duty of R2P is problematic when considered a "perfect" duty. While she is correct to identify a duty of HI as one of justice, she fails to follow the logical conclusion of Kant's writings that duties of justice require the instantiation of civil society for their universal fulfillment. Moreover, by misappropriating the object of coercion, she again fails to see how Kant's system requires public coercive institutions to ensure compliance of duty bearers.

Understanding the terminology and correct conceptual classification of a duty of R2P is conceptually and practically necessary. As Hobbes so eloquently acknowledges, "the manner how Speech serveth to the remembrance of the consequences of causes and effects, consisteth in the imposing of *Names* and the *Connexion* with them."[149] This reckoning of names with meaning facilitates understanding and provides guidance for future action, and this process begins once we grant that a duty of R2P is a provisional duty of justice.

The idea that a duty of rescue changes its nature once it is taken from the domestic realm to the international makes little sense. Which is why some, like Ripstein, argue that rescue ought to be undertaken by a state because it "is a need-based task that sustains the conditions of equal freedom," and is "a nonrelational duty owed to society at large, rather than to some particular individual."[150] If this is correct, then whether genocide, crimes against humanity or human rights violations are committed by a nonstate actor, a private person or a government ought to make no difference. Nor should it change the required response. A Kantian framework of justice would instantiate duties of rescue at the domestic level, and to remain consistent this framework should instantiate them at the international level as well. The structures are the same. How we do this, and what means we are authorized to use in undertaking this charge is the task of the next chapter.

3 Kant's permissive laws

> So force must be permitted, in order thereby to institute a right to preserve life. Here, too, therefore, the underlying maxim is that to institute a right, might precedes right, in accordance with a permissive law.[1]
>
> Vigilantius, Kant's *Lectures on Ethics*

Since *Recht* requires a priori that anything provisional (rights, duties or possession of external objects of choice) becomes "conclusive," that is, guaranteed through a system of public law, and a duty of R2P is a provisional duty of justice and must become conclusive or peremptory, we must consider how to accomplish this task. Kant's concept of a permissive law, or *lex permissiva*, gives us keen insight on how to do this. Moreover, its role and function does much to illuminate Kant's moral and political theory.

Kant's invocation of *lex permissiva* may appear simple, but the concept is actually difficult and problematic. This conceptual opaqueness has the potential to not only undermine many of Kant's more absolutist claims about doing one's duty, but threatens his entire discussion of justice as well. While *lex permissiva* puzzles scholars, it has by no means received ample attention yet. Those who do engage with the principle focus exclusively on two texts to explain it—"Perpetual Peace" and the *Metaphysics of Morals* (more specifically, the *Doctrine of Right*)—even though Kant discusses it in at least three other texts. What is more, two of these additional texts are concerned neither with politics nor justice (like "Perpetual Peace" and the *Doctrine of Right*) but with virtue. The failure of almost all scholars to discuss *lex permissiva*'s role in the realm of virtue is too important to overlook.

The chapter proceeds in two sections. The first surveys the current debate over *lex permissiva*, briefly canvassing the existing literature, but focusing mainly on Katrin Flikschuh and Joachim Hruschka's conflicting interpretations. Flikschuh and Hruschka's work is the most substantive in this debate, and so will be our primary focus. Flikschuh interprets the permissive law as a provisional solution to the antinomy of right. In contrast, Hruschka argues that it is a "power conferring norm" that provides a moral faculty (or power) to agents to establish necessary legal institutions. Such diverging opinions suggest that this debate is deeply important, not only to Kant scholarship, but also to those scholars attempting to use Kant's moral and political framework to solve real world problems, such as the debate over R2P.

The second section provides a new argument for *lex permissiva*, which clarifies much of the present debate. As I argue, Kant's *lex permissiva* is an exclusive disjunctive principle that one consults when one finds oneself in a "supreme moral emergency." The *lex permissiva* must be a disjunctive principle, operating as an "either but not both" proposition holding at one point in time, otherwise Kant's theory is incoherent.[2] A "supreme moral emergency" is one where following the dictates of morality or right, as if one were in the ideal world, would ultimately undermine the entire purposes of morality or right in the nonideal world.[3]

The debate

Incomplete versions: Gregor, Tierney, Szymkowiak and Brandt

Mary Gregor first noted that permissive laws have "to do with something that is permissible in the state of nature but forbidden by positive law," and that such laws are "found within ethics as well."[4] Gregor rightly stated that the permissive law applies to acts that "are not always morally indifferent," and that the "permissive law states the conditions under which a general prohibition does not apply."[5] Unfortunately, she did little to explain which actions are not morally indifferent and why there is a need for laws governing such "indifferent" acts in Kant's system. Furthermore, though she noted that permissive laws are found in ethics, her statement that permissive laws "give us a legal title to perform actions" does not seem to square with her other claims about them. If permissive laws give us a "legal title," then that title assigns to us a right, something that—by Kant's understanding—gives us the ability to coerce another person. However, the realm of virtue does not permit such coercion, and so it appears that a permissive law is something more than just a law that provides a legal title.

Ultimately, her discussion of Kant's permissive law in the realm of virtue is short, and she seems to define his permissive law differently here. She states:

> If some good end is to be achieved by the free play of inclinations, then it may be permissible to relax the restrictions that virtue generally imposes on them, even if there is some danger that the inclination, gathering strength from this exercise, might tempt one to vice.[6]

Yet such an interpretation is anathema to Kant's project because it is tantamount to consequentialism. A permissive law that permits otherwise prohibited acts based on the good ends "achieved" does not sound very much like Kant, and this explanation of a permissive law, as noted above, does not readily apply itself to her earlier explanation as something that provides us a legal title.

Another scholar who also grapples with Kant's *lex permissiva* is Brian Tierney. Tierney, a medievalist, is mainly concerned with understanding the role of permissive natural law through the writings of medieval and early modern political theorists, such as Gratian. His treatment of Kant's *lex permissiva* does take into account many of Kant's texts on the subject, especially the *Lectures on Ethics*, and the *Vorarbeiten zur Tugendlehre*. Like Gregor, Tierney reaches a conclusion that Kant's permissive law "must apply to acts that were not merely indifferent," and that Kant "went on to say that there could in fact be exceptional circumstances where a permissive law arising out of natural Right could authorize an act that would otherwise be forbidden."[7] Yet Tierney's treatment of Kant's permissive law ultimately comes back to the *Doctrine of Right* and the law's employment in the argument for the acquisition of property. His conclusion is that, historical context aside, Kant's use of *lex permissiva* "lead[s] on to paradoxes and problems."[8] These paradoxes and problems concern the justification of unauthorized unilateral acquisition of property, where he claims that

> if the act [initial acquisition] was unrightful in itself because it constrained the freedom of others, but was justified by the invocation of a permissive law, then a deeper problem arises. As Kant's argument develops, it seems that natural law is in conflict with itself.[9]

This provocative conclusion notwithstanding, Tierney's discussion of Kant's permissive law is rather vague. On the one hand, he seems to endorse the idea that the permissive law is an exemption, but on the other, that such an exemption renders Kant's entire *DR* incoherent. By taking the *DR* as the primary focus of his argument, he holds the postulate of practical reason with regard to right as *the* permissive law—and not *a* permissive law. The use of the postulate of right as a permissive law is only one instance of Kant's employment of this principle, and so the question of what *the* permissive law actually is, still remains.[10] Moreover, as he is trying to fit Kant's version of *lex permissiva* into historical context, the most he says in regards to identifying what exactly it entails is that historical arguments were "not quite adequate for Kant's purpose."[11] But if we are charitable to Kant and do not conclude that his writings are inconsistent and "insoluble," then, on Tierney's account, we are still left wondering what the permissive law is and why it is so important.[12]

More recently, Aaron Szymkowiak has also engaged with Kant's *lex permissive*. His arguments rely on Hruschka's distinction between "allowed" and "merely allowed" actions. Szymkowiak's argument for *lex permissiva* is that it is a function of Achenwall's hexagonal logic. Achenwall's deontic hexagon is a form of logic that has three possible areas for action: indifferent, permissible and commanded. So it is hexagonal because it has six possibilities: indifferent (or not); permissible (or not); commanded (or not). Achenwall, Szymkowiak argues, was concerned with rejecting the previous belief that acts could take only two forms: permissible or commanded. Achenwall wanted to show that some actions are also morally indifferent. Szymkowiak's position is that Kant invokes this deontic hexagon in his use of *lex permissiva*. This argument, though, is not substantively different than Hruschka's conclusion, and so we will not spend considerable time rehearsing Szymkowiak's arguments here.[13] This is so for two reasons. First, there is debate over whether Kant merely maps Achenwall's arguments on to his own or develops his own arguments for *lex permissiva* from a tradition, of which Achenwall was part. It is evident that Kant used the hexagonal logic; but that the content of the logical operators stayed the same as Achenwall's and did not change is not immediately clear.[14] Second, if such deontic logic was incorporated by Kant, and his treatment of it was fully in accordance with Achenwall (contra Tierney's point), it is odd that Hruschka, on whom Szymkowiak relies, would not have also invoked this in his own treatment of the permissive law. Hruschka's work on Achenwall *informs* his reading of Kant, especially since, as we will see, Hruschka argues that Kant's use of the term *licitum* (allowed) is Achenwall's, yet Hruschka does not identify deontic hexagonal logic as the *only* key to Kant's permissive law. The logic is important, but it is not the entire package. Ultimately Szymkowiak's argument does little to answer any substantive questions, and his treatment focuses solely on property acquisition and its relation to right. Thus, even if we took Szymkowiak's reading as correct, it still does not explain why a permissive law is necessary in Kant's moral system and how it ends up in the *Doctrine of Virtue*.[15]

Finally, Reinhard Brandt also presents an essay on Kant's permissive law.[16] Brandt's conclusion, though, is that Kant's *lex permissiva* is merely an exception to a prohibition, and so offers no further insight than Gregor or Tierney. Moreover, Flikschuh's argument for the *lex permissiva* incorporates Brandt's reading, and so we can engage with Brandt's notions by way of Flikschuh's more comprehensive account.

Flikschuh's permissive law

One way to discern Kant's notion of a permissive law is to identify the problem it is designed to solve. Flikschuh believes that problem is Kant's antinomy of right. "An antinomy is a conflict of reason in which two opposed philosophical positions derive conflicting conclusions from mutually accepted premises."[17] The antinomy of right, as Kant explains, arises when "reason is forced into a critique of itself in the concept of something external which is mine or yours."[18] In other words, the antinomy occurs when one begins to explain the possibility of rightful possession of "external objects of choice" (or, in common parlance: *property*). The antinomy of right, then, is a conflict between the freedom of the individual and the freedom of all arising from the unilateral acquisition of private property where both suppositions share the same premise of the Universal Principle of Right.[19] The antinomy is as follows:

> The *thesis* says: *It is possible* to have something external as mine even though I am not in possession of it.

> The *antithesis* says: *It is not possible* to have something external as mine unless I am in possession of it.
>
> *Solution*: Both propositions are true, the first if I understand, by the word possession, empirical possession (*possessio phaenomenon*), the second if what I understand by it is purely intelligible possession (*possession noumenon*).[20]

Empirical possession is dependent upon one having, e.g., physically holding an object. If I hold a book in my hand, I am the "possessor" of the book. However, as soon as Jane "wrests" the book from my hand, she becomes the "possessor."[21] Intelligible possession, or noumenal possession, "denotes a non-physical connection between [one's] innate right to freedom and external objects of [one's] choice."[22] This type of non-physical possession means we "have" an object but are not currently holding it. For instance, if Jane comes into my office and, unbeknownst to me, takes the book from my shelf, reads it, and then returns it to its former location, she has still wronged me.

The antinomy, as Kant writes it, is concerned with the use of the word "possession." He is concerned with the possibility of intelligible possession; that is, something over and above mere holding. Intelligible possession is necessary for the full and guaranteed exercise of a person's freedom. If it were not, possession would amount to the physical possession of the object, and that, in turn, would be dependent upon the morally arbitrary fact of a person's strength to retain it. The strong would be granted freedom because of their power, while the weak would be subjugated to the former's choices. Intelligible possession in principle, then, guarantees universal freedom for all.

However, there is an antecedent problem that Kant must solve before he can resolve the antinomy over "possession," and this is the way in which such "possession" comes into being. The problem is roughly this: the unilateral acquisition of an object in a state of nature puts that object beyond anyone else's possible use of it. In other words, by taking physical control of an object, one hinders the possible exercise of freedom of everyone else because taking that object out of the domain of possible use, *without the consent of all*, removes the opportunity of everyone else to choose that particular object. If Loki stakes off a water hole on an island, one of two sources of fresh water, and then attempts to protect the water hole as his because he was the first to find it, he has removed the opportunity for me to exercise my capacity of choice (in this instance). I now have no choice but to walk, however far, to the next water hole. Thus the unauthorized unilateral acquisition of an external object in a state of nature can be in direct tension with the freedom of everyone else.

However, the problem becomes even more difficult when an additional variable is added to the equation: the necessity of possessing objects of one's choice. As I argued in Chapter 1, external objects (private property) are necessary to one's freedom. For an agent to be fully free, she must make plans and pursue projects, and these can range from mere survival to perfecting her character. In any project an agent pursues, she must possess some type of external object (say, an apple to eat or books to read). Whether such possession is mere "holding" or "intelligible possession," on Kant's account any unilateral acquisition of such an object violates the freedom of everyone else. We are left, then, with a conundrum. If I want to be free, I must take external objects into my possession, but if I take external objects into my possession, I violate the freedom of everyone else (via the Universal Principle of Right).

Kant's solution to the antinomy is most puzzling: just divide the types of possession into empirical and intelligible. But why? This does not solve the antecedent problem of unilateral acquisition violating the freedom of all others. Moreover, such acquisition has three consequences (two of which we have seen already). First, the agent (as individual) exercises her freedom. Second, the agent (as part of a community) hinders the freedom of others by taking an object out of the domain of possible use. Third, and most perplexing, by claiming an external object as one's own, the agent now *imposes an obligation on others to recognize and refrain from using that object*. Now, we not only have the problem of possible intelligible possession (the antinomy), the antecedent problem of unilateral acquisition violating freedom, but also an *obligation* imposed on others by the (wrongful) act of unauthorized unilateral acquisition. Kant's ultimate solution to all of these problems is to institute the state whereby all provisional property acquired in a state of nature becomes "conclusive." The state makes possible intelligible possession, and further property laws regulate acquisition, inheritance and all other bundled property rights and laws.

Yet that explanation seems to rush through fundamental problems in Kant's account of property (and right). Furthermore, we have yet to see where the permissive law fits into all of this. Enter Katrin Flikschuh. Flikschuh's account is that the idea of a permissive law is a provisional solution to the antinomy of right and that the permissive law also provides the basis for political obligation.[23] On her reading, the permissive law provisionally authorizes "what is strictly speaking a violation of the universal principle of Right."[24] The permissive law allows for an agent to acquire unilaterally an external object without the authorization of all others (i.e., the antecedent problem).[25]

As Flikschuh correctly interprets, the empirical/intelligible and physical/nonphysical relationships of possession in the antinomy of right point to a fundamental problem with the concept of freedom. Moreover, she also notes that "Kant's abrupt statement of the antinomy of Right is exceedingly obscure and has given rise to much puzzlement." "Why exactly," she asks, "is there a conflict between these two conceptions of external possession, and what precisely is the solution supposed to amount to?"[26] She methodically works through the antinomy and finds that one can accept neither thesis nor antithesis, and that scholars who attempt to do either are incorrect. To accept thesis or antithesis violates a tenet of right, and so one cannot reasonably take a side. This is so because Kant's purpose is to find a solution to both, for choosing the thesis over the antithesis (or vice versa) fails to account for noumenal or phenomenal possession.

Flikschuh then examines Kant's use of "the postulate of practical reason with regard to Right" or, as she states, the *lex permissiva*, as a solution to the antinomy. The postulate asserts that "it is possible to have any external object of my choice as mine," and that once in my possession, all others have an obligation to refrain from using the object.[27] The solution to the antinomy permits acts of unilateral acquisition and counts such acts as legitimate. The postulate as *lex permissiva*, therefore, allows a violation of the Universal Principle of Right to establish the conditions for right (as it relates to the exercise of freedom). The postulate provides a solution, albeit a controversial one, to the antecedent problem of initial acquisition and the final problem of imposing an obligation on others, thereby solving the antinomy indirectly. The solution is indirect because Kant provides the postulate as the justification for empirical/phenomenal possession to be possible. Kant's direct "solution" to the antinomy is merely to restate the noumenal/phenomenal distinction in relation to property, but he must first employ the postulate to ground the antithesis.

Flikschuh follows Brandt's interpretation of permissive laws as "laws that provisionally authorise actions the commission of which are, strictly speaking, prohibited."[28] As she understands it, "Kant regards the commission of an act of injustice as a necessary condition of the possible establishment of the relations of justice between persons."[29] She claims that Brandt's analysis (and thus her own) "hinges on his reading of the postulate as a type of practical judgment peculiar to the concept of political agency."[30] While she does not elaborate on Brandt's concept of political agency, she takes it into her own account, for she claims that "permissive laws are tentative attempts at practical political judgment, the urgency and necessity of which subjects recognize and acknowledge, but the determinate form of which they are not as yet able to discern."[31]

On Flikschuh's account, Kant employs the concept of a permissive law in his argument for property acquisition because of human epistemic and practical limitations with regard to understanding right. In a state of nature, we cannot really "know" the principles of mine and thine because positive law has not come into existence. All we can know is that we are free beings, and as free beings we want and need to acquire property, but others threaten our acquisition of property because the only guarantee we have is our limited physical strength. Furthermore, we understand that as free beings we want to be left alone, and we ought to leave others alone, but we cannot take a step in either direction without violating either our freedom or someone else's. We are stuck between the proverbial rock and hard place to make a decision as to what right and freedom requires. The *lex permissiva*, therefore, offers a practical solution: it authorizes an otherwise impermissible act (unauthorized unilateral acquisition and the corresponding obligation to others to refrain from use) to establish the conditions of right.[32]

Furthermore, Flikschuh contends that because "reason wills that the postulate hold as a principle of pure practical reason ... then those whom the *lex permissiva* authorises to take external objects of their choice into possession must be acting within the constraints of reason. This means that their actions are subject to the demands of their possible justification to others."[33] In other words, once I understand that I am free, I thereby understand that other agents are also free. Once I understand that the acquisition of an external object of my choice limits the choice of others, I am then under an *obligation* of justice towards them because of *my* choice.[34] She notes that "the *lex permissiva* makes possible what one might call a recognitional shift in agents' perception of their situation, leading them from their unilateral claims to freedom to an acknowledgement of their duties of justice towards one another."[35] For Flikschuh the *lex permissiva* is a "provisional solution to the antinomy of right" as a "dark preliminary judgment."[36]

Hruschka's permissive law

In contrast to Flikschuh, Joachim Hruschka argues that Kant's permissive law is not designed to resolve the antinomy of right but to provide the necessary means (or authorizations) to establish particular legal institutions. In Hruschka's terms, the *lex permissiva* is a "power conferring norm"[37] because it grants us an authorization to establish "the legal institutions we need to be able to own and acquire property, to enter into contracts and acquire contractual claims, and to establish family relationships and acquire claim rights based on them."[38] Hruschka differs from Flikschuh mainly in two ways: i) he argues that the permissive law cannot be thought of as an exception to a prohibitory rule; and ii) he believes that it can be applied to more instances in the realm of right than merely the antinomy. This is important to note, as it broadens the possible applicability of *lex permissiva*, and suggests that further attention should be paid to this abstruse concept, given the divergent views about it.

To understand how the permissive law operates as a "power conferring norm" and how it establishes such institutions, we must first comprehend how Hruschka construes the meaning of "permissive." He claims that, for Kant, the concept of permissive can be either "allowed" (*erlaubt*) or "merely allowed" (*bloß erlaubt*).[39] He believes that scholars up until this point have missed this subtle distinction. According to Kant, Hruschka argues, allowed actions are "*not contrary* to what the actor must do," and so allowed "means the same as 'not prohibited.'"[40] In contrast *merely* allowed actions are something different. Merely allowed actions are "neither required nor prohibited."[41] This distinction is important, for if we were to distinguish between only prohibition and allowance it is unclear whether an allowed action is one that might also be morally required. Obviously, obligatory actions are, by their very nature, allowed, but the contrary does not always hold.

Hruschka then goes on to make a further distinction: some merely allowed actions are morally indifferent (*adiaphora*) while others require a permissive law, but are not themselves required.[42] He states that the latter kind of merely allowed acts "may need to be based on a rule," but that Kant does little to justify or to explain such an assertion.[43] Unfortunately, Hruschka does not correct this problem. He too offers little in the way of explanation of why a permissive law is required, but he does provide a full account of what such a law is.

Hruschka's explanation of the permissive law as a "power conferring norm," draws from Achenwall and Thomasius, as well as an early eighteenth-century philosophical dictionary by Walch. Hruschka's starting point is that the concept of a permissive law was not new with Kant, and that Kant had ample previous philosophical debate on this subject from which to draw. He then speculates that Kant would likely have been familiar with the "common" definitions, such as Walch's.[44] From Walch's definition of *permissio*, Hruschka suggests that Kant employs Achenwall's argument for a permissive law. Achenwall's permissive law, Hruschka states, "grants its beneficiary a moral faculty (*facultas moralis*)."[45] From here, Hruschka infers that Kant's understanding of a permissive law follows Achenwall's because Kant uses the word "*Befugnis*," which is typically translated as "authorization" but also at times as "*facultas moralis*."[46] From this etymological argument Hruschka draws two conclusions: (1) Kant's permissive law of practical reason relates only to *merely* allowed actions that one has license to do (such as establishing legal institutions like parental power and property rights); (2) that the permissive law "grants the beneficiary a moral faculty."[47]

This moral faculty permits something that otherwise would be morally, legally or politically impossible absent a requisite institution. Hruschka's example of such a situation is the act of buying condominiums in the United States during the 1960s. Since condominiums did not exist, buying one was not possible. However, once the law allows for such a thing as condominiums (and assuming there were condominiums built and available) people are granted a power (or a faculty) to exercise or not. "The law, we might say today, confers a legal power on its beneficiary," and so "[w]e therefore can call the permissive law a 'power conferring norm.' "[48]

His conclusions are drawn mainly from the *Metaphysics of Morals*, specifically the *DR*. As we have seen, Kant's use of permissive law in § 2 of the *DR* is aimed at justifying the possibility of acquiring property. Yet Hruschka rightly notes that although previous attempts have "incorrectly limited [their] application [of the permissive law] to property rights,"[49] Kant's use of the idea is broader than this. He argues that Kant's use is, rather, to establish the legal institutions necessary for right.

He is also careful to note that he believes Kant's arguments in "Towards Perpetual Peace" (*TPP*) are different from his arguments in the *DR*. Hruschka states that the long exegetical footnote in *TPP* defines permissive laws as "laws that provide exceptions to an 'assumed prohibition' ";[50] in other words, *TPP* formulates permissive laws as exceptions, tantamount to justifications.[51] This definition is closer to Flikschuh's. Hruschka's point is that in the *DR* Kant defines them as power-conferring norms, and that *TPP* does not employ the distinction between "allowed" and "merely allowed." He believes that Kant changed his usage in his later work, and that the *DR* was his final word. Therefore, we should follow the *DR* usage, as it is the final and most complete treatment of permissive laws.[52]

Yet why would Kant change his construal of *lex permissiva* between *TPP* and the *DR*? More importantly, if *lex permissiva* is, as Hruschka claims, a power-conferring norm that authorizes individuals to set up the necessary legal institutions for right, why would the *lex permissiva* make an appearance in Kant's *Doctrine of Virtue*, the second part of the *Metaphysics*? Certainly Kant is entitled to make changes to his own theory, but it is an odd shift for a philosopher so very concerned with consistency to have two separate meanings of the same concept solely for politics and then have it also show up in the realm of virtue—which is not concerned with legal institutions per se. Moreover, *TPP* was published only two years before the *DR*, but we have textual evidence in the Collins lecture notes that he was playing with this concept 11 years before *TPP*.[53] Thus, while Hruschka's work on the "allowed" versus "merely allowed" distinction sheds much light on the type of act to which a permissive law applies, his classification of permissive laws as power-conferring norms to set up legal institutions (and not exceptions), but it does not seem to provide the full picture. Too many crucial questions are left unanswered.

Permissive laws: disjunctive rules and conflicting *Rationes Obligandi*

While both Flikschuh and Hruschka provide keen insights into Kant's *lex permissiva*, they do not address the breadth of its use in Kant's thought. To fully understand the role of Kant's permissive law(s), we must therefore take into account all of the texts where he explicitly addresses the concept. Moreover, we must attempt to be at least a little charitable to the Professor from Königsberg, as he is not one to quickly change positions or tend toward inconsistency.

Once we take into account all of the nuances of his moral and political framework, we see that he regarded the *lex permissiva* as a principle that authorizes an agent to choose whether to engage in or forbear from a prohibited act (e.g., it grants an exception to a general law) for the ultimate purpose of sustaining reason and its ends. As I will argue, this permission is necessary for Kant's system to remain consistent. The permission arises in a particular situation, what I term "supreme moral emergency" (SME). An agent finds herself in an SME when reason commands a certain action, as if she were in an ideal world, but performing this action in the actual world would undermine the entire purpose of morality (the universal achievement of good willing through the exercise of practical reason, freedom and autonomy).[54] These rare circumstances threaten Kant's system with a fundamental conflict of reason with itself, thereby rendering his system incoherent. A permissive law, then, only comes into play when Kant's teleological concepts of nature and reason are opposed to one another in this way. What is fundamental to Kant's use of permissive laws is that it provides an opportunity for an agent to choose among different obligating reasons for action, and thereby extricate oneself from conflicting commands. Thus, there is not *the* permissive law, as some suggest, but in fact a *class* of permissive *laws*. For such permissions will be different depending upon the situation, and so we can have permissive laws of right as well as permissive laws of virtue.

Preliminary distinctions

To understand where Kant's concept of permissive law fits into his overall theory, let us provide a little background set-up. First, Kant divides his system into two realms: the noumenal and the phenomenal. The noumenal world is where man is considered an intelligible being, "i.e., as a being who must be declared independent of all influence from sensibility."[55] In other words, only man *qua* intelligible being is free because his actions are not determined by anything other than his own will; he is considered a first cause. The noumenal world is, therefore, the free world.

However, man is also considered part of the phenomenal world. Here man is regarded as a sensible being, i.e., man is "conscious of himself, his existence and actions, both through his outer senses and by means of his inner sense."[56] Phenomenal man is also affected by these senses, driven by them, so to speak, and, as such, is determined by them. Since phenomenal man is besieged by his feelings, inclinations and senses, his actions "are to be regarded as effects of preceding causes," and as he is not the author of these acts; responsibility for such acts cannot be "imputed to him."[57] The phenomenal world is not free but instead universally naturally determined.

The rub is that man is at once a noumenal and phenomenal being, or a being who is both free and simultaneously hindered (although actually not determined) by inclination. This dualistic framework is the reason why Kant formulates his theory as a set of imperatives. If man were solely a noumenal being, then he would be completely rational, a holy being as it were, and would always act in accordance with the moral law. However, man is not a completely or consistently rational being—he is influenced by his surroundings, his physical desires, and his senses, and his perceptions—and is capable of acting contrary to reason and morality. Reason must, therefore, issue the dictates of morality in the form of commands.

Second, there is an implicit distinction between the ideal and nonideal worlds. While the noumenal/phenomenal and ideal/nonideal distinctions do not map on to each other one to one, they do track rather closely. An ideal world is where all rational beings comply with the dictates of reason and morality. One might call this Kant's "Kingdom of Ends."[58] All agents comply with reason's dictates for the right reasons; that is, they comply because they understand what duty requires, and they take duty to be their motivating reason for acting. The nonideal world, on the other hand, is one where agents, for the most part, do not comply with the dictates of reason or morality for *the right reasons* and there is no "systematic union" or "connection" between human beings. Additionally, noncompliance can be the result of many causes. For instance, noncompliance might be the effect of rational miscalculation: I thought I was doing the right thing, but see after the fact that I did not have full information, and I made the wrong decision. Or noncompliance can be the result of the systemic conditions in which one finds oneself. For example, in a state of nature I might try to gain power over you, as I have no guarantees that you will not harm me if I do not. In this situation, complying with the dictates of reason, as if I were in a Kingdom of Ends, would more than likely harm me rather than help me. The point is that human beings as imperfect, finite, embodied beings, always, although not necessarily exclusively, inhabit the nonideal world.

We should also note that the nonideal world is a matter of degree. In most parts of the globe we witness widespread noncompliance with the dictates of reason or morality. In some parts, we do not. Noncompliance is not, generally, so widespread that we are in a "war of all against all," though. This may be due to the fact that we are either well-intentioned angels, or "a race of devils," or somewhere in between. But more likely, either by design or by luck, we have managed to institute systems that ensure outward compliance to a sufficient degree so that we can, for the most part, follow reason's dictates without much confusion or fear. This, of course, is the civil condition. The civil condition provides laws and protections in the nonideal world, and so the civil condition can ensure general compliance through enforcement. Indubitably there will always be some degree of noncompliance because the world is, after all, nonideal. However, through reform and education, mankind can continue to progress in hopes of approaching the ideal more closely.

A third distinction is between two forms of law in Kant's system: universal and general. Universal laws are "valid under all circumstances, so that an exception is therefore impossible."[59] General laws, on the other hand, "hold good in the great majority of cases," but not all cases, and so exceptions are possible.[60] Universal laws (*universales*) for Kant are those laws that provide underlying principles for general (*generales* or *allegemeinen*) laws. In other words, general laws are real-world instantiations or applications of universal laws. A universal law holds true without exception because it is a "supreme principle … and hence strictly universal."[61] General laws are the "real legislation" of universal ones.[62]

Kant employs an "universalizability" test for general real world laws. This test, however, is different from the classification of laws. Kant famously notes in his essay "Theory and Practice" that a legislator ought

> to frame his laws in such a way that they could have been produced by a united general will of a whole nation, and [these laws ought] to regard each subject, in so far as he can claim citizenship, as if he had consented within the general will.[63]

The test is for a legislator to check whether his laws are legitimate. Legitimacy of a law arises from whether it accords with right. As Kant claims, "all right consists solely in the restriction of the freedom of others, with the qualification that their freedom can co-exist with my freedom *within the terms of a general law*; and public right in a commonwealth is simply a state of affairs regulated by a real legislation which conforms to *this principle* and is backed up by power."[64] Thus, in *actual* constitutions, there are general laws tested for legitimacy via a thought experiment (considering universalizability).

An example might be helpful here. Let us take Kant's discussion of marriage. Marriage, Kant believes, is the only form of association where human beings reconcile the use of another person as a means (sexually) and with that person's freedom. This is so because one person gives full right over himself to the other in marriage and vice versa. Kant claims that "[m]atrimonium signifies a contract between two persons, in which they mutually accord equal rights to one another."[65] This full and complete giving and receiving can, for Kant, only be between two people. Monogamy is thus a necessary condition to matrimonial morality because one can only give oneself fully to one other person and thereby remain free. Reason wills this hold as a universal law.

However, what if one finds oneself in the unique position of being the last (married) male on earth, surrounded only by women? Kant might not be able to claim that monogamy within marriage holds as a universal law. This is because he also thinks there is an "end of nature," namely, procreation and continuance of the species.[66] In this case, Kant would claim that an exception must be made to the monogamy principle, thus allowing the man to take on many "wives" so that the species does not die out.[67] The tension arises between the dictates of reason and the unusual and extenuating circumstances of the empirical (noni-deal) world.

Although, in the case of the Last Man, how are we to know which law to follow, the natural law or the law of reason? This situation appears to involve a conflict of duties. The Last Man has a duty to his wife to remain monogamous, for the sake of both her freedom and his. He has made her a promise, and he does not want to use her as a means to an end. However, the Last Man also has a duty to ensure that the species does not die out. But Kant's system cannot admit of conflicts of duties. A conflict of duties in a rationalist system would mean the downfall of such a system, for one is obligated and not obligated at the same time.[68] This is why Kant declares that "[a] collision of duties and obligations is inconceivable (*obligationes non colliduntur*)."[69]

The way through the horns of the dilemma is to see that the Last Man's conflict is not one between duties; rather it is between the grounds of obligation (*rationes obligandi*).[70] Kant claims:

> However, a subject may have, in a rule he prescribes to himself, two grounds of obligation (*rationes obligandi*), one or the other of which is not sufficient to put him under obligation (*rationes obligandi non obligantes*), so that one of them is not a duty.—When two such grounds conflict with each other, practical philosophy says, not that the stronger obligation takes precedence (*fortior obligatio vincit*), but that the *stronger ground of obligation* prevails (*fortior obgligandi ratio vincit*).[71]

He further explains that "duty always contains a *ratio obligans*, or sufficient reason obligating to a dutiful act," but that an agent can have several *ratio obligandi*, that is "any other reason, insufficient [for a duty]."[72] While one may only have one duty, it does not mean that one does not feel a pull in the direction of the other *ratio obligandi*. One can still be upset, torn, or otherwise, but an agent has only one duty.

Thus the Last Man does not have a *ratio obligans*; he does not have an obligation. He has conflicting grounds (*ratio obligandi*). The permissive law presents itself here because of the circumstances: the ideal world and the non-ideal world conflict in such a way that following the dictates of reason may undermine the very existence of reason (in humanity). The permissive law does not tip the scales in favor of one *ratio obligandi* over the other; rather the permissive law opens up a space—for instance, it authorizes the Last Man to choose for himself whether he will take on more "wives" or not. Reason cannot obligate the man to forbear from performing act X, nor can nature obligate him to do X. He has strong reasons for each, but ultimately he must decide for himself.

One may object here and say that the Last Man has a strict obligation to his wife, as he made a promise to her prior to becoming the last man. The permissive law here is granting, if he so chooses, a temporary exemption to his self-incurred obligation. Once there are more men, the prohibition regains force. The Last Man has strong reasons to stay faithful to his wife (his promise of fidelity), but he also has equally strong reasons to perpetuate the species. Reason cannot dictate for him to violate his promise or to keep it and risk annihilating humanity, as there would be a conflict of duties as a result. Thus he has to choose. The permissive law, basically, exempts the Last Man from his duty to his wife, thereby making it not a duty, but a *ratio obligans*.

On my reading, reason requires a disjunction between the moral law, on the one hand, and the permissive law on the other. As Hruschka rightly points out, Kant, following Achenwall, divides his system into permissible acts (those that can be but do not have to be obligatory) and merely permissible acts (those that can only be *indifferent and not obligatory*). The permissive law governs the realm of some merely permissible actions, whereas the moral law governs the obligatory.[73] The moral law commands, and the permissive law allows. The permissive law in the Last Man cannot obligate the man one way or the other, for then the action would not be "merely allowed" but commanded. Hruschka correctly classifies merely allowed acts as those acts that are neither prescribed nor prohibited; acts that require a permissive law are a further subclass of merely allowed acts.

The definition of merely allowed applies to "indifferent actions," although, puzzlingly, Kant notes that "no special law would be required for" an indifferent act.[74] Morally indifferent acts are "indifferent" in relation to a moral law. For example, whether I decide to take my dog for a walk this morning or to stay home and drink coffee is neither commanded nor prohibited by the moral law. However, due to the fact that the permissive law arises only in SMEs, we might be hard pressed to claim that these actions are "indifferent," for they seem quite morally important instead. We have, then, a paradox: it seems we must grant that acts that require a permissive law are both indifferent (as the definition of merely allowed implies) and not indifferent (as the *DR* notes.) We can make sense of this seeming paradox on my reading because acts that require a permissive law are "indifferent" only in *form*. In other words, all morally indifferent actions are merely allowed insofar as they are neither in violation of nor required by the moral law. They are not, like the Last Man example, morally indifferent in *content*.[75]

Acts that require a permissive law are morally indifferent in that they are neither required nor prohibited. Reason cannot make them obligatory because if it did, it would undermine its teleological ends and come into conflict with itself. It would simultaneously command an agent to fulfill his duty D, regardless of whether fulfilling his duty D would undermine the entire purpose of morality in the real world. Thus we might want to say that merely allowed actions (*bloß erlaubt*) are, rather, *morally important* in the sense that they relate directly to Kant's moral teleology. We have to hold concurrently the dictates of the moral *telos* as well as the particulars of our situation. Thus, the content of an act that requires a permissive law is not "indifferent" to reason, but rather, due to the dualistic nature of a rationalist system, we must engage our practical reason and determine for ourselves—without command or prohibition—what to do.

Another example may be helpful here. Hruschka and Brandt claim that a permissive law allows for the coercion of individuals into a civil society. That is, coercion is legitimate to set up the juridical institutions necessary for *Recht*. Unilateral coercion, if we were to follow solely the Universal Principle of Right (UPR), is always illegitimate because it hinders the freedom of others. But to remain in a state of nature would despoil men of "all rights and abolish the very existence of laws," and would "erase the possibility of passing over into a condition of legal order."[76] We are thus left with two conflicting commands: follow the UPR and leave the state of nature by whatever means necessary. The rub is that without a permission to use such means, men could not fulfill their duty. Thus, the permissive law grants an authorization to use coercion to institute civil society.

An SME arises only when reason and the natural world dictate mutually exclusive actions simultaneously: X and not-X. The moral law (universally and ideally) states "not-X," while the natural law (and a tenet of reason itself) dictates "X." The moral law cannot command here; rather, what the agent requires is an authorization (to X or not-X) to do as he chooses. The prohibition (not-X) exists, but only in the ideal world *or* when the conditions in the real world reach a certain threshold (such as when the legal, juridical and coercive institutions of a state are in place). The prohibition exists but in a different time frame: the future. By contrast, the permission (X) exists in the "present." Only when conditions in the natural world either mirror or satisfactorily simulate the requirements of the ideal world will the prohibition gain force. Thus the moral law and the permissive law *cannot be at work at one and the same time*; they are disjunctive.

The necessity of a permissive law of practical reason is ultimately the result of the tension between the law of reason and the law of nature. This duality raises many problems for Kant: for instance, sometimes reason can dictate courses of action that would frustrate the ultimate purposes of reason itself, namely the universal condition of good willing. This is so because the empirical world presents human beings with unforeseeable situations, and these situations preclude us from following the dictates of morality. If we are to take Kant seriously on the dualistic nature of human beings, and grant that human beings live in a nonideal world, then we must accept the necessity of a permissive law of practical reason.

The reading that the permissive law is a disjunctive principle that authorizes agents to decide for themselves which dictate to follow is supported by textual evidence. Indeed, it is supported by every work where Kant mentions *lex permissiva.*[77] While few scholars refer to texts other than *TPP* and *DR*, many other scholars fail to take a comprehensive approach to Kant's writings on *lex permissiva.*[78] To remedy this problem, let us examine the entirety of Kant's published and unpublished works regarding the permissive law.

Lectures on Ethics

The first instance we have of *lex permissiva* is in student notes from Kant's *Lectures on Ethics* (*LoE*), in Collins's[79] note that there are laws that can be prescriptive, prohibitive, or permissive, "whereby actions are allowed."[80] We do not see this topic again until Mrongovius later notes that "*leges … permissivae*" are "prescriptive laws that forbid or allow."[81] Little is explained by these passages, and it is not until Vigilantius's notes of 1793–1794 that the fullest exposition of permissive laws comes to the fore. Vigilantius again reiterates the previous points, namely that there can be three types of laws, and that permissive laws allow something to an agent, except that Vigilantius provides us with further explanation. He states:

> For example, might must not replace right is a prohibitive [law], which is subject to an exception when all men are *put into a condition* where, by equal resistance to one another, they would *despoil themselves of all rights and abolish the very existence of the laws*; e.g., in *statu naturali*, where each takes himself to be defending the legitimacy of his own actions. Here, between them, *they erase the possibility* of passing over into a condition of legal order, and only the power of the stronger is then left, and thus might replaces right.[82]

Further:

> For if it be the case, that without might no right can be instituted, then might must precede right, whereas rule by right has to be the basis of power. If we take men in *statu naturali*, they are *ex leges*, under no legal order, and have no laws, only external power to keep them upright.… Should a prohibitive law be now issued, whereby it was not permitted to employ force, so that

> men might come into enjoyment of a *status civilis*, this would continue to uphold the state of lawlessness, and a condition, therefore, in which there would be no law, or no acknowledgement thereof. But *this is a state of affairs in conflict with the universal imperatives of morality*, and we thus have to assume that nature allows us, in this fashion, to bring man's free choice into the agreement with general freedom, by means of a universal law; and so here there is a natural law in effect, to permit the force employed.[83]

In these passages, we see that a permissive law must be present to ensure the *eventual* manifestation of universal freedom and morality. As we found in Chapter 1, universal moralization requires agents to enter into a rightful (civil) condition. If agents remain in a state of nature, then they erase the possibility of such progress. The state of nature is in direct opposition to the universal dictates of morality because agents in this condition have no guarantees or protections. The state of nature, therefore, presents agents with a supreme moral emergency, for if it persists any possibility of universal morality vanishes. The permissive law, then, permits agents to use coercive means to institute the civil condition should they choose to do so. They are not obligated to use these means, but should they decide to use them, it is permissible.

Vorarbeiten zu der Metaphysik der Sitten

In the *VMdS*, Kant takes another tack, but again with the same end in mind. He states:

> *Lex permissiva* is the law which allows something according to natural law, which is prohibited by civil law, e.g., to be one's own judge when insulted or having multiple women (polygamy with women) if there is only one man available or robbery in the danger of starvation …[84]

While this passage is only a fragment, we see again the situation of an SME. Reason cannot obligate a person to extinguish the very existence of reason. In the case of the Last Man, humanity would die out; in the case of a starving man, if he does not steal, he will perish, and so on.

One might object here that the starving man is only one individual, and so this situation cannot really be a supreme moral emergency. This is a fair objection. As this is only a fragmentary note, and it appears to be a casuistical question, it is difficult to discern Kant's entire meaning here; though it is important to note that numbers are not the main determinant of a supreme moral emergency. An SME is a situation that threatens the very possibility of reason and morality taking hold in the world. The state of nature is a very different situation, one that cannot be explained by "numbers." Now, if one is in a civil condition, where sufficient steps have been taken to ensure general compliance and safety, then an SME cannot result.

Doctrine of Virtue (*Tugendlehre*)

The meaning of *lex permissiva* is perhaps best indicated by Kant's explicit use of it in the *Doctrine of Virtue* (*DV*). Though he only mentions it twice, these two instances do much to explain this puzzling concept. First, he considers the duty of beneficence and questions whether one can ever exempt oneself from fulfilling such a duty. He thinks:

> For everyone who finds himself in need wishes to be helped by others. But if he lets his maxim of being unwilling to assist others in turn when they are in need become public, that is, makes this *a universal permissive law*, then everyone would likewise deny him assistance when he himself is in need, or at least would be *authorized* to deny it. Hence the maxim of self-interest would conflict with itself if it were made a universal law, that is, it is contrary to duty.[85]

We must note that in this passage Kant specifically addresses the concept of a "universal" permissive law. It is no surprise then, when he denies that such a law could exist. Once we recall that *only general laws can permit exceptions*, it is easy to see that the very concept of a "universal permissive law" is self-contradictory.

The most useful passage, though, is a short quip in one of his casuistical questions, where he toys with the question of whether a sterile couple is allowed to pursue sexual activities. While this example may seem extremely dated and puritanical, the way Kant formulates his answer is helpful for our present purposes. He asks: "Is there, in this case, a permissive law of morally practical reason, which *in the collision of determining grounds* makes permitted *something that is in itself not permitted* (indulgently, as it were), in order to *prevent a still greater violation*?"[86] In this brief note, Kant has again tied the permissive law to a fundamental tension between nature and freedom, where the permission involved seeks to maintain the ultimate purpose of the law of reason (universal moralization) in a nonideal world. While it is arguable whether this case is one of a supreme moral emergency,[87] Kant's characterization of a permissive law in this context provides much insight. It is "morally practical reason" that is employed to "prevent a still greater violation" of morality. Practical reason must separate the permissive law and the moral law because one cannot be obligated to perform two contradictory acts. Furthermore, he adds the crucial explanation of a collision of *ratio obligandi.* The couple has sufficient obligating reasons to X and not-X, but if reason is not to become "a pedantry regarding the fulfillment of duty,"[88] there must be a space where an agent is authorized (by a law) to choose for herself which course to take. Unfortunately, Kant offers no further advice to this couple.

"Toward Perpetual Peace"

Kant's discussion of a *lex permissiva* in "Toward Perpetual Peace" (*TPP*) occurs in two footnotes.[89] The first is the longer of the two and states: "It has previously been doubted, not unjustifiably, whether in addition to commands (*leges praeceptivae*) and prohibitions (*leges prohibitivae*) pure reason could provide permissive laws (*leges permissivae*)."[90] Kant goes on to claim that, indeed, there do seem to be permissive laws "that reason in its systematically analytic use sets out."[91] Any explanation, though, is not readily apparent, and the way Kant goes about responding is rather cryptic. He juxtaposes two cases to explain the possibility of a *lex permissiva*: the object of the law vs. the object of the permission, and natural law vs. civil (statutory) law.

First in regards to objects of law and permission, he states:

> For in general, laws contain a foundation of objective practical necessity, while permission only provides a foundation for certain acts that depend on practical contingencies. Thus a permissive law would necessitate an action that one cannot be compelled to perform, which, if the object of the law has the same sense in both cases, would entail a contradiction. But the permissive law here under consideration only prohibits certain modes of acquiring a right in the future (e.g., through inheritance), while the exception from this prohibition, i.e., the permission, applies to a present state of possession.[92]

Here, Kant separates "the object of the law," namely possession, into two temporal categories: present and future. The present time period here does not meet the requirements of right *in toto*, but it does satisfy a minimum condition.[93] Possession in the present may stand (i.e., is permitted) because "at the time (of the putative acquisition) [it was] accepted as lawful by public opinion in all nations."[94] However, due to the fact that the present condition in the international system possesses merely a modicum of right—and right, in its a priori universal form, requires full, public realization—a prohibition exists. The paradox is that prohibition and permission do and do not exist simultaneously. They do exist simultaneously in that right lays down a prohibition—"No independent nation ... may be acquired by another nation by inheritance, exchange, purchase or gift"[95]—while at the same time permitting putative possession of territory until a minimum threshold of international right exists. When the conditions for right line up with the dictates of the ideal, then the prohibition carries without the permission. Yet *presently* there must exist a permission, for the nonideal natural world has not attained the requisite features (international civil society with appropriate legal, juridical and coercive institutions) to issue a prohibition. For the sake of sustaining reason in the future, reason must permit something that it would otherwise prohibit.

The second case that Kant uses to explain a *lex permissiva* is its use in civil (statutory) law. Here, Kant claims:

> My desire here has been simply to draw the attention of proponents of natural right to the concept of a *lex permissiva*, a concept that reason in its systematic analytic use sets out and that is often used in civil (statutory) law, though with this difference, namely, *that the prohibitive part of law stands*

> *on its own, while the permissive part is not (as it should be) included in the law as a limiting condition, but is regarded instead as among the exceptions to it* … [F]or permissions arise only circumstantially, not according to a principle, that is, they arise only in considering specific situations. Otherwise the conditions would have to be stated in the *formulation of the prohibitive laws* and would in that way have to become laws of permission.[96]

A *lex permissiva*, it seems, has a function similar to, but distinct from, permissive statutory laws. Permissive statutory laws incorporate the exceptions into the prohibitive laws. But Kant's permissive law is separate from the prohibition. We can gain a clearer understanding of this reading by consulting the *Lectures on Ethics* (*LoE*) again. Vigilantius's notes have Kant explicitly stating that "if there are *leges permissivae*, they have to be accompanied with a prohibition."[97] Prohibitory laws, though, as we have seen, can be of two sorts: universal and general. Universal prohibitory laws are "valid under all circumstances," general prohibitory laws "hold good in the great majority of cases," and so "exceptions are conceivable."[98]

Returning to *TPP*, we can see that the primary text, which the explanatory footnote accompanies, makes a further distinction between strict laws ("*leges strictae*") and laws with latitude ("*leges latae*").[99] Whether Kant is thinking that *leges strictae* are analogous to universal laws and *leges latae* to permissive laws is beyond the philological capacity of us to fully determine. However, there does seem to be something that either hints at this, or at least makes a further distinction, that permissive laws are laws with latitude. Either way, the permission *accompanies* the prohibition and is legitimate based on the circumstance of a state of nature. The permission in *TPP* allows states to perpetuate a condition of injustice for the eventual sake of justice, for reason dictates that even though there is a state of nature amongst states, this is better than an all-out state of nature amongst individuals. A similar example is used in the *LoE*, where Kant claims that in a state of nature men have permission to use coercion to establish a legal order.[100]

We must make another important distinction: where Kant uses the term "exception," it is not the kind of casuistry that accompanies statutory laws. This explains why he juxtaposes civil statutory law to his version of *lex permissiva*. For example, in most states, there are laws prohibiting killing, *except* in cases of self-defense and, in some instances, capital punishment, or Trolley Problem-type cases. These are exceptions built into the rule, where one must look to each case of killing to determine whether it satisfies the conditions that allow a permission.[101] This type of exception, one that is built into the rule, would, for Kant, render the prohibition a permission.[102] However, Kant's use of "exception" is different. I take him to mean, *an area of a general law that does not apply in a special limiting condition (like a state of nature)*. This type of exception explains what Kant means by the use of "accompany," and the statement "the prohibitive part of the law stands on its own, while the permissive part is not … included in the [civil] law as a limiting condition."[103]

First, the use of "accompany" tells us that an object must be separate from another object, for one cannot accompany the other if it is part and parcel of it.[104] Second, Kant explicitly claims that the permission in civil law is not included as a limiting condition. A limiting condition (*einschränkende Bedingung*) here is distinct from an exception (*Ausnahmen*). A limiting condition ought to be thought of when formulating a prohibitive general law, but this condition, and the law that applies in it, is distinct from the prohibitive law itself. Making this distinction allows agents to know what situations trigger the permission *for everyone*. An exception, however, implies "freedom from a general duty or service *to which most others* are subjected."[105] Exceptions, or exemptions, *only exist for the person who possesses the relevant facts*. Permissions, on the contrary, apply *generally*. Thus an "exception," as permissive law, in *TPP* is a different kind of exception. Kant may be guilty of ambiguity, but his attempt to discern limiting conditions from typical exceptions is helpful.

This reading also makes sense of Kant's description in Collins's and Mrongovius's lecture notes that *leges permissivae* are laws that allow. They do not "contravene the law" because the act is "negatively good," that is, "not [in] conflict with the law of duty."[106] The permitted action occurs at a temporally different time, and reason cannot obligate X or not-X because it will undermine its ends or come into conflict with itself. Hruschka is correct in that the permissive law in *TPP* acts as justification, but so too does the permissive law in the *DR*.

The Doctrine of Right (*Rechtslehre*)

Scholars, such as Hruschka, look to the brief discussion of permissive laws in the "Introduction" to explain the later use in the sections of the *DR*. First, in the "Introduction," Kant states:

> An action that is neither commanded nor prohibited is merely *permitted*, since there is no law limiting one's freedom (one's authorization) with regard to it and so too no duty. Such an action is called morally indifferent (*indifferens, adiaphoron, res merea facultatis*). The question can be raised whether there are such actions and, if there are, whether there must be permissive laws (*lex permissiva*), in addition to laws that command and prohibit (*lex praeceptiva, lex mandati* and *lex prohibitive, lex vetiti)*, in order to account for someone's being free to do or not to do something as he pleases. *If so, the authorization would not always have to do with an indifferent action* (*adiaphoron*); for, considering the action in terms of moral laws, no special law would be required for it.[107]

We can immediately see from this passage that Kant's explanation of permissive laws points to the fact that permissive laws do not "always" have to accompany morally indifferent actions. This, of course, supports the present view that a permissive law is necessary for merely allowed and *morally important* acts.

The first clause of the last sentence suggests that permissive laws relate to actions that are *not* morally indifferent actions. The second clause reads "for considering the action [a morally indifferent action] in terms of moral laws, no special law [like a permissive law] would be required for it." This, of course makes sense, as morally indifferent actions would not need a law. Thus the question becomes: Which actions require a permissive law? As I have suggested, the actions that require a permissive law are those acts that, if one were to follow a precept of reason as if one were in an ideal world, would result in the undermining of reason (and its essential purposes) in the natural (nonideal) world. These acts become permitted because reason cannot dictate one way or the other.

The second widely cited use of the *lex permissiva* occurs in the *DR*'s section titled "Postulate of Practical Reason with Regard to Rights." Here Kant begins his argument for the acquisition of property rights and discerns whether "any external object of my choice" can be "mine."[108] On Kant's understanding, then, external objects can take three different forms: a thing, another's choice, or another's status.[109] What this ultimately means is that I can have possession of an object or thing, like the chair I am sitting on; I can have possession of another's choice, like a promise from Jane to help me move next Saturday; or I can have possession of another's status, such as the right (and duty) to take care of my children. All of these are "objects" outside of me, so they are external. Kant is concerned with the rightful possession of these objects,[110] and that, for him, requires proving that such possession is first possible.

He begins his argument by stating "an object of my *choice* is something I have the physical capacity to use as I please."[111] To use an object "as I please" means that no one else has possession of it; otherwise, I would have to go to that person and request to use it.[112] However, as we saw with Flikschuh's discussion and the antinomy of right, Kant wants to understand how we can reconcile possession of an object with the freedom of everyone. Kant states:

> This postulate can be called a permissive law (*lex permissiva*) of practical reason, which gives us an authorization that could not be got from mere concepts of right as such, namely to put all others under an obligation, which they would not otherwise have, to refrain from using certain objects of our choice because we have been the first to take them into our possession. Reason wills this hold as a principle, and it does this as *practical* reason, which extends itself a priori by this postulate of reason.[113]

Later in §16 Kant states that "provisional acquisition, however, needs and gains the favor of a law (*lex permissiva*) for determining the limits of possible rightful possession."[114] The last explicit reference to *lex permissiva* follows in §22, where he states that a "natural permissive law" provides a "favor" for the acquisition of a right to a person (really a person's status).[115] In each of these passages, Kant discusses acquisition of external objects or property. The latter two passages refer back to Kant's "Postulate of Practical Reason with Regard to Right" as a *lex permissiva*. I forgo much exegetical interpretation on these last three instances of *lex permissiva* because Flikschuh's argument and interpretation appear correct. However, we must look to whether the postulate and the *lex permissiva* are the same thing, as some seem to suggest, or whether the postulate is just that, a postulate, and, as such, merely an *instance of* a permissive law.

In favor of the present reading, Kant explicitly states that "the postulate can be called *a* permissive law." The postulate is one instance of a permissive law. Possession of objects must be possible because I must use objects in the pursuit of my projects. Some projects may also require that I do not have merely the use of these objects, but sole possession of them. Reason requires this. However, the UPR states that if I exercise my freedom and take an object, then I am effectively taking something that another agent may also use. I restrict her freedom because I have limited her capacity to choose.

The even stickier wicket is the second and third clauses of the first sentence: "which gives us an authorization that could not be got from mere concepts of right as such, namely to put all others under an obligation, which they would not have otherwise have …" I am interested neither in the coherence of Kant's argument for property nor whether first occupancy and *res nullis* justify initial acquisition. What does concern us here is the use of the postulate as a permissive law. These second and third clauses provide us further insight into *lex permissiva*, and they also seem to tidy up some lingering questions about how I can obligate others without their free assent.

First, Hruschka is correct here; a permissive law does provide an authorization to do something. That is, it provides for a faculty, and that faculty gives us an authorization (or an allowance) to choose to do (or not do) something. We should expand his point further, though, and say that this faculty is due to reason, that is *practical reason*, and not "mere concepts of right as such."

For Kant, an a priori deduction of "mere concepts of right as such" (like the *DR*) takes as its starting point assumptions about the moral worth of human beings, their innate right to freedom and three noncontingent facts about the empirical world (time, space and the spherical shape of the earth's surface). This deduction is therefore concerned with determining what is "right," what is necessary for right, and what holds in the ideal world. It does not take into consideration contingent facts. If we were to try to derive a permissive law from this framework, we could never do so *because* a permissive law is necessary due to the tension between the ideal and nonideal worlds, which is due to contingent facts. Concepts of right *as such*, are ideal, but permissive laws are necessary because of nonideal contingencies. If one is not allowed to factor into the equation contingent facts about the nonideal world, one could never see the need for or deduce a principle designed to mitigate the effects of such a world. One needs to move beyond the ideal in order to understand the necessity of a permissive law.

Thus we must move beyond "mere concepts of right as such" to the realm of practical reason. Practical reason is exercised in

> the practical sphere [where] it responds to inclinations by generating principles of action or maxims, taking the objects of empirical desire into account in setting ends, selecting policies of action for their achievement, and forming an idea of our happiness in relation to which actions can be judged regarding the agent's self-interest.[116]

This is why Kant claims that "Reason wills that this [postulate] hold as a principle, and it does this as *practical* reason."

Even if we grant that it is practical reason requiring a permissive law, one that allows agents to choose to act in a certain way, it is still not clear why any of those actions would impose an obligation on others. In the case of the postulate, Flikschuh argues that it is reflective judgment that places an obligation on us, and I think this is, in a sense, correct. If a permissive law is thought of as a principle that authorizes an agent in a nonideal world to choose which action to take when reason threatens to undermine its own existence, then one sees that by consulting a permissive law an agent is required to use his practical reason and judge whether to act or forbear from action. The permissive law encourages practical reason's exercise and thus reflective judgment. This, we could say, has the result that reason imposes an obligation on us, and it does this as practical reason. However, I think this reading is a bit of a stretch. If Flikschuh is purporting to make a "Kantian" (as opposed to Kant's) argument, then this stretch is not a problem; if, however, she is attributing this argument to Kant, that is another matter.

The obligation, at least in the instance of the postulate, is incurred by the fact of possession of an object, and is not incurred by the reflective judgment of others. I stated earlier that Kant's argument for original acquisition of property is not the main focus of this chapter. However, the issue of obligation is a "thorn" for Kant *in this matter*, that is, the matter of rights to external objects of choice. The necessity of a permissive law does not entail that such a law always imposes an obligation on others (as the cases in ethics make manifest). Vigilantius explains:

> Between *having the right* to do this or that, and *having a right* to something, Professor Kant distinguishes as follows. A subject may be granted license to do a thing, and yet it may contain merely the possibility (namely, where the right appears by reason of the object, as opposed to any actual object of right); but in that case the subject still does not *possess the right to do* anything. [It is merely provisional right] This is equivalent to the term *jus illi competit*, i.e., he has permission to act, i.e., he does no wrong in engaging the action, e.g., to take possession of a thing that belongs to nobody. But a subject *has a right* as soon as he has something in regard to whose use he can do or omit as he wills. Here an object is present, and not merely the right to act thus, in and for itself. To have a right therefore already presupposes an acquisition, and thus the possession of a thing, or a promise on another's part, over which promise or thing I am able to dispose and of which I can make use.[117]

The obligation incurred is not due to the postulate as a permissive law. The obligation is (provisionally) incurred because of the necessity of civil society. Thus Hruschka is correct on this point: it is "Kant's assumption of the universal united will ... in anticipation of the move to a civil social order (*bürgerliche Gesellschaft*) or state that imposes an obligation to recognize the property rights of others."[118] To this I would add that the obligation is *provisional*, in that I have strong reasons, all things considered, to recognize others' property rights, though "I am ... not under [an] obligation to leave external objects belonging to others untouched unless everyone else provides me assurance that he will behave in accordance with the same principle with regard to what is mine."[119] The obligation does not become perfect until I am in a civil society; however, the obligation is initially and provisionally imposed once a person takes possession of a specific object of her choice.

Flikschuh is correct that reflective judgment is part and parcel of practical reason. We come to know the moral law by the "fact of reason," which is our own self-awareness that also gives rise to respectful awareness of others. We then act morally when we conform our maxims to the moral law, and doing so requires that we take others into consideration via reflective judgment. However, this is not how we come to have an obligation to recognize and refrain from other's property.

Conclusion

Kant's *lex permissiva* does not apply only to his arguments for property. Indeed, Hruschka is correct to point this out. Kant's use of it spans, and is necessary for, his entire moral theory. This is why one must look at Kant's works comprehensively, and also why each scholar's interpretation is correct in some way. Only by synthesizing this body of commentary, as well as looking at the entirety of Kant's work, can we come to see the full picture.

Flikschuh is correct to acknowledge that the postulate, as an instance of a permissive law, is a solution to the antinomy of right. Possession of external objects of choice is necessary for the exercise of reason and freedom, but such initial acquisition threatens the UPR. The postulate as a permissive law authorizes such acquisition, and only the institution of civil society can fully reconcile the freedom of each with the freedom of all. Moreover, Kant's typical explanation of solving an antinomy by dividing the problem into noumenal vs. phenomenal distinctions does little to solve the antinomy of right because the antinomy is the result of this very division. Reason and freedom are faced with the possibility of "practical annihilation"; they are in an SME.

Hruschka, likewise, presents us with many correct readings of Kant. A permissive law is necessary to institute civil society, to first acquire property, and to delay premature constitutional reform. Permissive laws obtain in these situations and authorize agents to choose whether to establish such institutions or reform them. However, permissive laws do not apply only in the realm of right. As we have also seen, permissive laws apply in virtue too.

Moreover, Hruschka's original insight into the merely allowed/allowed distinction, and further subdivision of merely allowed actions into morally indifferent actions and morally indifferent actions that require a permissive law, is central to the present reading. Though, while Hruschka does not think that permissive laws are "morally indifferent" but a class of merely allowed actions, I contend that they are "indifferent" in a sense; that is, they are neither required nor prohibited by the moral law. They are not, however, "indifferent" in the everyday sense in that they have no moral import. Quite the contrary: acts that require a permissive law are morally important actions, but due to the issue of consistency, they cannot be required nor prohibited. Hruschka's interpretation lays this foundation, but he does not go far enough. He limits his application of *lex permissiva* to the establishment of legal institutions, and this, as we have seen, is not the whole story. Permissive laws exist in ethics too, thus their power must be more than to "introduce or license certain rights."[120]

It is not the case, therefore, that Kant employs two different concepts of permissive law (one in *TPP* and one in the *DR*). As I have argued, the concept of *lex permissiva* is the same in each instance Kant uses it. However, in each text, he describes the features of the permission differently, and each permission has a different object in its view. Does this mean that Kant is guilty of not being crystal clear? Certainly. Does he fail to provide us with one fully explicated account of *lex permissiva*? Absolutely. However, as I suggest, each of his uses points to the same fundamental problem and the same solution.

Until now, no one has provided the entire picture of the permissive law and given a resounding answer to the question of its purpose. As interest in Kant's political philosophy grows, scholars are encountering his use of *lex permissiva* more and more. Indeed, this is seen by the recent attention paid to it. Nevertheless, these arguments are still myopic in that they do not attempt to locate the *lex permissiva* in Kant's overall moral system. These scholars remain, at present, tied to the arguments in *TPP* and the *DR*.

This reading of the *lex permissiva* is the first step in understanding the constraints of justice in the real world. If we are to let Kant guide our understanding of what justice requires—such as the protection of human rights—we must fully understand many of the conflicts that can result due to the nonideal character of our world. In the next chapter we will see exactly how this plays out in relation to R2P. We will do so by first applying the argument for *lex permissiva* to the case of a provisional duty of R2P. Second, we must contend with the major objection to my argument for *lex permissiva*: that it opens up a realm of permissiveness that is too broad for Kant's theory to support and that the case of a duty of R2P highlights this excessive broadness perfectly.

4 Permissible coercion

> They rounded up all the villagers. They separated men from women. To the women they said, "You may go to the border," and they put us men in two big rooms. They said, "Now NATO can save you," and they started to shoot. And when they finished shooting they covered us with straw and corn and set it on fire. We were one hundred and twelve people. I survived with one other man.[1]

> When we arrived, I looked at the school across the street, and there were children, I don't know how many, forty, sixty, eighty children stacked up outside who had all been chopped up with machetes. Some of their mothers had heard them screaming and had come running, and the militia had killed them, too. We got out of the vehicle and entered the church. There we found 150 people, dead mostly, though some were still groaning, who had been attacked the night before. The Polish priests told us it had been incredibly well organized. The Rwandan army had cleared out the area, the gendarmerie had rounded up all the Tutsi, and the militia had hacked them all to death.[2]

Later in the day, when Major Beardsley went back to that same Rwandan village, he did not see survivors; the militia managed to clear all roadblocks and kill the remaining people.[3] Moreover, Mr. Krashishi's experience in Kosovo was not the exception but the rule: both of these heartrending events occurred at the hands of states or the hands of state-sanctioned representatives. These states, or their functioning rulers, selected a portion of the population to systematically murder. Their crimes were carried out with impeccable organization and coordination. Indeed, to kill so effectively on such a large scale requires such organization and coordination, and because of this, too often these crimes are perpetrated not by nonstate actors (though this is certainly possible) but by states—governments—against the people they are supposed to protect. In situations like these, situations where the possibilities of law, order and protection vanish, we must ask whether morality itself is in peril. Indeed, in such extreme circumstances, we ought to ask ourselves: Should we follow the precepts of law and justice, or are we faced with a situation so "unusual," so "horrifying," that different actions—perhaps traditionally impermissible actions—are required?[4]

Winston Churchill once said:

> The letter of the law must not in supreme emergency obstruct those who are charged with its protection and enforcement. It would not be right or rational that the aggressive Power should gain one set of advantages by tearing up all the laws, and another set by sheltering behind the innate respect for law of its opponents. Humanity, rather than legality, must be our guide.[5]

This is the sentiment that underlies a Kantian supreme moral emergency (SME). Instead of norms or the rule of law requiring disobedience, as in the Churchill example, it is now juridical precepts that must sometimes be disobeyed, not for just any reason, but for the sake of morality itself. Human beings, imperfectly rational animals that we are, are sometimes faced with conditions (some of our own making, some not) that threaten our very existence and humanity.

There are a variety of circumstances in which SMEs might arise (for instance, Kant's Last Man example or the threat of global destruction due to nuclear war). It is our job now, though, to discern whether the international system presents us with another example of an SME. In other words, does the amount and variety of R2P crises communicate that the (non)juridical condition of international society threatens the ability for justice to take hold in the world?

I argue the affirmative. The international system is a state of nature, and due to its nonjuridical status *and* the frequency and severity of human rights violations, the international system finds itself in an international supreme moral emergency (hereafter iSME). This iSME is analogous to the domestic supreme moral emergency (hereafter dSME) witnessed between individuals in a state of nature. In a state of nature between individuals, people must, for the sake of justice and morality, form a civil society to protect their basic rights. Functionally, the situation in the international system is no different. As individuals must found a civil condition, so too must states. The only difference between the arguments for state formation at the individual level and at the state level concern Kant's "Presumption of Badness."

The argument proceeds in three sections. Section I examines the Presumption of Badness and the other conditions that trigger the dSME. It argues against Byrd and Hruschka's use of Kant's presumption to justify coercion of states into a "state of states," noting that a presumption cannot hold against artificial moral agents (such as states). Section II posits, however, that the same conditions that trigger a dSME also give rise to an iSME. The important difference between the two concerns only the use of empirical evidence to make a *conjecture* about the intentions and future behavior of states. Finally, Section III contends with objections that the international system has progressed to a degree that makes coercion of states illegitimate.

Up to this point, I have tried to remain true to Kant's texts by providing substantial exegetical support for the argument for a provisional duty of R2P and what I take to be Kant's understanding of *lex permissiva*. At this point, however, we must diverge slightly from interpretation of Kant's texts and provide Kant*ian* prescriptions to address the requirements of a duty of R2P. Obviously, Kant did not address the evils of genocide and gross crimes against humanity, and his stalwart faith in the domestic state ultimately weakens portions of his theory's applicability to current international affairs.

The logic of justice

> Well, I've now come to what we likened to the greatest wave. But I say what I have to say, even if the wave is a wave of laughter that will simply drown me in ridicule and contempt.... Until philosophers rule as kings or those who are now called kings and leading men genuinely and adequately philosophize, that is, until political power and philosophy entirely coincide ... cities will have no rest from evils ... nor, I think, will the human race.
>
> (Plato, Republic[6])

> The Platonic Republic has become proverbial as an example—and a striking one—of imaginary perfection, such as can exist only in the brain of the idle thinker; and Brucker ridicules the philosopher for maintaining that a prince can never govern well, unless he is participant in the ideas. But we should do better to follow up this thought and, where this admirable thinker leaves us without assistance, employ new efforts to place it in clearer light, rather than carelessly fling it aside as useless, under the very miserable and pernicious pretext of impracticability.... Now although a perfect state may never exist, the idea is not on that account the less just, which holds up this maximum as the archetype or standard of a constitution, in order to bring legislative government always nearer and nearer to the greatest possible perfection.
>
> (Immanuel Kant, *The Critique of Pure Reason*[7])

Since reason requires that justice become universal, and a state of nature presents us with an SME, the permissive law of practical reason allows agents to force all others into a civil condition. This conclusion is not controversial; however, when the same logic is applied to the international system, coercion is typically judged to be impermissible, and a state of nature, while undesirable, is not anathema to the pursuits of justice.[8] Indeed, the vast majority of Kant scholars adamantly object to the use of coercion in international politics, claiming that Kant could not condone such measures. In sharp contrast to this position, Byrd and Hruschka passionately claim the contrary: that Kant's theory actually requires the coercion of states into a "state of states" (*Völkerstaat*). How can such disagreement over such a fundamental issue exist? The simple answer is that Kant put too much faith in the domestic governments and viewed threats to freedom as primarily external, not internal, to the state. It is these background assumptions that hinder application of Kant's theory to present-day international politics and so result in the kind of division seen above. Once we identify these assumptions, though, and find that they do not hold, we see that the international system is in a position analogous to the one witnessed between individuals in a state of nature. The iSME is analogous to the dSME and the permissive law applies.

There are several conditions that must be met for a state of nature to trigger an SME. For it is possible that not all states of nature are *ipso facto* threats to the ends of reason. To see this more clearly, let us recall Kant's command that we must exit the state of nature. The civil condition is the only condition that removes private judgment and enforcement from individuals, where law supplants the practice of "might makes right" and protects every person universally. The command to exit is known as the *Exeundum* Principle, and the reason for doing so is formulated in another principle. Let us call it the Universal Requirements of Justice. However, the civil condition is not merely about justice; it is also a necessary stepping-stone for morality to take hold in the world. Without the protection of laws, culture and education cannot take root, as people are not in relative safety to pursue these enterprises. Without culture and education, morality is a distant hope.[9] According to Kant, men must become moral beings. We can call this the Principle of Teleology of Reason. There is an assumption that Kant makes about the nature of men that simultaneously gives rise to and threatens all of these principles: the Presumption of Badness. The Presumption states that men are naturally evil, and unless a person gives "equal assurance" that she will refrain from doing wrong, one ought not to hope otherwise.[10] Such assurance, for Kant, is entering into civil society.

The Presumption plays a central role in Kant's formulation of the other principles. For, if men were (i) not naturally evil, and (ii) equal in regards to their power and strength, then the other principles would be moot. Men would obey the moral law and respect each other's rights naturally; they would be perfect angels. If, however, men are (i) evil and (ii) unequal in regards to their power and strength, then the other principles are a priori necessary. "[G]iven the depravity of human nature" men must work at becoming moral beings.[11]

Basically, Kant believes that human beings are nasty selfish creatures and will not exit the state of their "lawless freedom" voluntarily. Due to this, we may presume their recalcitrance and not "wait for actual hostility" to coerce one out of a state of nature, and thus "one is authorized to use coercion against someone who already, by his nature [i.e., evil], threatens him with coercion."[12] In order that men do not "erase the possibility of passing over into a legal condition" (a condition which provides assurance and protection of rights), reason prescribes a permissive law that authorizes agents to coerce all others into civil society.[13] The permissive law thus allows agents to use impermissible means to achieve the ends of reason, and it is the combination of all of these principles that results in an SME. All are necessary, though not sufficient conditions, for the presence of an SME. More specifically, if all four principles are not met, then an SME results.

The Presumption of Badness

The Presumption of Badness is really the crux of the argument for whether the international system presents us with an SME. This is so because it justifies the coercive move between individuals to found a civil society, and it gives substantive character to Kant's theory of a state of nature. Moreover, the Presumption also provides a ground for the necessity of man's moral progress. In other words, the Presumption grounds the *Exeundum* Principle and gives further meaning to the Principle of Teleology of Reason. Given this, it is important to understand whether the Presumption applies throughout Kant's political theory, or if it plays a role only in the beginning stages of it. If it is the former, then there may be justification for the coercion of states into an international civil condition or at least the formation of a juridical simulacrum. If it is the latter, then there is not only a possible resolution to the dispute between Kant scholars on the issue of coercion in international affairs, but a deeper understanding of how the modern state mitigates the need for violence and thwarts the possibility of an SME arising between states.

Since Kant takes a state of nature between individuals to be analogous to that of a state of nature between states, we might find that this alone is justification for coercion of states into a cosmopolitan civil condition or federation.[14] Regardless of the type of agents (individuals or states) who find themselves in a state of nature, the condition is untenable because it is "opposed to … not a … social [society] but rather the civil [society]."[15] If the states of nature between men and states are analogous, then we might also claim that the juridical imperative to leave a state of nature might also be the same in both. That is, if individuals must leave the state of nature, so too must states. This interpretation is supported, not only by logical consistency, but also by Kant's remarks at the beginning of the *Doctrine of Right* where he explicitly claims that the later sections of his work (those of international and cosmopolitan right) can be "easily inferred from the earlier" sections.[16] The *Exeundum* Principle operates in both conditions.

Byrd and Hruschka take this line of justification in their work on Kant's state of nation states (*Völkerstaat*), citing the Presumption of Badness as their primary justification.[17] As Kant explains in the *Religion*, all men are presumed to be evil and, given the chance, they will choose to disobey the moral law and attempt to satisfy their appetites instead. As evidence of this viewpoint, Kant cites man's fall from grace. The "fall" was simultaneously both an evil and a good act. It was a deliberate choice to put self-interest above the commands of God (and so proved man's nature), and it was therefore evil because it privileged self-interest above duty. Nevertheless, this same act also proved man's capacity for good, as it displayed his faculty of choice. It is the very faculty that gives man his humanity and the possibility to degrade it. Thus, Kant believes that man is "evil from his very nature," and so without guarantees like the rule of law, there is no need to wait for actual harm to occur before one can rightly coerce others.[18] This right to coerce others into a civil condition is a result of the fact "that we have a right (in the state of nature) to exercise preemptive and preventive defense."[19] The best way for individuals to protect their rights is to enter civil society, and so states, if they too find themselves in a similar situation, should follow the same logic as well.[20]

Given the fact that Kant claims that a state of nature between individuals is analogous to that of a state of nature between states, and given his remarks about the "inference" of arguments in the *DR*, Byrd and Hruschka are led to the conclusion that the Presumption must also apply to states in the international state of nature and are authorized to coerce other states into a *Völkerstaat* (despite Kant's remarks in "Perpetual Peace" about the impermissibility of coercing states into a world state).[21] They believe that Kant's remarks in "Perpetual Peace" are not his final answer to the question of instantiating a universal conception of justice, and we should instead take Kant's last word is his *DR*, written two years after the essay on peace.

It is not immediately apparent, however, that we should follow Byrd and Hruschka's use of the Presumption to legitimate coercing states in an international state of nature. Indeed, we should be skeptical of applying the Presumption by rote to the international system, for the different classes of agents (individuals and states) matter greatly.[22] A state, as a moral agent, can have intentions, and responsibility can be imputed to it for its actions. However, to claim that such a state is *by its nature* evil obscures the distinction between human beings as moral agents and moral agents *simpliciter*. In other words, states and human beings are types of moral agents, and not all moral agents necessarily have evil natures (as Kant believes angels are moral agents too). A human being may, by his nature, be evil, but that fact does not mean that *all* moral agents are evil. The Presumption, as it works in Kant's theory, only applies to human beings (especially given his use of the "fall" as evidence), and cannot be automatically applied to states.

One might object that states are merely entities constituted by human beings, and so it is human acts and decisions that must ultimately determine the general moral character of state conduct. Indeed, Kant seems to admit to this position. In *Perpetual Peace* he notes that "the depravity of human nature … is revealed and can be glimpsed in the free relations among nations (though deeply concealed by governmental restraints in law-governed civil society)."[23] Moreover in "Theory and Practice," he claims that "human nature never seems less lovable than in relations among entire peoples."[24] This, taken in conjunction with his assertion that "as nations, peoples can be regarded as single individuals," appears to cement the view that nations are nothing more than the sum of their parts.[25] If nations can be regarded as collectives of individual human beings, and these single individual nations are regarded as moral persons, then, *modus ponens*, states should be regarded as evil.

This position is one where we take Kant to be a radical individualist, and so any type of moral status granted to states is merely by way of the individuals (with their human natures) that compose them. This argument entails, therefore, that the Presumption holds for states as well, and so coercing states into a state of nation states is legitimate. States find themselves in an iSME because the Presumption cannot be rebutted due to the condition of a state of nature, and since the Presumption cannot be rebutted we are left with an imperative to leave the state of nature for the sake of universal justice and moral progress.

While this conclusion would be helpful for establishing that the international system is currently in an iSME, the argument is unpersuasive. First, this conclusion is not so easily reached. In the *DR*, the Vigilantius lecture notes of 1793, *The Conflict of the Faculties* and "On the Proverb: That May be True in Theory but is of No Practical Use" Kant's position is that states, courts, legislatures, executive branches, humanity and ideal beings such as God or angels are all moral persons.[26] Here, Kant appears to be claiming that if one has the status of a moral person, then this is merely about having the capacity for intention and action. In other words, if one is a moral person, then one can be held responsible for one's acts; that is, responsibility can be attributed because acts are imputable to the agent. It is not the fact that human beings occupy positions within these offices, but the offices (or authorities) themselves are capable of agency.

Second, all of Kant's other assertions about the moral personhood of states, courts, executives, etc., his definition of a person ("a subject whose actions can be imputed to him"), and his explicit claim that "moral personality is therefore nothing other than the freedom of a rational being under moral laws" and is therefore separate from "psychological personality," which is "merely the ability to be conscious of one's identity in different conditions of one's existence," leads us to believe that a state cannot be merely reducible to the people within it.[27] For Kant, the kind of moral agency that courts, executives etc., exercise is more like the modern notion of corporate moral agency. Just as corporations are held legally and morally responsible for certain misdeeds, but not the individual shareholders, states too are held responsible (in interstate disputes). Government officials may be held responsible in their official capacities, but they are not held responsible as private citizens. This is analogous to a board of directors being held responsible for a corporate policy, and not the Chief Executive Officer being held privately responsible. Leaders can only be held responsible for their failure in their public roles.[28]

Despite Kant's musings about the ability to observe human nature more fully in the relations amongst states, his account of the person and moral personality is so minimal that states and juridical institutions are capable of moral responsibility. That means that Kant's political theory endorses what we now call corporate moral agency. This is so because he holds that governments and their juridical powers are capable of acting freely; that is, they have autonomy.[29] These entities are capable of intention and action, and due to this fact they also have rights accorded to them.[30]

It is not our concern to enter here into the debate about the best account of responsibility and whether one should hold a corporate (collective) or individualist account. There are good reasons on both sides of this debate to accept or reject the other.[31] What concerns us is what Kant's political theory can sustain for his prescriptions of justice. While he does not endeavor to provide a full and complete explanation of how states and their juridical institutions can have intentions, make choices, have ends and act to bring them about, he does at least assert that they do.[32] Such an admission, then, means that *he* is not a radical individualist.[33]

If states are corporate moral agents and not reducible to the individuals that compose them, then they are artificial corporate moral agents. They are capable of forming an intention, having an end, and acting to fulfill that end, but they do not have an inherent nature.[34] Moreover, states are entities that live on long past the lives of their constituent members. They "have an identity over time" and they have "continuity."[35]

What this means for Byrd and Hruschka, then, is that if states have no inherent nature, then we cannot presume them to be evil. We cannot make a presumption. For example, if we look at the moral character of Japan in 1941, it is significantly different from the character of Japan today. Thus if we are to judge the character of a state, or, more precisely, a government, we must instead look to empirical evidence to see how it acts over time. We must not make an a priori presumption, but must make an a posteriori conjecture.

As they note:

> Conjectures are preliminary judgments about facts or circumstances. They are individual judgments and not generally valid propositions. They are descriptive and have no normative character. If I am in a room with no windows, I may conjecture about whether it is raining outside. My conjecture might be based on a weather report I heard in the morning or noise I hear on the roof that sounds like rain. This conjecture is purely factual—that it is in fact raining—and has no normative content. It is valid only for me, because others might conjecture differently about the weather at the moment. And it is only preliminary; as soon as I get to a window I may change my mind.[36]

Since the Presumption cannot hold for states, as artificial agents, I contend that something else is required to form preliminary judgments about the possibility of an iSME: empirical evidence. If State A is to hold a belief about State B's intentions or character, State A must come to hold this belief based on observed events. As Kant asserts, "a state is permitted to prosecute its right against another state … when it *believes* it has been wronged by the other state."[37] This wronging can take several forms: threats, active violations or a "publically expressed will (whether by word or deed) [that] reveals a maxim by which, if made a universal rule, [would render] any condition of peace among nations impossible."[38] In each of these cases, states do not have to wait to be *attacked*, but they do have to wait for states to "undertake" to do *something* that would thereby threaten them.[39]

One might counter that Kant specifically states: "This is a wrong to the lesser power merely by the condition of the superior power, before any deed [*Tat*] on its part."[40] I submit that the focus should be on the type of "wrong" under consideration. The condition of a state of nature is "wrong in the highest degree" (i.e., it is a non-rightful condition where violence is the only way to secure one's rights), and so while this condition "wrongs" all who are in it, that "wrong" cannot be imputed to one state in particular. In other words, the condition is wrong because of all states' refusal to exit the state of nature (i.e., act in accordance with the *Exeundum* Principle).

Moreover, as the rest of the text in this section shows, Kant suggests that State A has reason to fear State B because of its *actions* (either by State B's increasing its territory or creating more power or a higher status). To undertake a preemptive or preventive attack, another state must feel or perceive itself to be threatened by another state. Threats can only be made when someone actually *does* something. The state of nature amongst states aggravates the insecurity of each, but to be justified in attacking one state there must be some reason to attack, even if that reason is merely self-preservation rather than self-defense.[41]

While Byrd and Hruschka argue that conjectures cannot apply to Kant's arguments about Right, this is incorrect. The Presumption, they note, carries the normative force needed to justify coercion of a state into the *Völkerstaat.* However, this conclusion seems to run against everything Kant says about non-intervention, free federations of states, and the absence of sovereign or coercive powers in international leagues. Byrd and Hruschka's position seems to beg the question when it comes to the role of coercion. At one stage in their interpretation the right to coerce appears always present, for the mere condition of a state of nature combined with the Presumption authorizes an agent to coerce. However, if this were the case, then it is odd why Kant explicitly notes that the federation of free states (*Völkerbund*) is not, and indeed cannot be, coercive.[42] How, then, can the structure of Kant's argument justify coercion at the individual level (*Staat*) and cosmopolitan levels (*Völkerstaat*) but not at the interstate level (*Völkerbund*)? How does the *Völkerstaat* acquire coercive power if the *Völkerbund* forbids it?

The simple reason is that coercion into the *Völkerbund and Völkerstaat* is impermissible if we follow Kant's assumptions and logic. Indeed, the majority of Kant scholars are correct in this matter. However, if we do not take Kant's assumptions as correct, then we are left with a different task: determining whether coercion is permissible in the international system (e.g., whether the international system is more alike to the individual state of nature than previously thought). The issues, then, are the assumptions Kant makes about the civil condition and international behavior. These assumptions are: that existing states protect individuals sufficiently and secure their basic rights; and that the largest threat to states' and people's rights is external.[43]

If we grant that domestic states do protect rights—*sufficiently and generally*—then there is no need to coerce countries into a transnational state, and the Presumption of Badness is moot.[44] This is the view that states have "outgrown" the need for coercion because they already have an internally lawful structure.[45] Thus attempting to coerce states further risks undermining the protections present at the domestic level. If, however, domestic states fail to protect and secure basic human rights, then, regardless of their internal order, they are not fulfilling the role for which they are intended. Moreover, if we find that the greatest threats to states' and peoples' rights are not external, such as from wars of conquest or mere aggression, but are instead from internal civil breakdown, the normative prescriptions Kant makes in regards to the *Völkerbund* and *Völkerstaat* may also not hold.

If Kant's assumptions are no longer empirically valid, then we might want to look back to his earlier discussions of domestic state formation to guide the requirements for transnational justice because it is in this portion of his theory that we gain the most clarity on issues of justice in a state of nature. Kant does not provide us with detailed prescriptions for international and cosmopolitan right, but, as Byrd and Hruschka note, Kant's arguments in the first section of the *DR* (on private right) ought to apply in each subsequent section (public right, international right, cosmopolitan right). What's more, while the Presumption may not hold for states, we may still be able to use an analogue of it to determine whether states are acting "evilly." If states are acting in such a manner, we can instead make a conjecture about their future behavior. This conjecture, taken in conjunction with the structural features of a state of nature, would thereby show that the international system is in an iSME.

The state of the world: then and now

Since states are artificial moral agents and the Presumption of Badness cannot be automatically applied to them, we must look at empirical evidence to make preliminary judgments about whether states are also "evil." If they are not, then the majority of states uphold and protect the rights of their peoples, and threats to states' and peoples' rights come from the outside. We can then conclude that Kant's arguments about international coercion still hold and we are not in an iSME. We cannot justify coercion of states into a juridical condition. If, however, the majority of states do not uphold sufficiently the rights of their peoples, and the greatest threats to states' and peoples' rights is internal, then we ought to conclude that Kant's arguments about the impermissibility of coercion in international relations do not hold, and we should return to his earlier arguments about individuals in a state of nature.

While it is true that Kant did not provide lengthy arguments about state failure, collapse or internal threats, he did reply to Hobbes about the relation of a government to its people. This is the most direct insight we have into Kant's arguments about the threat posed by a government to its people. He claims that a sovereign domestic state "has no wish to do [its citizens] injustice."[46] He argues further:

> [I]f [a citizen] assumes that the ruler's attitude is one of good will, any injustice which [the citizen] believes he has suffered can only have resulted through error, or through ignorance of certain possible consequences of the laws which the supreme authority has made.[47]

On this account, the ruler (or sovereign) cannot possibly wish to do harm to its citizens. Kant's famous remedy for any perceived injustice is to allow for "freedom of the pen" so that the citizens might inform the ruler of the injustices suffered by the people (so that he can correct them).[48]

Unfortunately, after the horrors witnessed in the twentieth century, this response is at best naive and at worst dangerous. Kant's first assumption, that the majority of governments uphold and secure sufficiently the rights of their people, appears empirically false. The present-day reality is that well over half of the world's governments systematically and intentionally violate the rights of their peoples. Such violations are not violations of political rights, but basic human rights that have included such rights against torture, killing, disappearing and other fundamental rights pertaining to external freedom. To place full faith in the power of the pen to redress wrongs is nothing but blind hope. The pen is an insufficient safeguard against government propaganda dispersed over radio and press to incite violence against groups of people. Moreover, freedom of the pen cannot stop nonstate actors from perpetrating crimes against the populace when the state is too weak to enforce its "laws." Top-down reform cannot happen in these instances because either "the top" desires to annihilate a portion of its people or there is no "top" to address.

That the majority of the world's states do not protect sufficiently the rights of their people is no secret. For example, looking to the 2012 Failed State Index, we see that 125 states (out of 178 measured) are either at the "warning", "high warning," "very high warning" or "alert" risk for failure.[49] The Index is based on content analysis that flags certain economic and political indicators for each country. The software (Conflict Assessment Software Tool) triangulates these data with other major events in country, such as political or natural disasters. The Index finds that almost two-thirds of the world's states are in trouble.[50] For our purposes though, I have separated the economic factors from the Index to get a better picture of the number of states failing, or under severe pressure towards failing, as measured by human rights problems. After reorganization, 29 states are on "alert", while an additional 90 are on "warning." The findings are summarized in Figure 4.1.

When one focuses solely on state legitimacy and stability, omitting all human rights and economic indicators, the trend continues to grow: 42 states are in the "alert" position and 86 are on "warning."

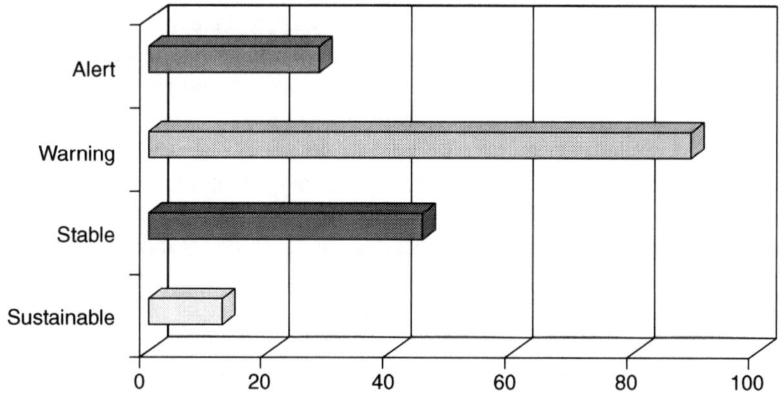

Figure 4.1 Risk of state failure due to human rights violations/concerns.[51]

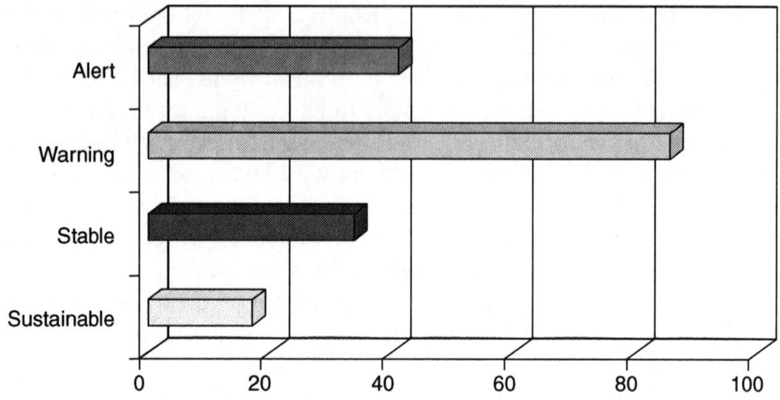

Figure 4.2 Risk of state failure due to political intability and lack of legitimacy.[52]

Well over half of the world's states are in a crisis or near crisis with regard to protecting human rights, instability and illegitimacy. Although these data are imperfect, and many of the indicators interact or influence one another, such methodological objections do not detract from the conclusion: Kant's assumption that the world's states are satisfactorily protecting rights is not true; only a minority of states adequately do so.

The international system, as Kant notes, is a state of nature, though he believes that even its fragile juridical condition is better than nothing at all. These recent empirical findings suggest that the majority of states are not that far removed from an individual state of nature, in that the law is either absent, defunct or used to persecute minorities.[53] According to Kant, the domestic state is the first bastion of protection for individuals' rights; if it collapses, or fails to fulfill its purpose, then *individuals* find themselves back in what amounts to a state of nature. However, this state of nature is not the somewhat peaceful society of states, but a state of war, where the enemies can take the shape of governments, nongovernmental organizations or fellow citizens. When a domestic state fails to protect the basic rights of its citizens, it can no longer be considered a "civil society"; its people are left in a juridical vacuum.

This juridical vacuum exists because the state system (in Kant's theory and in international relations) has been set up to engage only with other states on the assumption that most individuals have adequately removed themselves from a state of nature. However, as we have seen, this assumption is incorrect. Many individuals, including refugees, internally displaced persons, stateless persons and targets of genocide, ethnic cleansing and crimes against humanity, have no protection from a home country and have no place to seek redress or protection.[54] Moreover, the Westphalian system that privileges territorial integrity and state sovereignty precludes other states from "interfering" in domestic matters to the detriment of human rights, R2P notwithstanding.

How does Kant fare with his second assumption that the greatest threat to justice and rights comes from external war? Not too well, as it turns out. Today, data suggest that the greatest threat of war comes from intrastate war and not interstate war. Fearon and Latin find that between 1945 and 1999 there were roughly five times as many intrastate as interstate conflicts, with three times as many states involved in intrastate conflicts, and almost five times as many deaths as a result of those internal conflicts.[55] While this study ends in 1999, the current data available continue to support their findings: out of the 23 conflicts since 2000, 19 of these were intrastate wars.[56] The current trend in international conflict is an easy one to predict: threats come mainly from the inside. Kant's belief, or rather hope, that a state's ruler cannot possibly intend harm is false.

Of course there were internal conflicts during Kant's time, the French Revolution being the most prominent; but from his writings, the reader is left to assume that the greatest threat is external strife, war *between* states.[57] As he notes, war is "the destroyer of everything good," and it threatens to undermine the moral progress of mankind.[58] That is, it seems, why Kant is so adamant about the necessity of a republican constitution. Republican constitutions are "the best among all others to banish war,"[59] but the "problem of establishing a perfect civil constitution depends upon the problem of law-governed *external relations* among nations."[60] Internal composition and civil strife do not threaten humanity's moral progress, and it seems that Kant does not address these factors.

The simple fact remains that civil war, not external or interstate war, is the greatest threat. Ignoring the implications that the majority of the world's conflicts are internal and continuing to espouse a doctrine of nonintervention, despite the staggering numbers of deaths from these conflicts, threatens to undermine not only Kant's writings on the importance of humanity, but his theory's applicability to present-day affairs, especially the doctrine of R2P. While many of Kant's ideas are timeless (e.g., humanity as the highest value that guides and limits our actions or the need for laws to regulate behavior and protect our rights), others are now antique. The political landscape changes, as Kant thought it would, but such change does not necessarily follow his prediction of peaceful republican constitutions emerging all over the globe. To be sure, external threats still persist, but internal war is equally, or more, threatening to the moral progress of humanity.[61] Internal war threatens not only the lives of the people but also the structure of the domestic and (future) international juridical system, threatening citizens with degeneration to a state of nature. Therefore, if we are to apply Kant's writings today, we must take account of these empirical facts; we must not only relax some of Kant's strict maxims on nonintervention and coercion between states but revisit his arguments laid out in his theory of private right.

An international SME

It should now be apparent that the international system is in an SME analogous to the one witnessed in the individual state of nature. Because Kant's assumptions about the protection of basic rights by the domestic state are incorrect, the system he has built upon them cannot fully maintain itself. In other words, we should not agree with Kant that what is morally required is "only a voluntary coalition of different states which can be dissolved at any time, not a federation (like that of the American states) which is based on a constitution and can therefore not be dissolved."[62] This is because Kant's argument is based on an empirical falsehood. Kant's argument that a congress of states cannot have coercive powers, and any act against a state would constitute an act of aggression (thus triggering legitimate reciprocal coercion, i.e., war) does not hold. Rather, the current international situation places us in a condition where the use of coercion to establish an institution to maintain basic human rights is permissible via Kant's permissive law.

Returning to Kant's earlier arguments about private right in light of the Presumption and three principles, and applying them to the international state of nature, creates a drastically different picture. First, while the a priori Presumption cannot hold for states (as it stands), we can justify an a posteriori conjecture of government self-interest.[63] This conjecture is justified by empirical evidence that the majority of the world's governments do not uphold the basic human rights of their peoples and that such internal wrongdoing is the cause of most war-related deaths. The conjecture posits that governments do not act justly toward other states or, when domestic juridical institutions are weak or absent, toward their own citizens. This conjecture, taken with the other three principles reveals an iSME.

Reason requires that justice be universal in form and that humanity continually progress toward moral perfection. Moral perfection is only gained via culture found in civil society.[64] Alas, many states are threatened with instability, failure and collapse, and this failure and collapse threatens man's moral progress because it undercuts the means for moral progress. The problem is only compounded when one looks to international society for help. As many of the problems associated with R2P highlight, states are reluctant to undertake such actions for the sake of another state's people. The international "legal" system is a system of private right, and so each agent (state) is judge in its own cause. International society as currently structured is not—indeed cannot be—sufficient for the type of moral progress Kant requires. Moral progress requires the gradual expansion from the individual and his community, to the state, to interstate relations, and finally to a universal and cosmopolitan relation of peoples. This progress can be seen as a series of concentric circles, at the center of which is the individual and his community. Without the center, nothing further can be done. Thus, if domestic civil society fails to provide the conditions necessary for progress, such as securing basic rights, then we cannot rely on a larger society of states to do so.[65]

An iSME is present in the current international system. The prevalence of R2P crimes and crises show the juridical failings of this system. Indeed, international society recognizes these acts as the gravest and most atrocious crimes that can be committed against persons. This recognition is a first step; and a further positive step is, of course, the attempt to secure the rights of peoples by instituting treaties and transnational courts. However, the treaties and courts have no teeth to them; coercive mechanisms (that can either force states to halt their crimes against their people or force other states to intervene in a target state) are lacking. Right entails the authorization to use coercion, and the current state of affairs in the international system proves that if there is to be right, and not merely the power of the strongest, then formal juridical institutions with power must be present. That international society must found such institutions is a dictate of reason for the sake of not only R2P, but rights protection and moral progress as well.

While the international system may not appear to be in an iSME, it in fact is. The threat of civil breakdown and violence is all too near, and because the system lacks what Michael Walzer calls "the rivets of authority," individual (and state) rights can only attain a provisional status.[66] States must exit the state of nature and establish an institution capable of securing the basic rights of peoples everywhere. Justice cannot exist merely for the morally lucky; states are, therefore, authorized under a permissive law of practical reason to coerce other states into joining such an institution.

This is not to say that this is the only solution. States could be coerced into something much broader, such as a global state; however, as we will see in the next chapter, such coercion into a world state may prove inefficacious. For Kant, this "sure-to-fail" maxim would, therefore, be unjust. The maxim would not always be wrong, say if the conditions in the system improved, but presently such coercion would be bound to fail and create more strife. Thus, coercing states into a "surrogate" that can protect the rights of people everywhere is a necessary step. Much like individuals in a state of nature may coerce others into a domestic civil condition, states too can coerce other states into an analogous institution. As Kant notes, states have a right "to constrain each other to leave this condition of war and so form a constitution that will establish a lasting peace," and if states have this right, they must also have a right to establish an institution that will enforce the international laws currently in place and monitor the behavior of states toward their peoples.[67] Sovereignty is not sacrosanct—it is a privilege that is dependent upon the state fulfilling its obligations towards its people.[68]

Objections

Some might object that my characterization of the international system as being in an SME is exaggerated, and so the permissive law does not apply. The critic might argue that the international system is actually further along the juridical path than in Kant's time, and that such progress puts us closer to, not further from, a condition of international public right. This forward movement, therefore, makes a supreme moral emergency a distant possibility and not an immediate concern. Indeed, she might concede that idea that the international system is still a *statu naturali*, but this bleak Hobbesian picture is losing accuracy because the society of states is governed by international law, adjudicated by international courts and tribunals, and executed, in a sense, by the United Nations.

At first blush these observations all hold true, even though these "juridical" mechanisms are not properly juridical in Kant's sense. But more importantly, the opposite is true. States actually seem to subvert the "progress" they claim to have made, as they perpetually refuse to give up a certain degree of sovereignty and establish a transnational institution with universally coercive capabilities. Thus, while the current international system is a society "compatible with rights," it is still not a rightful society, and attempts at forming and implementing international institutions have done little to regulate state behavior and protect basic human rights.[69] The international system might be "governed" by international "law" (treaty and customary), and it may have transnational courts to adjudicate disputes between states or persons, but it does not "secure against violence" the rights of "human beings, peoples, and states."[70]

Kant's notion of public right is "the sum of the laws which need to be *promulgated generally* in order to bring about a rightful condition." In other words, it is a "system of laws for a people, that is a multitude of human beings, or for a multitude of peoples, which because they affect one another, need a rightful condition *under a will uniting them*."[71] What this ultimately means is that established and promulgated laws must be general in form (i.e., applicable to all people) and they must be backed by a "public lawful external" coercive mechanism (i.e., enforcement of the laws must not depend upon any one individual's strength). The question "What makes right?" then, is not so simply answered as "those rules set up by a legislator (or legislature)." For Kant, right requires the legislative authority, but that authority must be "public" in the sense that "the people" authorize it to make laws (either through appointed or elected officials or through direct voting).

However, the legislative authority is not the only requirement for public right. There must also be separated executive and judicial authorities. Kant claims that:

> These [authorities] are like the three propositions in a practical syllogism: the major premise, which contains the law of that will; the minor premise, which contains the command to behave in accordance with the law, that is the principle of subsumption under the law; and the conclusion, which contains the verdict (sentence), what is laid down as right in the case at hand.[72]

Right, for Kant, cannot really be public law without the other two authorities present. Thus international law, constituted by agreements (treaties) and generally observed rules (norms or *jus cogens*), does not satisfy the Kantian conditions of public right.

Customary international law requires that there "must be widespread and uniform practice of states, and states must engage in the practice out of a sense of legal obligation, [and] this second requirement, often referred to as *opinio juris*, is the central concept of customary international law."[73] Treaty law, in either its bilateral or multilateral form, is an easier case because the rules of the treaty are made public and the parties to the treaty know explicitly the terms of agreement. However, this is not to say that states commit or comply with treaties more often than not. There is a large literature on the reasons for state commitment and compliance that falls into roughly two schools of thought: rational choice (interests) versus liberal-ideational (norms) as reason for compliance.[74] The first school of thought, represented by the likes of Eric Posner and Jack Goldsmith, argues that states commit to or comply with treaties out of their own self-interest (coincidence of interests) or fear of retaliation (coercion). The second school of thought, represented by those like Harold Koh and Andrew Moravcsik, argues that states commit and comply with treaties because of the power of the ideas, where "states internalize norms and act in accordance with them because they understand them to be correct or appropriate."[75] Oona Hathaway argues for a middle ground between the two sides in her "integrated theory," which places emphasis on domestic regime type, domestic actors, self-interest and structural consequences.[76] While the debate over why states do or do not comply with international law is certainly important, from a Kantian standpoint it misses the point. For Kant, the rules outlined in a treaty or the patterns of behavior in *jus cogens* are not really law, for they lack the fundamental characteristics of publicly promulgated rules, laid down by a legislative authority. Furthermore, they lack a requisite enforcement mechanism and, in the case of dispute, an authoritative judiciary.

Even though transnational courts are present in the international system, they lack the Kantian requirement to settle "irreversible" decisions.[77] The office of the judiciary must be able to "apply the law, and to render to each what is his with the help of the executive authority," by pronouncing final judgments that cannot be appealed.[78] The transnational courts currently in place do not fulfill this requirement for two reasons: noncompulsory jurisdiction and the lack of enforcement mechanisms (i.e., "the help of the executive").

The first issue, noncompulsory jurisdiction, is no surprise.[79] The International Court of Justice (ICJ) is the principal judicial organ of the UN, where states, and only states, can bring suits against other states. While all members of the UN are parties to the Court's statute (by function of signing the Charter), its jurisdiction is not compulsory.[80] Simply stated, only states that expressly recognize the jurisdiction of the ICJ can: (1) bring suits or be sued; (2) have judgments enforced against them (typically by the UN Security Council). One of the oft-cited cases involving jurisdictional problems is the *Avena* case (*Mexico* v. *the United States of America*), where the United States did not inform the Mexican Consulate that the accused (Ernesto Medellín Rojas, *et al.*) were arrested, tried and convicted in US courts. Under the Vienna Convention (signed by both Mexico and the United States), the Mexican Consulate has a right to review the case, visit and correspond with the accused and appoint representation. In *Avena*, Mexico was not made aware, and so in 2003 Mexico brought a suit against the United States. The United States, however, continued to deny the jurisdiction of the ICJ even in the face of a judgment against it. The end result was that the United States ignored the judgment by the Court, and in 2008 executed Medellín. In 2008, Mexico again brought the issue before the ICJ for interpretation. Ultimately, the ICJ, while acknowledging that the United States had "failed to discharge its obligation" to Mexico (upholding the 2004 judgment), dismissed the further claims by Mexico that the United States violated the 2004 judgment on the grounds of lack of jurisdiction.[81]

The US response to Mexico was the result of an international legal loophole. Mexico requested interpretation by the ICJ under Article 60, which claims that if there is a dispute between parties over the meaning and scope of the judgment then whatever the Court decides is "final and without appeal." The United States then changed course and replied that it agreed with the judgment, and was aware of its obligation to comply with it, though the United States differed on its view of how the obligation was to be discharged. The Court, therefore, claimed it lacked jurisdiction under Article 60 to interpret the judgment of 2004 because the United States had backtracked and agreed that it had an obligation; though, of course, the United States patently failed to uphold the judgment of 2004 by executing Mr. Medellín. The take-home message in this case is that a party to a case can easily flout the judgment of the Court by first claiming that domestic rule of law does not allow implementation; second, by withdrawing from any treaty that subjects a state to adjudication; and third, by using loopholes in the ICJ's constitutive articles. Thus, an already tenuous and fragile area of jurisdiction is weakened even further.

The second transnational court, the International Criminal Court (ICC), created by the Rome Statutes, is separate from the UN, and it prosecutes crimes (listed under the Rome Statutes) committed by individuals. States and individual agents (persons or organizations) can call attention to situations of possible Rome Statutes violations, though the procedures and evidentiary proof appears to be different in each case.[82] In the event that a state or the UN refers a *situation* to the ICC, the ICC is to proceed with investigation unless there is no reasonable basis under the Rome Statutes. If an individual or a nongovernmental organization (NGO) receives a *communication*, the ICC is not to initiate an investigation unless there is a reasonable basis under the Rome Statutes. It appears that individuals and NGOs carry a heavier burden of proof when submitting communications to the Office of the Prosecutor. Again, the Court's jurisdiction is noncompulsory.[83] As of this writing, 121 countries (out of 196) are party to the ICC and accept its jurisdiction.

While it appears that a good majority of countries acknowledge the ICC, unfortunately three of the largest and most powerful do not: the United States, China and the Russian Federation. It also happens that these three countries make up the majority of the Permanent Five (P-5) members on the United Nations Security Council (SC). The obvious result is that if a person is to be charged with violating the Rome Statutes, *irrespective of the State's jurisdictional acceptance or the place of the crime*, then the charge can only come via a recommendation of the SC. However, with three of the P-5 currently refusing to acknowledge jurisdiction, it is possible, indeed probable, that if such a suit were brought against a national or ally of one of these countries, the UN would not, or could not, submit a referral. The referral of Colonel Muammar Gaddafi in 2011 to the ICC via the SC versus the failure of the SC to issue a similar referral of Syria's President al-Bashar in 2011–2013 is a case in point.

More subversive still is the practice of the Bilateral Immunity Agreement (BIA). A BIA is an agreement that the United States (US) makes with another country where: the US and the other country agree not to surrender nationals of either country to the ICC; where the other country agrees not to surrender US nationals to the ICC; where the country will continue to receive US foreign aid as long as the country upholds the BIA with the US; or cases that are "unconfirmed" where the agreement has not been disclosed by the US State Department and thus the outlines of the agreement are unknown.[84] The US now has BIAs with 95 signatories to the ICC, most of which are repeated human rights violators.[85] This tactic, it is claimed, "is an attempt to undermine the ICC's universalistic role."[86]

Aside from the two largest transnational courts, some, such as Eyal Benvenisti, insist that domestic courts are capable of forming an "international judicial alliance" where "[domestic] judges can force governments of strong as well as weak countries to adhere to a set of international values or constitutional norms that otherwise would not receive universal consent."[87] Others, like Posner and Goldstein, however, argue that such a notion is "certainly odd and has no known adherents" in practice.[88] What is of interest to us is whether the current structures of the ICC, the ICJ, or even a hypothetical international judicial alliance can satisfy (or come close to satisfying) Kant's requirement for public right. The answer is that they cannot.

These institutions, real or hypothetical, are the exact opposite of what Kant requires for a judicial system. For Kant, "the moral person that administers justice is a court (*forum*) and its administration of justice is a judgment (*iudicium*)."[89] Judgments, in Kant's terminology, are publically "laid down as right;"[90] that is, Kant's court holds jurisdiction over all parties in society, and this jurisdiction is coupled with the capacity to coerce parties to fulfill its judgment. Moreover, the authority of the Kantian judiciary is to be held with the people, who appoint "administrators" such as judges to "apply the law, and to render to each what is his with the help of the executive authority."[91] International society, with all questions of international law aside, lacks the requisite features of a "people" establishing a court with universal jurisdiction and an executive to administer or enforce judgments.

While individual states are those "moral persons" that make up the society of states, this society is not properly called "a people." The society of states is merely a collection of agents each pursing its own purposes, where sometimes those purposes have a "coincidence of interest" and sometimes not.[92] For Kant, a public condition of right can only be established through a "will putting everyone under obligation, hence only a collective general (common) and powerful will," in other words, an omnilateral will.[93] It does not appear that the international society of states fits this description.

One might still object that since the majority of states signed the UN Charter, and the UN established the ICJ, there is, therefore, consensus by the society of states to place authority in this judicial body. Unfortunately, as we saw before, this is not the case. Many states refuse to recognize the jurisdiction of the ICJ (when brought to suit), and thus they do not recognize its authority to pronounce supreme and "irreversible" judgments. One might retort that the ICC also came into existence by the voluntary act of a majority of states, and so this body, at least, has the authority and jurisdiction required under a Kantian framework. Yet again, this too is wishful thinking. There is no mandatory jurisdiction for states, and, even more problematic, states (such as the United States) have figured out a way, through BIAs, to sidestep jurisdiction in those states that have recognized the jurisdiction and authority of the ICC. Despite the diplomatic maneuvering, issuing of statements, signing of treaties or the meetings of heads of state, we seem to fail to recognize or to admit the existence of the elephant in the room: a refusal to limit state sovereignty and provide coercive power to a transnational institution undermines the possibility of universal justice. Thus, Posner's claim that the proliferation of ineffective transnational judicial bodies "is a sign of the weakness of the international system, not its strength" appears correct.[94] States continue to create judicial bodies, but "then find they cannot control them," and "rather than submitting to their jurisdiction, they set up even more courts or more arbitration panels—ones they think the *can* control."[95]

Finally, the oft-cited lack of coercive power is the largest and most problematic factor for international right. The lack of a centralized, public and authoritative coercive mechanism means that any attempt at founding an international juridical condition absent such a force is doomed to fail on Kantian grounds. As "right and the authorization to use coercion therefore mean one and the same thing," and authorization must come from a "collective general (common) and powerful will," international society fails to be a genuine condition of public right.

A critic might still point to the fact that public and centralized enforcement is not necessary for international law to be "really law,"[96] as "international law is enforceable in the same way that domestic law is enforceable," namely by some sort of "legally imposed sanction."[97] The sanction "remove[s] one or more of [a state's] entitlements," and that entitlement is a "legally recognized right."[98] This private enforcement of international law can take several shapes, such as economic and political sanctions, as well as all-out war. While this argument from private enforcement might appeal to many international lawyers, it is unpersuasive from a Kantian perspective because private enforcement of public laws is not sufficient for the rule of law.

According to Kant's criteria, public right, that is public law, must be enforced by an authoritative and *external* mechanism. Individual enforcement by states is an internal mechanism and such enforcement is dependent on a state's strength (much like the individual's strength in a state of nature); right, in this situation, always amounts to might. Moreover, the argument that state practice has evolved to a point where states now have entitlements obscures the distinction between society and civil society. For Kant, agents in society can be guided by a set of primary rules (natural right), but these are not legal in character.[99] What makes these rules legal (i.e., entitlements) is their public determination, which are both externally enforced and arbitrated by a neutral judge. The international system cannot be called a condition of public right because agents privately enforce their private judgments with regard to their "entitlements."

All of this is not to say that the international system is not "rule governed;" indeed it is. There exist rules for the seas, rules governing trade, war, diplomacy, and a variety of other activities. There also exist international institutions, where states come together to decide on existing rules and implement new ones. Though, in most instances, when states actually make agreements (either multi or bilaterally), states often would have either complied with those rules anyway because it is already in states' self-interest, or states have no intention of complying with the rules and sign a treaty for some other reason and then defect.[100] There is no external way to make states comply with the rules, and so the state of international affairs fails to be a juridical condition.

What all of this shows is that the international system is currently witnessing an iSME. The system is not a civil society, and the background assumptions Kant makes about the progress of states and the direction of threat are false. Given that the system is in an iSME, and that many of the R2P crises are in states that are failed or collapsed (dSMEs), we find ourselves in a morally compounded situation. On the one hand, R2P victims more than likely lack a functioning domestic civil society, while, on the other hand, they are emplaced in a nebulous international society that also lacks the requisite institutions to protect rights.

The reaction portion of R2P, therefore, becomes increasingly important. For if individuals cannot rise up to found their own functioning domestic civil society and the "government" that is *de jure* or *de facto* in place is violating their rights, then the only redress is to look to outside help. However, if such help is to be reliable and protect individual rights generally and sufficiently, more is required than unenforceable agreements and impotent juridical institutions. As it stands now, R2P is nothing more than a "covenant without the sword;" it is "mere words."[101] The international system, then, due to its structural features of private right, the empirical conjecture that states will not uphold human rights, and the moral imperatives of the *Exeundum* and Teleological Principles, finds itself in an iSME. Thus a permissive law of practical reason applies and coercion used to force states to exit this condition is permissible.

Conclusion

The debate over whether Kant permits coercion in the international system points to tensions between his political theory and the real world. While this may seem unimportant from a practical point of view, it is in fact quite significant for theorists and practitioners of international justice. If coercion is permissible, it is due to the fact that a permissive law of practical reason allows the use of otherwise impermissible means for the sake of preserving reason and its ends. In other words, if we are to ever protect peoples from genocide, crimes against humanity and other violations to their external freedom (i.e., fulfill a duty to protect), then we must remove the insecurities and barriers to cosmopolitan justice.

While some might disagree that the international system is in an SME analogous to the one witnessed in the state of nature between individuals, this judgment is misguided. It is certainly true that if we follow Kant's arguments throughout the *DR* and his explicit assertions in *TPP*, we see that coercion of states into a federation of free states or world state is deemed illegitimate. However, this is due to his background assumptions that governments do not wish harm to their own citizens and that the greatest threat to the domestic state comes from other states. If we do not hold these same assumptions, but change them on the grounds of empirical evidence to the contrary, we see that Kant's arguments about the impermissibility of the coercion of states lose traction.

Byrd and Hruschka are, therefore, correct in one sense: the Presumption of Badness is a key feature to legitimizing the move from a state of nature between individuals to a civil condition. The Presumption can only be overridden in civil society. However, they are incorrect to apply this same argument to the relations between states. States are artificial moral agents and as such have no inherent nature. We cannot make a presumption about all states. Rather, we must, based on factual evidence, make an a posteriori conjecture. This conjecture is subject to change if states change their behavior. While such behavioral change might be difficult, that it is not to say it is impossible. The acceptance of R2P points in this direction. Thus instead of taking the nature of states to be a brute fact, with all of the potential behaviors that follow from it, we should view the states and the system more like Alexander Wendt: "anarchy is what states make of it," and for us, they should leave it.[102]

Lamentably, the empirical evidence points to the fact that any conjecture we make about the motivations and intentions of states is that they are similar to individuals in a state of nature: evil. Evilness here, though, originates from the very concept of freedom. It is through one's free choice to ignore the moral law and act instead according to self-interest that one acts evilly. States, as artificial moral agents, must then be observed to know what their self-interests are. And given the empirical evidence, protecting the rule of law and rights of their citizens is not amongst many of states' interests. Byrd and Hruschka thus reach the correct conclusion but by way of faulty argument.

As the Failed State Index shows, 70 percent of the world's states are in danger of "failing" due to their poor human rights records. About 72 percent are considered to be failing because of instability and illegitimacy. Certainly not all states perpetually violate the rights of their citizens, but this number is by no means the majority.[103] Because of this fact, we see that many peoples vulnerable to the actions of their states have no protections or guarantees, and they will do whatever they feel is necessary to secure themselves, whether by fleeing and becoming refugees, internally displaced persons or stateless persons, or initiating civil war. Kant's assumptions, therefore, are factually incorrect. States can and do wish harm to their peoples, and the threat of civil breakdown looms large.

States in the international system can establish the conditions necessary for justice, and they can create an institution to help discharge a duty of R2P. While certainly a difficult enterprise, we should not "fling it aside." Furthermore, aiding states in this pursuit is Kant's permissive law. As we will see in the following chapter, while *lex permissiva* authorizes coercive mechanisms, only the most efficacious mechanisms should be used to establish the juridical institutions necessary to fulfill a duty of R2P and thus transition a provisional duty of R2P to a peremptory one.

5 Provisional to peremptory

Institutionalizing a duty to protect

> It is true of course, that we have no judicial precedent for the Charter. But international law is more than a scholarly collection of abstract and immutable principles. It is an outgrowth of treaties and agreements between nations and of accepted customs. Yet every custom has its origin in some single act, and every agreement has to be initiated by the action of some state. Unless we are prepared to abandon every principle of growth for international law, we cannot deny that our own day has the right to institute customs and to conclude agreements that will themselves become sources of a newer and strengthened international law. International law is not capable of development by the normal processes of legislation, for there is no continuing international legislative authority. Innovations and revisions in international law are brought about by the action of governments such as those I have cited, designed to meet a change in circumstances. It grows, as did the common law, through decisions reached from time to time in adapting settled principles to new situations. The fact is that when the law evolves by the case method, as did the common law and as international law must do if it is to advance at all, it advances at the expense of those who wrongly guessed the law and learned too late their error.
>
> Robert H. Jackson[1]

Chief Prosecutor for the Nuremberg Trials, Robert Jackson, uttered these words to legitimize the Tribunal's, and his, authority to prosecute the military and political leaders of the Nazi regime. Jackson's strategy was to work within existing international customary law, claiming that the Nazi regime was a criminal organization that planned to break the laws of war and the law prohibiting aggression. Where his arguments pushed the limits of international law was in his inclusion of "crimes against humanity" in the charges. Prosecuting the Nazi regime for crimes committed against people in its own sovereign territory changed the face of international legal history. Such changes, advanced "at the expense of those who wrongly guessed the law," continue still. However, it is not only that international law evolved at the expense of those who guess wrongly and thus break it; it also evolved at the expense of victims such as the Jews in the Holocaust, the Tutsi in Rwanda or the Albanians in Kosovo.

From the Nuremberg Trials, the famous "never again" slogan arose. Nations claimed they could no longer stand idly by while mass numbers of people were brutally slaughtered. Indeed, nations signed international agreements denouncing crimes against humanity, genocide and gross violations of human rights. Some might say this attitude towards rights violations became the norm. Yet it seems that much of the progress was made only from 1945 to 1948.[2] Little more has been accomplished since this time to move international law forward to secure those rights.[3]

Throughout this book I have suggested that a duty to protect must be institutionalized. Institutionalization is required because it is a duty of justice in a state of nature, which renders it provisional, and provisional duties must become peremptory. This requirement is not prudential, nor is it expeditious, but is a logical requirement of a universal theory of justice. The way forward must show us the requirements, not only of such an institution, but also of the necessary reforms in the existing structure of international legal organizations. This is so because problems and duties of justice are necessarily linked, and so one cannot merely create one new institution without looking to the rest. Indeed, creating such an institution will not solve all problems of international justice, and there will still be difficulties governing the practice of R2P; however, these reforms can ameliorate the effects of private right *for the matter of R2P* by mirroring, as best as possible, the juridical requirements of public right.

The following chapter is organized into two sections. The first section argues that an R2P institution (R2PI) should be established to promulgate public rules to govern the practice of R2P, thereby solving the ubiquitous problem of indeterminacy regarding the scope of a duty to protect. The institution should have the ability to monitor human rights violations (in all countries) that have the potential to determine that a humanitarian crisis is taking place. Furthermore, it should provide a centralized information network to the United Nations and society of states. However, it must be autonomous from the UN. The institution ought to mirror the position of National Human Rights Institutions (NHRI) at the international level. Once in place, the UN should execute its rules, and when individuals or states do not comply, a strengthened International Criminal Court (ICC) or International Court of Justice (ICJ) should adjudicate controversies about non-compliant individuals or states. Moreover, I suggest that, to execute effectively the rules of the R2PI, the UN ought to have a rapid-reaction volunteer military force. The second section explains how such reforms can satisfy Kant's requirements of protective, commutative and distributive justice, thereby rendering a provisional duty of HI peremptory.

Governing the practice of R2P

> Civilization asks whether law is so laggard as to be utterly helpless to deal with crimes of this magnitude by criminals of this order of importance. It does not expect that you can make war impossible. It does expect that your juridical action will put the forces of international law, its precepts, its

> prohibitions and, most of all, its sanctions, on the side of peace, so that men and women of good will, in all countries, may have "leave to live by no man's leave, underneath the law.[4]

The most contentious issue within R2P's umbrella is the use of force. For this reason, much of the debate about military intervention persists and any steps taken towards implementing R2P amount to little more than legal prestidigitation. In other words, most states no longer question "whether international actors should intervene in one way or another, but how."[5] The "how" remains the sticky wicket.

Since the UN's adoption of R2P (and its subsequent lack of institutionalization), states have inconsistently, and perhaps arbitrarily, applied the concept. Such haphazard application worries some that R2P will become little more than a "Trojan Horse," used to justify any state's foreign policy, while others purport that additional attempts at application will ultimately yield more coherence on the concept and thus limit misapplication.[6] Despite this difference in beliefs, any attempt to generate public rules governing the practice of R2P, and military intervention in particular, has received little support.

One of the main barriers to institutionalization is the General Assembly's (GA) stalling tactic. On the one hand, the GA continues to push back scheduled debates on implementation of R2P. On the other hand, it simultaneously claims that any further implementation of R2P can only occur after such debates. One such issue to be discussed is Secretary General Ban Ki-Moon's desire to create a joint office of the Special Advisers on Genocide and R2P. However, such a merger could only take place after the GA has had a chance to read the Secretary General's reports on R2P and, more crucially, come to consensus.[7] Unfortunately it seems to be that the only actor in the UN who desires change is Ban, as Special Adviser Edward Luck is now no longer in his post, and the organization continues to drag its feet or blatantly stonewall any progress.[8]

While political will is, of course, the solution to almost any international political problem, many of the difficulties associated with R2P are due to the duty's current lack of institutionalization. In other words, states recognize they must do something to protect basic human rights of all peoples, but how, when, where and whether they can be coerced to do so is still unclear. Thus the duty to protect is undertaken only in the broadest possible scope and according to a state or a coalition of states' conception of what is right. Thus R2P is debated and executed in a condition of private right.

We see this most clearly in three circumstances. First, there is the UN Security Council's refusal (or inability) to come to agreement about military intervention (as in the case of Darfur). Second, there is the attempt of various states to justify their actions under the auspices of an undefined and noninstitutionalized principle of R2P (as in the case of Georgia). Finally, there is the abject failure of the UN and states to uphold the R2P principle at all (as in the case of Somalia, and more recently Syria). This tendency to act on private conceptions of right is underscored even further if one views R2P as "a political commitment to prevent and halt genocide and mass atrocities accompanied by a policy agenda in need of implementation."[9] Without implementation, states will continue to abuse (either purposefully or not) the concept and the problems of indeterminacy, and compliance, will never be overcome.

An international R2P institution

Institutionalizing a duty to protect is, ultimately, a question of strengthening international governance and all of its accoutrements. As a duty of R2P is a provisional juridical duty, it requires bolstering the *juridical*. Unfortunately, the normal avenue for creating international law, i.e., the time-honored process of voluntarily creating bi- or multilateral treaties, is interfering with the institutionalization of R2P.[10] Member states within the UN refuse not only to make necessary reforms to the organization but to even debate such reforms. If we are to extricate ourselves from this quagmire, we must be more inventive with (re) making the rules of international law. To do this we might look to a coercive maneuver within the existing avenues of international law to establish a R2PI.[11]

We know that Kant's *lex permissiva* permits agents to use coercion to establish a civil condition, and, conceptually, this coercion could take any form: military intervention, "coercive diplomacy," monetary threats, revoking of aid packages etc. Practically speaking, however, using such means to create an R2PI would at best be ineffective, and at worst might provoke such a harsh backlash that it could incite total war. The efficacy of such a move is still quite important theoretically, as well as practically.[12] Few states would abide being strong-armed, as they would see this as a move to dominate global society. It appears that in principle Kant's theory justifies a coercive course of action, but in practice considerations of prudence dictate. This result puts us back between the horns of the dilemma: coerce states or do nothing.

If we are to find a way out of this conundrum, then it appears to be only through the (rather problematic) nonjuridical status of international society and its accepted rules for regulating behavior in this condition of private right. To do this, we can attempt to coopt an emerging practice of domestic legal change. This emerging practice is a nonvoluntary approach to international law creation, and not, as some would have it, a process of "soft institutionalization."[13]

In a recent insightful article, Jean Cohen argues that the UN Security Council (SC) is illegitimately legislating for the international community.[14] She claims that traditional means for law making in the international system, i.e., bi-or multilateral treaties, are being circumvented. Instead of seeking state consent, the SC issues resolutions that require member states to change their domestic legal systems to conform to whatever the SC deems appropriate for the "peace and security" of the international system. To wit, the SC is legislating for the world without member states' express consent. Cohen cites Resolutions 1373, 1540, 1730 and 1566 (resolutions governing the fight against terrorism and the acquisition of weapons of mass destruction) as the main means by which the SC is operating. She argues that:

> the Security Council arrogates to itself the competence to identify not particular, but general, permanent yet amorphous threats to the existing order, and responds by legislating for the international community as a whole, thereby informally amending the Charter, usurping constituent authority, and radically changing the way international law is made and its function.[15]

Cohen believes that by extending its scope of action and authority, the SC is illicitly amending the Charter, which can only be legitimately accomplished by a two-thirds vote in the GA and a unanimous vote by all five permanent members in the SC.[16] She posits that the SC is extending its powers beyond the scope originally defined in the Charter.[17]

While Cohen is quick to note that she believes such legislation is illegitimate and harmful to the protection of state sovereignty and international law, I do not think we should be as dismissive of this process. First, the SC claims it is working within its enumerated Chapter VII powers.[18] The argument runs something like this: when the Charter was created, member states did not foresee such global threats as are currently witnessed, and so the SC's exercise of its powers has expanded to meet such threats. Through an evolving order, the SC has extended its reach, but only to fulfill its mandate. Another line of argument for the SC's arrogation of legislative powers is roughly as follows: while the SC is stretching the boundaries of its powers, this is necessary to get member states to institutionalize in their domestic constitutions adequate mechanisms for the protection of their governments and peoples.[19] Without the SC issuing resolutions under Chapter VII, its decisions would not be binding and states would be free to ignore them. Exercising power in this way is the only way to ensure universal compliance. The SC has merely found a way to make secure, as best as it can, rights of states and peoples; it has become an international Romulus, so that the international system can later be ruled by a Numa.[20]

It is via this avenue of Chapter VII powers that I suggest the SC forms a subsidiary, yet not dependent, organ for the institutionalization of a duty of R2P. It is important that this organization be authorized by, but autonomous from, the UN. One very fruitful avenue to pursue is to mirror the model of domestic organizations known as National Human Rights Institutions (NHRI). These NHRI were developed to occupy a "unique position … between government … and civil society."[21] These institutions act as "middle grounds" between governments, peoples and NGOs, while remaining separate from them all.[22]

While NHRI receive funding from their domestic governments, they act as watchdogs, holding their governments accountable for human rights abuses. As Anne Smith notes about the independence and functions of NHRI:

> The institution must be independent of government control, including financial control. It should have an appointment process providing political independence and a body composed of persons broadly representative of those bodies involved in the protection and promotion of human rights. It should have adequate funding to fulfill its functions effectively and be given as

> broad a mandate as possible in order for it to be able to promote and protect human rights. Other features include adequate powers, including the right to initiate investigations without referral from a higher authority or receipt of an individual complaint, the power to access information, prisons, and other places of detention, and the power to compel witnesses to testify.... [A]n institution should be able "to perform its functions without interference or obstruction from any branch of government or public or private entity."[23]

Interestingly, NHRI are often created by domestic states to ensure the states' compliance with international human rights norms. This might seem somewhat paradoxical, as I am recommending the establishment of an international organization to monitor not only domestic governments but the UN as well. International organizations require monitoring of their compliance with international human rights norms too.

The R2PI's functions should be broad: it must promulgate public rules for the practice of R2P; it must have the ability to monitor domestic governments to ensure compliance with those rules; and it must be able to act as an ombudsperson for the UN.[24] Most important for our purposes is the first task: promulgating rules. Such rules ought to be formulated not by the GA, but by those "men who possess most wisdom to discern, and most virtue to pursue, the common good of the society;" in other words, by individuals who are experts and who can play advisory roles, such as the Special Adviser on Genocide, and any potential new Special Advisor on R2P.[25] Because this body will ultimately promulgate rules for the practice of R2P, which is a global practice, the institution ought to attempt to be representative of global society. Those involved in the promulgation of rules should "make no law which will not have its full operation on themselves and their friends, as well as on the great mass of the society."[26] Thus, the formation of rules should come out of a consensus reached by a community of global experts, and all states are equally subject to these laws.[27]

Such rules could, of course, be lifted from the ICISS report "The Responsibility to Protect," or one could use the Rome Statutes (as I have suggested) as a starting point.[28] How such rules are operationalized is open to debate. The crucial point is that an organization be established with the authority to promulgate them. The removal of private judgment is paramount.

One might object here that the GA is exactly this kind of body, and so the formulation of rules governing the practice of R2P ought to be done there. Much like legislative bodies throughout the world, the delegates to the GA come together to discuss issues, make recommendations and the like. Moreover, the GA is a smaller body than most legislatures, and so coming to consensus might be easier too. Indeed, if we were to even try to think of global society represented anywhere, it would be the GA. Unfortunately, there is one special difference between states' legislatures and the GA: power. The GA is only empowered to "discuss" issues. It cannot issue any binding law on member states, but can merely make recommendations. Furthermore, it is more frequent that when the GA does make a recommendation or a resolution, these suggestions are the product of backdoor and nontransparent dealings. The world's "legislative" body issues nonbinding recommendations that do not even arise from a formal vote.[29] The GA is ultimately a powerless and nontransparent body.

Some might object that the best-situated authority within the UN is not the GA or the SC, but actually the Secretary General. Anne Orford takes this route. She convincingly argues that the challenges of R2P are not new, and that they are due to the twin problems of locating proper political authority and providing security and protection to peoples. This is indeed not far from the Kantian account provided here, as Hobbes (one of Orford's primary philosophical sources) provided similar prescriptions. Hobbes was concerned with the establishment of the state as the principal means of guaranteeing natural right, and the absolute state, represented by the Leviathan, provided those mechanisms. The Leviathan became the one and only authority to promulgate law and settle rights disputes, and so individuals in the state of nature consented to institute such a system to ensure their lives and rights were protected.

Where Orford takes Hobbes' account is in relation to rights protection and disputes in the international system as a precursor to the doctrine of R2P. She argues that it has been the job of the Secretary General to fill power vacuums in international authority and create pathways for rights protections. Citing Dag Hammarskjöld's civilian protection practices in the 1950s and 1960s, she argues that the executive authority within the UN can undertake broad measures, "such as administration, surveillance, fact-finding, quiet diplomacy, management, capacity-building and policing," and draw particular jurisdictional boundaries where other international bodies cannot.[30] Hammarskjöld's expansions of not only the Secretary General's powers, but also the powers under the UN Charter, were the result of decolonization and the Cold War. R2P, she claims, is no more than a coherent doctrine applied to these previously inconsistent practices.[31]

While Orford's account is certainly noteworthy, and she correctly identifies the problems of proper authority and jurisdiction as inherent to rights protection and a duty of R2P, she does not link the remedies to these problems with the other three requisite authorities (legislative, judicial and coercive force). Her claim is merely about "understanding these practices [executive action] as a specific from of governance (administration) with a particular history" that can then "help to make the political stakes of international executive rule intelligible."[32] She is rightly skeptical of functionalist accounts of international law, and she accurately draws attention back to the fundamental questions of authority and status. But she shies away from linking the other necessary authorities to her argument about executive action.

More problematic, though, is that her claim that R2P provides the "normative foundation of the form of authority that has been created through the practices of policing and administration conducted in the decolonized world of the 1960s" actually begs the question of authority. Claiming that the 2001 ICISS report provided the normative foundation for authority already in practice is anachronistic and confused. For how could the international executive, as represented through the Secretary General, lack a normative foundation for his practices if they are undertaken as part of his very authority? The doctrine of R2P does not somehow provide more normative force to the actions of Hammarskjöld, and it does not actually bestow any new or more authoritative powers on the office of the Secretary General now.

It is therefore necessary to create a new institution to fulfill the international community's duty to protect, and that institution should be endowed with the authority to promulgate public binding rules. We can skirt the two traditional avenues of international law creation by utilizing the SC's ability to pass resolutions requiring a change in domestic legal regimes. The SC is the only UN body that can require member states to change their existing domestic laws. By passing a resolution that requires states to support such an institution, the international community is, in a sense, forced to be free. As the only international body with the authority and power to make such universal decisions, the SC is the most capable agent to do so, and capability here ultimately rests not solely on military prowess but a modicum of authority.

The ICC and the ICJ

> Until it is possible to remove from the interested states the prerogative of resolving questions of law and transfer this permanently and universally to an impartial authority, all further steps along the road to world peace are to be excluded.[33]

Hans Kelsen's suggestion, that international courts have mandatory jurisdiction, is not a new claim. Kelsen argued for this in 1944, and others have since followed suit.[34] But what reforms are necessary for the world's two courts? First, the ICJ is a court constituted to settle contentious cases between states, and it is rare that a state commits gross crimes against humanity or genocide against citizens of another state. Thus, reforms to the ICJ are not as practically, legally or morally pressing.[35] Contrarily, states established the ICC specifically to prosecute these very crimes (genocide and crimes against humanity), and so we should focus our attention there.

Besides the problem that the ICC ought to have compulsory and universal jurisdiction, one of the continued thorns in the side of the Court is the principle of complementarity (PoC). The PoC set out in Article 17 of the Rome Statutes provides the rules according to which a case is admissible to the ICC. The PoC favors local prosecution; only when such prosecution has not occurred, because a state is unwilling or unable to prosecute, or because prosecution proceedings are being used to "shield" a perpetrator, may the ICC prosecute.[36] The ICC is supposed to be a "court of last resort."[37]

The PoC in theory is unproblematic. However, in practice it is the source of much dispute. Three such problems are: misapplication of the PoC; "interests of justice" arguments; and "shielding" proceedings. The first problem is the easiest to resolve. Darryl Robinson, drafter of the text that became Article 17, recently argued that most international law scholars completely ignore almost half of the text of the Article.[38] He explains that Article 17 is really a two-step test of inadmissibility of a case to the Court. The first step is to assess whether national proceedings are being prepared or ongoing, and then the second step is to assess the quality of those proceedings. Robinson notes that international lawyers and scholars ignore much of what the Article says, and they collapse all distinctions into what he calls the "slogan version," where the Article is made to look as if "unable and unwilling" (one of the second-step tests) is the hallmark condition for ICC jurisdiction. Robinson's plea is for international lawyers and scholars to pay closer attention to the wording of Article 17. By doing so, they will see that the role of the ICC is complementary to domestic legal institutions. In other words, sovereignty is not at risk because the ICC is a court of last resort: when there is effective prosecution at the domestic level, the ICC has no need to intervene.

The second problem is more difficult. This problem concerns the "interests of justice." To illustrate, let us use the case of Uganda. Without going into great historical detail, the problem is roughly this: Uganda referred a case to the ICC to try members of the Lord's Resistance Army (LRA), and after the ICC issued arrest warrants for the prosecution of several LRA leaders, Uganda began peace talks and attempted to sign peace treaties with the rebels.[39] Treaties were not, ultimately, signed because several of the leaders failed to show up to the signing ceremonies due to the fear that they would be arrested and sent to the ICC for prosecution. Thus one of the stumbling blocks to peace has been the ICC's refusal to dismiss the arrest warrants. Another has been Uganda's refusal to support the ICC after it requested the Court's help. The question, therefore, is whether the ICC should continue to prosecute members of the LRA despite local calls for amnesty. The underlying tension is not necessarily between peace and justice but between differing conceptions of justice. Some believe that the ICC should continue with prosecution, while others think that continuing prosecution is "a form of international law legalism; in other words, the pursuit of formalistic universal justice comes at the expense of meaningful local mechanisms of justice."[40] When the prosecutor has discretion to determine whether a case ought to be pursued "in the interests of justice," it is not immediately clear whose conception of justice he ought to follow.[41] Robinson states that the drafters of the Rome Statute did not want to deal with the problem of dueling conceptions of justice and would rather leave it up to diplomats.[42] Unfortunately, diplomats are not addressing the case in Uganda, and the "creative ambiguity" left in the statute only creates further problems.

The Kantian solution is to enforce the Rome Statutes universally and limit prosecutorial discretion. Although it may be hard to accept, Uganda is a case of strict universalizability. Uganda referred the case to the ICC, and the ICC investigated and found that the LRA leaders had committed war crimes and crimes against humanity. The ICC then issued arrest warrants for its leaders. Some might argue that Uganda's referral was merely a political ploy, but whatever its motivations, as a sovereign member state it was within its rights to do so.[43] Uganda believed that utilizing the ICC was the best course of action, so it must then abide by its ruling and support the ICC. If the maxim of referring cases and then dropping them for reasons of political expediency were universalized, the ICC would be robbed of legitimacy and efficacy.

The final problem concerns the "shielding" of perpetrators. Shielding goes far beyond a domestic government setting up sham prosecutions (thereby satisfying the first-step test of admissibility in Article 17). Shielding can also take the form of a state not complying with the ICC's demands,[44] as well as the form of other member states failing to observe their obligations under the Rome Statutes.[45] The current case against Sudan's President Omar Hassan al-Bashir is representative of all of these problems. When a state as recalcitrant as Sudan flouts the rights of its people, as well as dismissing any authority of the ICC, it is an affront to the pursuit of justice. Unfortunately, the ICC can do nothing in response. The chief prosecutor can issue arrest warrants, or he can remind states of their R2P obligations, or even write op-ed columns in newspapers, but the fact remains that nothing can be done.[46] The Court lacks power to enforce its proceedings, as it requires states to do the enforcing. This is because the ICC finds itself within

> a system of justice [that] exists within the system of states and is subject to all that this interstate system entails. The ICC depends on elements of this interstate system for its success, and to secure the cooperation of the states within this system, contains elements that reinforce the authority and sovereignty of the state.... This is balanced against, and sometimes contradictory to, the universality to which the ICC aspires.[47]

To remedy the problems of shielding (broadly construed) is to remedy the problems of rendering final and binding judgments capable of enforcement. The ICC must have the means available to execute arrest warrants and to hold states accountable for their noncompliance.

United Nations Rapid Reaction Force

Arguments for a volunteer UN Rapid Reaction Force (RRF) have gained scholarly favor over the last few years.[48] Indeed, scholars continue to refine their arguments for such a standing army, debating the numbers required, the placement of such a force in the UN organization, who should provide financial, military and logistical resources, and how to limit abuses of and by an RRF by providing concurrent institutions of accountability. Many of the participants in the debate over intervention agree on one thing: in the past, undertaking interventions has been increasingly difficult because states did not want to put their soldiers in harm's way to save the lives of distant strangers. An RRF, they now argue, is required to solve the problem of member states' lack of "political will" to intervene. Such a force should be small and capable of rapid deployment anywhere in the world and sustainable for a short period of time.[49] Moreover, proponents of an RRF claim that by making this force voluntary, and not subject to any one state, the RRF will be truly cosmopolitan, an army for the protection of *human* rights.[50]

While not wanting to repeat much of what has been said before, discussing whether there ought to be 200,000 or 600,000 troops is not of theoretical importance. What is important is discerning why a cosmopolitan RRF is logically required, not only to help a provisional duty of HI to become peremptory, but by the concept of *Recht* as such.

Recall that Kant claims that:

> A rightful condition is that relation of human beings among one another that contains the conditions under which everyone is able to *enjoy* his rights, and the formal condition under which this is possible in accordance with the idea of a will giving laws for everyone is called public justice.[51]

In other words, only in a condition where individuals' rights to external objects of choice (persons, promises and objects) are secure can public right exist. Such "enjoyment," or security, requires an authoritative coercive force capable of ensuring each his own.[52] This force, which Kant calls "power" (*Macht*), must be capable of "constraining everyone else with whom he comes into conflict."[53] Only when this force is present, and working according to universal standards, can each person's rights be secured. By universal standards, I mean laws that a people could decree for itself.[54] If a people could not agree to a law, through a test of hypothetical universalization, then that law fails to protect each person.

Coercion is "limitation of freedom by the will [*Willkür*] of another,"[55] but public, lawful and "irresistible"[56] coercion is necessary a priori for the protection of rights. The coercive power must be irresistible, in terms not just of its overwhelming force, but of its legitimacy. In terms of a domestic constitution, individuals create such a force to protect equally each person's rights under the law; what is required internationally should be no different.

An international force, capable of systematic enforcement of public rules and judgments, is necessary to provide all human beings with the capacity to "enjoy" their rights. This necessity is part and parcel of the metaphysics of Kantian justice, and not merely a political expedience. That scholars repeatedly identify such a solution shows that, intuitively, we are aware of its importance. This argument, then, answers the question of why. An RRF is therefore not just a standing army; it is the necessary coercive mechanism capable of protecting each person in his freedom, equality and independence.[57] Public "rules" or agreements on the "Responsibility to Protect" are, likewise, hollow words without an institutionalized military force capable of enforcing such rules.

There is a question of whether such a force would also be authorized to carry out arrest warrants that the ICC issues, thus acting as a police force as well as a military one. This may be politically tricky, as there are not many institutional mechanisms in place to ensure the supremacy of international law, but I see no moral reason why not. If a country has signed on to the Rome Statutes and has not furnished the accused to the Court, then the PoC should apply here as well. If a state has not signed the Rome Statutes, jurisdiction (for prosecution and police action) could be satisfied when the Security Council recommends the case to the Court. This is of course assuming that the Court undergoes no significant changes in universal jurisdiction.

An RRF ought to be under the direction of the UN, for at the moment there is no other international body capable of global representation. In the case of an emerging humanitarian crisis, the R2PI should make a recommendation to the SC for the deployment of the force. In the event that the SC is caught in a quagmire due to the P-5 veto, the decision should be referred to the GA for a vote. The ICISS report on R2P suggests such a procedure in the case of a SC stalemate, and I see no reason why such a procedure should not be used to direct the RRF as well.[58] Since the SC's main function is to provide for the peace and security of the world's states, it ought to be the principal organ to issue directives. To guard against the same problems witnessed now with regard to R2P, the GA should be an alternate avenue for checking the veto power in the SC.[59]

One could perhaps object that referring a situation to the GA will always result in forbearance of the use of force because the GA is made up of both Kantian republics and non-republics. There are a plethora of types of states in the GA: Western liberal democracies, transitional democracies, despotisms, autocracies, and a score of states who fear intervention in their territories. Thus any vote would result in a lack of protection. While all these facts and conjectures are certainly true, the response to this objection is that the SC would, of course, necessarily know as well. This gives the SC reason to guard its power and come to agreement on the use of force without having to delegate any of its power to the GA. In practice though, it is perhaps possible that the GA would authorize protective actions. With the recent events in Syria, the GA did manage to pass a nonbinding resolution condemning the violence perpetrated against rebels and civilians by the Assad regime.[60]

Providing a "Surrogate" or making a Provisional Duty of R2P Peremptory

Of course, a duty of R2P cannot become fully peremptory until something like a state of states (*Völkerstaat*) is established, but such a duty can be institutionalized and become enforceable. It can approximate, in what amounts to a Kantian state of nature, a peremptory duty of R2P. We can do this by employing similar reasoning to Kant: to set up a surrogate institution to secure rights in the interim.[61] The institution, coupled with a reformed ICC and implemented cosmopolitan RRF, is a surrogate to the state of states. Instead of requiring a sharp and drastic move, and risking the emergence of a "soulless despotism," we can instead approximate the requirements of public right.

The requirements of public right, Kant explains,

> can be divided into *protective justice* (*iustitia tutatrix*), *justice in men's acquiring from one another* (*iustitia commutativa*), and *distributive justice* (*iustitia distributiva*).—In these the law says, *first* merely what conduct is intrinsically *right* in terms of its form (*lex iusti*); *second*, what [objects] are

> capable of being covered externally by law, in terms of their matter, that is, what way of being in possession is *rightful* (*lex iuridica*); *third*, what is the decision of a court in a particular case in accordance with the given law under which it falls, that is, what is *laid down as right* (*lex iustitiae*).[62]

These three forms of justice are formally necessary. They must exist as institutions in the real world.[63] These institutions are "public law giving, the free public market, and the public judiciary."[64] *Any system of public right must have these three (separated) authorities*, and anything short of these requirements means that one finds oneself in a condition of private right.

Iustitia tutatrix

Iustitia tutaxtrix is "protective" because it promulgates laws publically, and therefore takes private judgment about rights out of the hands of private persons. The protective form of justice corresponds to the legislative authority in a community. For Kant, public law contains "the a priori principles of reason about what law should be, but it also gives them effect in the world of experience because it is enacted and enforced."[65]

The establishment of an R2PI, as an institution that can authoritatively lay down public rules for the practice of R2P, can fulfill the requirement of *iustitia tutatrix.* Promulgating public rules that settle issues of when, where and how a duty of R2P ought to be discharged removes states' private judgment over these questions. Moreover, the creation of a volunteer RRF settles the question of "who" ought to intervene.

Iustitia commutativa

The commutative form of justice governs transactions between individuals in the marketplace. As Kant argues, people cannot have external rights to things, but only rights against people, and so the marketplace is an extremely important concept in our dealings with others.[66] Each time I decide to buy an apple or to make or accept a promise, my right to an external object of my choice is affected. My right is affected because it is dependent upon the recognition and actions of others. Therefore, the role of commutative justice is to regulate property and contract law in the real world between acting individuals.[67] The kind of authority corresponding to commutative justice is, therefore, the executive.[68]

Regulating the exchange of external objects of choice may not appear to be the role of the executive, but Kant's argument depends on his understanding of the role of subsumption in a practical syllogism. As Byrd and Hruschka explain, the major premise in the syllogism would be the law; the minor premise would be a particular case involving a dispute about the law. The conclusion would be a judgment that a neutral and public judge renders on the particular case (i.e., in determining whether the case applies under the major premise.) The executive authority comes to the fore when the laws laid down by the legislature or the judgments rendered by the judiciary must be executed. In other words, *the executive is in charge of setting up the requisite institutions for law*. For example, if the legislative authority claims that landowners must sign a registry, then one of the executive's functions is to create that registry. Thus, in the marketplace, the executive must make the necessary arrangements to govern the buying and selling of external objects of choice.

In terms of fulfilling a duty to protect, the executive in this case would be the UN Security Council. Its role would be to use its authority to issue binding resolutions on member states and force them to support the creation of an R2PI. The SC would create the institution required to fulfill the international community's duty to protect.

Contrary to Orford, the Secretary General is not the proper authority for this action. The Secretary General has no power to make arrangements to execute law or judgments. It only has power to "bring to the attention of the Security Council any matter which in his opinion may threaten the maintenance of international peace and security" and to appoint staff in the office of the Secretariat.[69] The Secretariat has the *potential* to exercise executive functions, but only when the General Assembly or the Security Council explicitly authorizes it to do so. The office itself is not one of executive authority. In the case of the General Assembly, much of this power is relegated to matters internal to the organization, such as setting up new offices. In regards to R2P, the actual creation of the institutions necessary to discharge a duty to protect could happen only via the SC. Only the SC has the authorized powers to do so; that is, to issue binding resolutions on member states and to create the necessary mechanisms required for peace and security. In reality, the Secretary General is typically deemed the "UN's chief politician, diplomat, and mediator," and has no power to create new institutions, issue binding resolutions or statements, or do much more than make recommendations and "bring attention" to particular issues of international concern.[70] While Hammarskjöld was certainly a formidable and noble Secretary General, his actions (and the conferment of powers on him) may have been the result of a tumultuous period in international society's history and not a systematic and expanding office within the UN.

Iustitia distributiva

Finally, the role of distributive justice is to "award to each what is his in accordance with the law."[71] In other words, when rights are in dispute the role of a neutral judge is necessary to determine whether the object of choice belongs to Party A or Party B in accordance with the public laws. Thus, the corresponding institution to distributive justice is the judiciary.

Strengthening the ICC to render public and final judgments, capable of enforcement via an RRF, would satisfy Kant's requirements for distributive justice. The ICC would have not only the crimes listed in the Rome Statutes to "subsume" under its judgment, but would also have any other public rules laid out by the R2PI under its jurisdiction. Moreover, with the formation of a RRF, that force would be subject to the same international humanitarian law that governs all states' armed forces. Placing cosmopolitan soldiers under the jurisdiction of a cosmopolitan court would provide accountability for any crimes undertaken during an operation. Currently, there is no means for such accountability within the UN, and this continues to place strain on the organization.[72]

Universality and reciprocity

As Byrd and Hruschka argue, Kant employs three different "models" in his explanation of the transition to international and cosmopolitan law.[73] They argue that Kant ultimately requires the second model, a state of nation states (*Völkerstaat*) for the realization of cosmopolitan justice. However, due to the lengthy process of gradual reform, Kant writes in "Perpetual Peace" that a league of nations (*Völkerbund*) should be the penultimate target. States have "a duty to strive toward the constitutional perfection of one single state of nations in an effort to approximate perpetual peace," but "we cannot completely attain our goal," even though "we can come as close as possible to attaining perpetual peace."[74]

The need to establish an R2PI, along with reforms to the ICC and the creation of a voluntary UN RRF, would place the international system further along the continuum towards international public right. Such reforms go beyond a mere *Völkerbund*, which is concerned only with "maintaining and securing freedom for a state and simultaneously for the other states in the league."[75] The *Völkerbund* cannot acquire any power over its members, and each state must consent to join the league.[76] The R2PI, by contrast, would be set up via the powers delegated to the SC by UN member states. This institution would have authority to promulgate public universal rules by which member states must abide. Moreover, it would have authority to monitor states' treatment of their citizens. If leaders, militias or any other individuals within a state commit gross crimes against humanity, the institution has power to call for protective coercive measures to stop such abuses and to make recommendations to the ICC for prosecution. Most importantly, state consent to abide by the R2PI would not be required because the SC could use its powers to issue a binding resolution requiring all states to join it. A *Völkerbund* has power only to secure the rights and freedoms of states; an R2PI is concerned with securing the rights and freedoms of individuals within states.

As Kant informs us, the transition from provisional to conclusive right[77] requires that every person:

> provides me with assurance that he will behave in the same principle.... This assurance does not require a special act to establish a right, but is already contained in the concept of an obligation corresponding to an external right, since the *universality*, and with it the *reciprocity*, of obligation arises from a universal rule.[78]

An R2PI promulgating universal rules that ensure reciprocity satisfies such a condition. Since it is concerned with universally protecting the basic rights of human beings, regardless of where they happen to be born, the rules it promulgates cannot "infringe upon natural right, (i.e., that right which can be derived from a priori principles for a civil condition)."[79] Further, a UN RRF provides the requisite "accompanied power" to give force to the public laws and the settled judgments.[80]

It is only when the legislative, judicial, executive and enforcement authorities are present that one's rights can be fully secured. We must theorize about how to establish such authorities in the international system, especially as states are very reluctant to curtail their powers, even for the protection of human life. Kant understands the dangers of such reluctance, so we must continue to remember his command: "When you cannot avoid living side by side with all others, you ought to leave the state of nature and proceed with them into a rightful condition, that is, a condition of distributive justice."[81] But such a move does not need to result in a *Völkerstaat*; we can create another "model" to ensure the protection of human rights and to discharge a duty of R2P.

Conclusion

> In order, therefore, that the social pact may not be an empty formula, it tacitly includes the commitment, which alone can give force to the others, that anyone who refuses to obey the general will shall be compelled to do so by the entire body; this means nothing else than that he will be forced to be free.
>
> (Jean Jacques Rousseau, *The Social Contract*, Chapter VII)

The notion that man must be forced to be free or compelled to obey the dictates of law for the sake of freedom is paradoxical. Freedom appears to be, by its very nature, the antithesis of coercive acts. But this is to take a very strict understanding of law and freedom. Lawless freedom is that type of freedom that is not rule governed, and it threatens to undermine the freedom of everyone else. This is why Kant follows Rousseau's understanding about force and freedom. Without the ability to order our lives and pursue our projects independent of the arbitrary will or domination of another, any freedom that we experience is fleeting. Those who attempt to remain in a condition of such lawless freedom threaten the rest.

It is therefore the task of law, indeed the very idea of law, to increase the freedom of each by regulating the conduct of all. The "law demands that there be rules, that they be made known, and that they be observed in practice by those charged by their administration."[82] Thus the very idea (*Idee*) of law requires three substantive parts: the protective, the commutative and the distributive. All three are necessary for the realization of universal justice. Law's nature, therefore, does not change. We do not say that what is necessary for law in the domestic state is different than what is necessary for law in international society. The features remain the same.

Thus if we value freedom, and we value the rights that being free entails, we must recognize our responsibility to protect. The doctrine of R2P is an attempt to balance the freedoms of people against the freedoms of states. States cannot be the only rights bearers in international society, for their rights are dependent upon providing protection to their peoples. When they manifestly fail to do this, the idea of justice does not merely vanish. It remains. Yet it remains in a condition of provisionality, where further actions are necessary. These actions require the setting up of juridical institutions. The practice of R2P, the fulfillment of a duty of R2P, and the limits of R2P can only be governed once these institutions are in place.

Thus, while we might say that institutionalizing a duty to protect solves many practical problems, this is not the whole of the matter. Institutionalizing a duty to protect, that is, creating and reforming institutions, is necessary a priori for the realization of justice. While forcing the international community to accept the rule of a transnational institution and court is no easy task, and any attempt at pushing a larger agenda is doomed to failure, we must still attempt to provide a surrogate for universal public right.

To make a provisional duty of R2P peremptory, we must establish an R2PI that effectively promulgates public rules, for this will achieve the requirement for protective justice (*iustitia tutatrix*). Moreover, using the SC's ability to issue binding resolutions that require member states to join and to abide by an R2PI fulfills the requirements for commutative justice (*iustitia commutativa*). Reforming the ICC to have universal jurisdiction with a capacity to enforce judgments against violators of R2P satisfies the need for distributive justice (*iustitia distributiva*).

To ensure compliance, an external authoritative coercive force, an RRF, must also accompany these reforms. Kant famously said that "there is connected with right by the principle of contradiction an authorization to coerce someone who infringes it."[83] It is only by resisting, with force, a "hindrance to freedom" that can one be free, and it is only when such resistance is universal, guaranteeing the rights of all, that there can be universal freedom. A cosmopolitan military, designed to protect human rights, would be such a force.

Ultimately, I am sure that much of what I have said here will be construed as a mere "pious wish." Indeed, as Kant observed in 1795:

> Reason can provide related nations with no other means for emerging from the state of lawlessness, which consists solely of war, than that they give up their savage (lawless) freedom, just as individual persons do, and, by accommodating themselves to the constraints of common law, establish a *nation of peoples* (*civitas gentium*) that (continually growing) will finally include all the peoples of the earth. But they do not will to do this because it does not conform to their idea of the right of nations, and consequently they discard in *hypothesis* what is true in *thesis*.[84]

The logic of justice requires that states move beyond their lawless freedom and submit to public coercive laws. Not merely for the regulation of their affairs, but for the protection of individuals within their borders. This is true in thesis, and we must continue to work towards its realization.

6 Conclusion

The Responsibility to Protect and the real world—Libya and Syria

Two of the most recent R2P crises, Libya and Syria, are representative cases of the discrepant effects of possessing a juridical duty in a condition of private right. Namely, while one case appears a victory for the protection of human rights, the other vitiates such success. The variance with which the "international community" discharges its responsibility to protect is certainly due to the problems of lack of political will, case selectivity and power politics, but these problems themselves are the result of the failure to establish institutions of justice in the international system. The problem is ultimately systemic in nature, and so requires a systemic solution. As long as the international system lacks the juridical requirements for Kantian justice, international humanitarian assistance and universal human rights will always remain merely "provisional."

By examining two of the most prominent and contemporary cases pertaining to R2P—one where the doctrine was invoked and the international community reacted swiftly to stop human rights abuses and one where the doctrine was invoked and the international community stood by and failed to stop such abuse—we can see the structural causes of state behavior. These two cases, similar yet distinct, provide us with a comparison to draw out the details of each, giving weight to the empirical arguments of why intervention occurred in one, but not the other.[1] More importantly, though, by examining these two cases we also see why such empirical arguments are not sufficient for an explanation of a duty of R2P, but ultimately require a theory of justice.

Libya: the success of R2P

The spring of 2011 saw a spread of popular protests throughout the Arab world. From January through February, protests spread from Tunisia to Algeria, then on to Egypt, Lebanon, Jordan, Bahrain, Iran, Yemen and Libya. Protests in Iraq, Morocco, Saudi Arabia and Syria soon followed. Several states managed to quash rebellions and protests rather quickly; others made small political changes or paid out, in political science and economics jargon, "rents" to citizens in hopes to manage dissatisfaction. In Libya, the Gaddafi regime reacted swiftly and violently to protests, urging supporters to attack the "cockroaches" and "greasy rats" questioning his rule and inciting sedition and rebellion.[2] He declared that he would go "house by house" executing all who stood in his way, ridding and cleansing Libya of its rebels.[3] The world had evidence that he would indeed follow up with such threats, for, only 24 hours prior to his televised rant, two Libyan air force pilots defected to Malta after being ordered to bomb civilian centers.[4] The events that followed in the days after Gaddafi's now infamous speech showed the possibility of effective and rapid reaction to threatened mass atrocities.

On February 22, merely six days after the beginning of the protests and violent crackdown, the League of Arab States (LAS) suspended Libya from its organization. That same day the UN Security Council (SC) issued a statement condemning the violence inside Libya and calling for an immediate cessation of hostilities against civilians. Within another 24 hours the African Union (AU) had issued a statement also condemning the violence against the protesters while simultaneously recognizing their right to "political reform, justice and socio-economic development."[5] The Organization of the Islamic Council (OIC) followed suit, and within days the UN Human Rights Council established a commission of inquiry and called for the General Assembly to suspend Libya from the Human Rights Council, which it did several days later.

The momentum continued to increase, and the Security Council unanimously adopted Resolution 1970 on February 26. It supported and echoed many of the previous statements by regional organizations, by condemning the attacks against civilians, but it also added that the SC suspected such acts "may amount to crimes against humanity" and explicitly drew attention to the Libyan regime's "responsibility to protect its population."[6] Far from using mere words, the SC used the resolution to refer the situation to the International Criminal Court for investigation, establish an arms embargo, impose travel bans on Gaddafi, his sons and several members of the regime, freeze assets of several regime members, and create a sanctions committee to monitor these coercive measures.[7]

During this period, the rebel opposition established itself as the Interim National Transition Council (NTC). Members included Libyan diplomats who defected from the regime, officers and enlisted personnel from the Libyan armed forces, and opposition leaders, tribal leaders, academics and businessmen.[8] Establishing its base in Benghazi, the NTC quickly started to close ranks and claim that it was the interim government of Libya, thereby delegitimizing the Gaddafi regime and claiming itself to be the sole representative of the Libyan people.[9] Within weeks the NTC began courting foreign governments for aid for its cause, seeking money, arms and recognition. By March 10, France, Italy and the European Union (EU) foreign affairs head Catherine Ashton had opened a dialogue with the NTC. By this time the Gulf Cooperation Council also recognized the NTC as the official representative body and urged the LAS to do the same. On March 14, the US Secretary of State, Hillary Clinton, held a late-night closed-door meeting with a leading figure within the NTC, Mahmoud Jibril, in a hotel in Paris.[10] The next day, President Obama held a meeting with senior officials outlining options for intervention in Libya.[11]

On March 17, the Security Council passed Resolution 1973. It passed with 10 votes in favor, zero votes against, and five abstentions (Brazil, China, Germany, India and Russia). The resolution defined the situation in Libya as a threat to international peace and security, thereby triggering Chapter VII powers in the UN Charter. The SC demanded an immediate cessation of violence and attacks against civilians, as well as authorizing "all necessary measures … to protect civilians and civilian populated areas under threat of attack in the Libyan Arab Jamahiriya, including Benghazi."[12] To do this, the resolution established a no-fly zone inside Libya, enforced an arms embargo, including preventing further provisions of mercenaries to the Libyan army, banned flights of all aircraft unless approved in advance by the AU's High Level Committee on Libya, continued asset freezes and travel bans denoted in Resolution 1970, and established a Panel of Experts to oversee various measures undertaken in compliance with Resolution 1973.[13]

While the resolution outlined broad powers to protect civilians and disable the regime's ability to continue its onslaught, the consensus on how the no-fly zone ought to be enforced was vague at best. Several of the SC powers explicitly questioned how to fulfill this duty to protect. Russia held the opinion that "the quickest way to ensure robust security for the civilian population and the long-term stabilization of the situation in Libya is an immediate ceasefire."[14] Moreover, China voiced "serious difficulty with parts of the resolution," particularly how the use of force would be governed, and Germany continued to be wary of the use of military force in that it might prolong the conflict or increase the likelihood of loss of life.[15] India's stance was clearest of all: "We also do not have clarity about the details of enforcement measures, including who will participate and with what assets, and how these measures will exactly be carried out."[16] The scope of duty was, ultimately, left open.

While member states raised their concerns about who would enforce the resolution's mandates, and how, for all intents and purposes it was assumed that NATO would at least play a significant part. As early as March 8, NATO began surveillance flights over Libya, and two days later began moving ships into the Mediterranean. By the time Resolution 1973 passed, the United States was already preparing plans for air strikes on Gaddafi's forces. On Saturday, March 19, the US launched "Operation Odyssey Dawn" (OOD), attacking Libyan air defense installations in Tripoli and the coastal areas south of Benghazi.[17] For less than two weeks the United States provided "the bulk of military assets and firepower, logistical support and overall command and control," assuring a swift and devastating blow to Gaddafi's capabilities.[18] Yet, due to public sentiment about the use of force for humanitarian purposes abroad, as well as limitations in US federal law governing the President's powers to authorize the use of force without Congressional approval, the United States quickly handed over the operations (excluding electronic attack, aerial refueling, lift, search and rescue, and intelligence, surveillance and reconnaissance) to NATO on March 31.

The Alliance's control, now termed "Operation Unified Protector" (OUP), lasted roughly seven months. It flew 26,000 sorties, damaging or destroying

6,000 military targets.[19] Ending in October 2011, and enjoying the support of non-Alliance members such as Qatar, the United Arab Emirates, Jordan, Morocco and Sweden, Operation Unified Protector was hailed a "success." The Alliance managed to turn the balance of force in favor of the NTC, helping them to capture Tripoli and Sirte, and many claimed that genocide and mass crimes against humanity were averted.

During the initial phases of OOD and OUP, the mandate of enforcing a no-fly zone quickly started to expand into regime change. Political settlement between Gaddafi and the rebels was seen as impossible, and cries for the ruler's ouster became louder and louder. Even Simon Adams, executive director of the Global Center for the Responsibility to Protect, began to equivocate on whether the removal of Gaddafi was justified or within the bounds of R2P's doctrine or not.[20] Such "mission creep" embodied the worries of Russia, China and India, inadvertently paving the way for future reticence on R2P enforcement action.

In less than six weeks, the international community was able to rally unprecedented support to protect the people of Libya. Moreover, the SC reacted swiftly, passing not one but two resolutions taking coercive measures against Gaddafi and his regime. The United States and its allies were also able to scramble the necessary assets to undertake ODD and OUP. The speed with which a duty of R2P was undertaken was impressive, and showed what the international community, or at the very least a coalition of willing states, is able to do.

Syria: the "failure" of R2P

At the beginning, the situation in Syria appeared to follow a similar path to that of the other Arab Spring protests. On March 18, 2011, protests calling for expanded political freedoms erupted in five Syrian cities. The clashes between protesters and regime security forces soon turned deadly, though, when five protesters were killed in the city of Daraa.[21] Within several days, security forces had killed six more protesters, prompting thousands to take to the streets to march in their funeral procession. More protests began to spread, condemning the regime's brutal violence and crying out for political change.

Yet Syria's President, Bashar al-Assad, did little more than prevaricate. On the one hand, he quickly dismissed a majority of his cabinet, promising political reform and blaming the unrest on "foreign conspirators."[22] Yet on the other hand, within hours of his decision on March 29, he televised a speech promising harsh treatment for any dissent. Protests continued to mount each passing week, and at each event regime security forces opened fire. Within a month of the start of the uprisings, the regime killed an estimated 500 people.[23]

The deteriorating situation quickly brought international attention, with the Under-Secretary for Human Rights briefing the SC that the regime was targeting civilians. Within weeks, the United States froze Assad's assets and the EU imposed arms embargoes and travel bans on Syria and its leading elite.[24] Momentum towards international action appeared to be growing, though at a slower pace than in the case of Libya.

At this point, Assad's response to the brutality was to blame security forces, citing "poor training" as the reason for all of the bloodshed. All the while, he ordered these same forces to use machine guns and tanks to bombard rebel towns and villages. Over the next several months, Assad continued his cat-and-mouse game regarding political reforms. These moves stalled much movement from the international community, and it was not until August, amid mounting body counts, that the SC issued a "Presidential Statement" condemning the violence inside Syria but simultaneously supporting its right to sovereignty. With this statement, any formal discussion of intervention for the purpose of protecting civilians was dismissed.[25]

During this period, the Syrian people began to fight back against the regime's security forces. From June through December, local men formed themselves into armed rebel militias, aiming at disrupting Assad's attacks. These local fighters comprised the majority of the opposition fighters, and to this day they still do. The local militia were not, however, the only fighting forces. On June 10, a Syrian army lieutenant, Hussein Harmoush, defected during an operation against civilians, claiming that his current mission was not to bombard the Syrian people, but to protect "the protesters who are acting for freedom and democracy."[26] Harmoush's defection ignited the "Free Officers Movement," and in July another defected officer, Colonel Riad Assad, announced the formation of an additional officer corps: the "Free Syrian Army" (FSA). The Free Officers Movement and the FSA ultimately joined forces in September when Harmoush was captured by the regime. The result was a patchwork of opposition fighters, poorly trained and poorly armed, and very much unlike the unified opposition within Libya.

On November 2, as fighting between the regime and rebel forces continued to mount, Syria agreed to an Arab League peace plan outlining the cessation of violence, the retreat of the military, the release of all political prisoners and the granting of access to human rights groups, the media and Arab League monitors.[27] Many waited with bated breath to see whether the seven-month conflict would finally draw to an end. Unfortunately, within days, it was apparent that Assad had no intention of abiding by the agreement, and on November 12, the Arab League suspended Syria's membership. Meanwhile, the United States and the EU continued to impose sanctions on Syrian imports and freeze assets of the Assad family and elite, and Turkey's government became increasingly critical of Assad's behavior.

Assad's strategy throughout was to agree to political concessions while concurrently attacking civilians. Thus, in response to the Arab League's suspension, he agreed to yet another peace deal and allowed monitors to enter the country for one month. True to form, Assad reneged on his concessions. Before the end of the one-month monitoring mission, he adamantly rejected a call to hand over power to his vice president and create a national unity government, and continued the assaults on his people. Within days of these statements, the Arab League suspended its monitoring mission due to "worsening conditions."

As the situation continued to deteriorate, another two months went by before the SC was able to draft a resolution on the situation inside Syria. That draft demanded that all sides to the conflict (regime and rebel forces) cease hostilities, and that the regime release all political prisoners, withdraw all armed forces from cities and towns and guarantee the freedom to hold peaceful demonstrations.[28] On February 4, 2012, the SC failed to pass the resolution. Thirteen Council members supported the resolution, but Russia and China exercised their vetoes.

By the end of the February, the UN and the Arab League could do no more than press diplomatic pressure. At this point, Secretary General Ban Ki-moon appointed Kofi Annan as the "Special Envoy" to the Syrian crisis for a period of six months. The hope was that Annan would be able to negotiate a peace deal with the rebels and Assad, or at the very least find a diplomatic solution to end the violence. Within weeks Annan submitted a "Six Point Peace Plan" to the UN. He began earnestly politicking with Moscow and Beijing, attempting to gain support for his efforts. On April 4, more than one year since the beginning of the violence, Annan announced that Assad agreed to the plan, and a ceasefire would begin on April 12. Unfortunately, it quickly became apparent that the regime and the rebel forces had no intentions of abiding by the plan, and fighting continued.

With the increasing levels of violence in March, the government shifted its tactics of using only security forces to attack civilian populations. In a move to further intimidate and demoralize the civilian population, the regime began using and inciting "shabiha," or sectarian civilian pro-Assad militia.[29] These armed "thugs" threatened and killed civilians in an attempt at breaking the opposition.[30] By May, the shabiha were fighting alongside regime security forces. In efforts to terrorize the population, the Syrian army would first bombard towns, then, after the shelling, would send in the shabiha to summarily execute the remaining civilians. One of the worst massacres of the conflict occurred on May 25, when the shabiha were said to have killed 108 civilians, including 49 small children, in the region of Houla.[31]

Annan's peace plan lay in shreds. The international community continued to debate about what "could be done" in Syria, but little movement to end the violence occurred. By August, Annan had resigned as Special Envoy, citing a "lack of follow-through" by the international community and "finger-pointing and name-calling in the Security Council."[32] It took little more than a week to appoint a new Joint Special Representative to Syria, Lakhdar Brahimi.

Brahimi quickly set out to meet with Assad, and in mid-September 2012 he sat down with the ruler in an attempt to negotiate yet another ceasefire. Brahimi managed to negotiate a four-day ceasefire between the regime and the FSA to commence on October 26. The plan enjoyed the support of Russia, China and Iran, Syria's main allies, and, to date, was the last in a long line of diplomatic efforts to end the conflict. Unfortunately, the ceasefire lasted just four hours.[33]

While international action to halt potential crimes against humanity within Libya occurred within a mere six weeks, the situation in Syria continues to deteriorate at an alarming rate and at the time of this writing over 60,000 Syrian civilians are dead.[34] The regime has perpetrated heinous crimes, including torture, mass killings, and rape.[35] An estimated 700,000 Syrians have fled into neighboring countries,[36] while the Red Crescent estimates that 2.5 million are now internally displaced persons (IDPs) living inside the country.[37] The IDPs are living in camps supplied by Syrian activists, with little or no foreign aid. They lack tents, food and blankets, and with winter on the way, the situation only looks bleaker.[38]

Furthermore, the violence has spilled into neighboring Jordan, Lebanon, Israel and Turkey. Stray bullets and bombs landed in Turkey in October 2012, killing five Turkish civilians.[39] In response, Turkey undertook a week-long shelling campaign against Syrian forces. In November 2012, Turkey then requested that NATO provide it with Patriot missiles to line its border with Syria, thereby attempting to deter further aggression (inadvertent or otherwise) by the Assad regime.[40] By December 5, NATO had approved the request.[41] At present, the civil war in Syria continues to destabilize the region, and there are further fears that the violence spilling out of Syria might ignite the region in sectarian strife.

Complicating the situation is a fear that Assad will use chemical weapons against the opposition fighters and remaining civilians. In July of 2012, the Obama administration issued public statements warning the Assad regime that if it were to use such weapons, it would be "held accountable," though there is no indication of what such punitive measures might look like.[42] In response to Obama's statements, the regime insisted that the chemical weapons cache was safe, and that it would never be used against noncombatants. However, with the continued fighting and escalation of violence, many continue to worry that such guarantees are empty, especially given that the regime began concentrating its stockpile at five air bases. As of December 2012, these movements prompted further harsh warnings from the United States and the UK.[43] Thus, with the increasing possibility that the rebels will eventually oust Assad, some worry that he will become more desperate to maintain power, and thereby perpetrate more monstrous crimes. Such a worry is not unfounded, as Assad has increasingly upped the ante at every stage of the conflict; recently, he began using Scud ballistic missiles on rebel strongholds, in addition to his cluster bombing entire towns and villages.[44]

Not to be forgotten amongst the fighting is the political side of the conflict. First, there is continued infighting between major powers in and outside of the Security Council. With the February 2011 resolution veto, Russia and China became the target of increased vitriol.[45] Much feet dragging and finger pointing ensued, and it was only recently that the United States and Russia seemed to be in agreement that Assad ought to be removed from power to end the conflict. An early December meeting in a luxury Dublin hotel between Secretary of State Clinton, Russian Foreign Minister Sergey Lavrov and Lakhdar Brahimi signaled some hope that Russia's shielding of the Assad regime may soon come to an end. That hope is still rather fleeting, though, as Secretary of State Clinton noted afterwards that "It was an important meeting, but just the beginning," and

> I don't think anyone believes there was some great breakthrough. No one should have any illusions about how hard this remains, but all of us with any influence on the process, with any influence on the regime or the opposition, need to be engaged.[46]

Much in keeping with the tenor of these informal meetings, Lavrov issued a public statement a week later claiming that "we are not conducting any negotiations on the fate of Assad," and that "all attempts to portray things differently are unscrupulous, even for diplomats of those countries which are known to try to distort the facts in their favor."[47] Thus gridlock remains in and outside of the UN.

Second, bickering within and between the Syrian National Council (SNC) and other opposition leaders has left any unified front fragile at best. The SNC, made up primarily of exiled technocrats, envisioned itself as the principal negotiating body for the opposition and its goals. Unfortunately, due to its horizontal structure, much squabbling and disunity prevailed.[48] The SNC is rivaled for leadership against another group, the National Coordination Committee for the Forces of Democratic Change (NCC, or sometimes known as the "National Coordinating Body" or "NCB"). The NCC, led by Hassan Abdel Azim, consisted of mainly independent political activists, dissidents and left-leaning secular political parties. As the dispute became more militarized, the NCC took a back seat to the political maneuvering, and it refused to attend "Friends of Syria" conferences in Tunisia, Istanbul and Paris. The NCC and the SNC disputed whether to negotiate with the Syrian regime, and the issue of Assad's ouster remained a contentious point.

Until recently, the NCC saw any international interference, in the form of support or military intervention, as illegitimate.[49] While the SNC looked to recognition from Western powers, particularly France, Britain and the United States, the NCC entered into dialogue with powers such as Russia, China and Iran. The divide between the SNC and the NCC looked increasingly political, beyond merely their internal disputes.

With increasing worry over the deep divisions within the Syrian opposition, Secretary of State Clinton denounced the SNC for its failures as the "visible leader of the Syrian opposition."[50] She decried the SNC's fractured and politicized rulers, and called for further inclusion and unification of the opposition groups. Within weeks, the SNC and the NCC met in Doha, where they agreed to form a new coalition body, called the "National Coalition of Syrian Revolutionary and Opposition Forces." This new umbrella organization is an attempt not only at bringing together the dysfunctional political parties, but at subsuming the disparate military forces as well. The new unified coalition's plan for the military forces is to form a "Revolutionary Military Council," thereby institutionalizing one body to oversee differing rebel militias, the FSA and other defectors.[51]

To do this, the coalition elected Sheikh Ahmad Moaz al-Khatib, a former imam of the historic Umayyad mosque in Damascus, as its president. Progress is still uncertain, however, as the unified opposition is still struggling to "agree on a slate of governing leaders that would unite what is still a loosely allied organization, trying to weave together local councils, splinter organizations, disparate opposition groups and the loyalties of the armed units."[52] In an effort to show support, though, the EU quickly recognized the new opposition coalition as the legitimate representative of the Syrian people.[53] Several weeks later, in early

December, President Obama followed.[54] Despite these achievements, the conflict still rages and there are no public plans for outside military intervention. At the time of this writing, there are still hopes that diplomatic pressure will ultimately work to end the conflict, with Brahimi attempting to renegotiate a revival of a June 2012 communiqué supporting a political transition inside Syria.[55] The Geneva Communiqué united Russia, China, France, Great Britain, Turkey, the United States and the Arab League in calling for a peaceful solution to the conflict. However, such a transition is mired in dispute due to the question of Assad's tenure as president. Assad has publicly claimed he will not leave office, and the opposition continues to vow that it will not cease fighting until he does so.

Unlike the extremely swift response to the situation in Libya, the Syrian crisis has dragged on for 21 months and is ongoing. Many leaders deplore the situation inside Syria, but few are willing to do much more than wag a disapproving finger at Assad. Some claim that Assad's allies, consisting mainly of Russia and Iran, dissuade Western powers from intervening in the crisis, and since the 2011 failed SC resolution little headway has been made within the UN's main enforcement body.

The exception and the rule: the first sense

We have before us two cases, similar in some respects, different in others, with two very different responses from the international community. Libya, a North African Arab state, ruled by an autocrat for over 40 years, witnessed a series of popular uprisings. The protestors demanded political freedoms and change. The regime, in response, cracked down violently, attempting to quash the nascent rebellion. In response, the international community, within a series of weeks, mounted a political and military campaign to protect the Libyan people under the rubric of the Responsibility to Protect. Sorties by US and NATO forces took out Gaddafi's military capacities; Western powers armed and trained opposition fighters, and within seven months, the regime fell.

Syria, a Middle Eastern Arab state, ruled by an autocrat for over 40 years, witnessed a series of popular uprisings demanding the same freedoms and changes. In similar fashion, the regime responded violently and swiftly. Where the differences emerge, however, is in the international community's responses. In Libya we see the ability of the UN and the SC to act decisively, with the Permanent 5 (P-5) abstaining from using its veto, while still registering complaints or worries. With Syria, we see two of the P-5 exercising their vetoes, and any further ability for coordinated international responses thwarted. Certainly the situation in Syria is dire, and while the world reminds Assad of his "responsibility to protect his people," those calls fall on deaf ears. So why do we see the intervention in one case and not another?

As Alex Bellamy notes, the intervention in Libya is the exception rather than the rule when it comes to international politics governing human protection. He cites three reasons for the exceptional circumstances in Libya: the "extraordinary clarity of the threat of mass atrocities," the "extremely short" time frame, and the roles played by the regional organizations of the OIC, the Gulf Cooperation Council (GCC) and the LAS.[56] These are certainly contributing factors to the international community's ability to act so swiftly. However, we should also add that the situation was also more tractable militarily. Libya is geographically very different than Syria, with its low coastal plains and lack of mountainous terrain. This geography is amenable to monitoring and gathering intelligence, as well as tactical bombing campaigns. In Syria, on the other hand, cities are nestled amongst the mountains, thereby complicating any attempt at intelligence, surveillance and reconnaissance, as well as bombing campaigns.

Inside Libya, we also have more favorable demographics, with a population at roughly 6.6 million. Inside Syria, the population quadruples. With a larger population we find not only denser population centers but also a larger balance of forces. Syria's military is more than eight times that of former Colonel Gaddafi's, with raw numbers showing Syria's airpower to be twice the strength of Libya's former air force. Assad has nine times the number of operable tanks, four times the amount of land weapons, and three times the amount of towed artillery.[57] There is, frankly, much more to contend with in terms of manpower and military capability.

Most importantly, we see that the opposition forces inside Libya were geographically concentrated in Benghazi, and they controlled portions of the country, had a clear and identifiable body in the NTC, and were being attacked with the regime's air power. Until recently, in Syria none of these factors held. The Syrian opposition was not one unified body but a series of groups, and we are still waiting to see whether the newly unified front holds. Furthermore, the Syrian rebels did not control any large portion of territory, but instead fought to control areas of cities, often fighting block by block. At the outset, the regime also primarily used security forces armed with machine guns to disperse crowds. Only over a series of months did Assad begin to employ tanks and then fixed-wing aircraft. Even now that Assad's regime is facing the newly unified opposition, and that he is committing not only war crimes but also crimes against humanity, might we claim that the situations are starting to parallel with regard to the desirability of enforcing a no-fly zone.

The politics of intervention, however, also play an important role in determining the exceptional nature of one over the other. While the support of the OIC, LAS and GCC were weighty considerations in the Libyan case, they did not provide the same influence with Syria. Similar to Libya, the LAS and the OIC suspended Syria's membership,[58] and the GCC denounced the regime and recalled its ambassadors.[59] Despite these similar actions, though, the regional powers have not seen the same support for a coercive solution to Syria. This is surely due to the existence of friends and allies of the different regimes. Gaddafi certainly isolated himself politically, managing to "insult and alienate many leaders across the Middle East and Africa", and "his regime's previous support for international terrorism had alienated the West."[60] Syria, to the contrary, is allied with Iran and Russia, two powerful international players. Russia's ability to thwart international coordination in the UN, as well as Iran's ability to deter outside intervention by the West, has seemingly assured Assad's freedom of movement to target and kill his own people. Thus the empirical factors surrounding the two cases explain much in the way of why the international community was able to not merely invoke R2P, but to react as well. These empirical factors, however, do not explain why we will continue to see agents haphazardly fulfilling their duty to protect.

The exception and the rule: in the second sense

The Libyan and Syrian cases represent the exception and the rule in another, more fundamental sense: states self-selecting to fulfill a provisional duty of R2P. The Libyan case is, for all intents and purposes, an exception to norm of self-interest maximizing states in a condition of "lawless freedom." The Syrian case, unfortunately, is the rule. Powers are reticent to engage in costly conflict for distant others, especially when they cannot convince their own peoples of a successful outcome,[61] and without international authorization—or perhaps motivation—intervention is even less likely. Essentially, R2P takes a back seat to the interests of the major powers, and they will only fulfill their duty to protect when it does not conflict with these interests and is politically convenient for them to do so.

These factors, however, are the result of a provisional duty in a state of nature. Possible or potential interveners must self-select to fulfill their duty, and there is no enforcement mechanism to coerce agents to do so should they fail to act. Thus politics and prudential considerations will continue to provide the lion's share of considerations because of the incomplete nature of the international system of justice. A state of nature means that each is judge in his own case, and due to this, it is only when one deems it as within one's power (and interest) that one acts.

Furthermore, when evaluating what "ought to be done", as in the Libyan case, the scope of a duty to protect is left open. To be sure, the R2P doctrine provides a series of coercive mechanisms to apply in a sequenced fashion, and the response to Syria followed these exact "coercive measures short of intervention." We witnessed individual states and regional blocs issuing political, economic and military sanctions, freezing assets, issuing travel bans, and enacting arms, oil and banking embargoes. Moreover, Syria was expelled from regional organizations, and many states and organizations recalled diplomats and representatives. When it comes to actions that include intervention, the scope of a duty to protect is wider still. As Resolution 1973 authorized "all means necessary" to protect civilians, nothing more particular was forthcoming. How to protect civilians, who would protect civilians and what assets would be used to do so was left the discretion of the intervening state(s). When the scope is wide, as it is in the case of a provisional duty of R2P, we cannot adequately judge whether the obligation has been fully discharged. Of course we can identify when there are manifest failures, but short of this, judgment is problematic. Thus, in the Libyan case, we are left wondering if the Alliance fulfilled its duty to protect, or if by inadvertently killing Libyan civilians in bombing campaigns it failed to do so. With Syria, we might claim that the international community manifestly failed to protect the 60,000 people already murdered. Or, we might claim that the international community discharged its duty, as many powers followed the particular punitive measures short of intervention. Since we have nothing more than our private judgment in this matter, the most we can do is assign moral blame.

Moreover, a provisional duty of justice identifies only capable agents as duty bearers. Because each R2P situation is inherently different, we cannot identify a priori a set of possible interveners. In one situation, one set of capacities, say former ties due to former colonization, might provide a possible intervener with greater ability to moderate a dispute or intervene. In another crisis, perhaps sheer military size and training might be the determining characteristic that enables an intervener to end mass atrocities. In a condition of private right, each R2P situation will leave judgment about who ought to do what open, and identifying the duty bearer to the private judgment of states and individuals. Only when there exists a public authoritative body, with a monopoly on the coercive force, can we remove the private nature of assigning a duty to protect. Moreover, we can then hold those duty bearers to account and force them to fulfill their obligations. Until this time, we will continue to see rather ad hoc responses, the kind witnessed with Libya and Syria.

This conclusion might seem unsatisfactory to some. Ability as a sole criterion for identifying possible interveners appears to leave unanswered many questions about what such ability entails, such as whether a minimal level of ability would suffice or if one must be successful (at least prospectively) to be deemed "capable." Such a worry is partially justified. On the one hand, we can assuage it by claiming that prospective success is not required for a duty bearer. A Kantian account of a provisional duty of protection is not consequentialist in nature, and so it is not required. Moreover, we can also respond that any state supplying an obviously ineffective or minimal force to an R2P situation cannot be said to be fulfilling its duty. If Liechtenstein sends ten soldiers to intervene in Syria, this obviously will not be an effective R2P response. Efficacy is an important element in determining the capacity to respond in R2P situations, and attempts at denying that efficacy plays a role in Kant's moral and political theory are incorrect.

Yet given that the international system is a state of nature, there is no other characteristic to identify possible interveners. In domestic civil societies the rule of law reigns, and so legislatures can create a variety of laws to deal with the assigning of certain duties of rescue. There can be public or private fire stations, police or militia. The state can craft laws governing how, when and from whom such responses are required. In the state of nature this is not the case. That does not mean that a duty to rescue is therefore nonexistent, however. What it means is that the duty falls to those capable of fulfilling it.

Some, like Joel Feinberg, argue that to hold this account is to hold something akin to contributory group-fault responsibility that is simultaneously collective and distributive:

> [E]ach has a duty to attempt rescue so long as no more than a few others have already begun their efforts. In short, everyone should use his eyes and common sense and cooperate as best he can. If no one makes any motion at all, it follows that no one has done his best within the limits imposed by the situation, and all are subject at least to blame.[62]

Given that there is no public institution to take a duty of R2P and make it peremptory, capable agents must act in the way that Feinberg notes. All those capable of acting should coordinate as best as possible, and if they do not, they are subject, at least, to blame. Thus, absent reform or attempts at coordination efforts, R2P will continue to be ad hoc and selectively applied because there are no formally institutionalized mechanisms for it to be otherwise.

The conclusion that we require further institutionalization to extract ourselves from this situation might seem self-evident to some or practically unfeasible to others. This, though, is no more than a sign of how we have internalized the need for juridical institutions to uphold rights, as well as a sign of how we understand the difficulty of establishing such institutions. Such difficulty, however, should not be evidence of this argument's uselessness. Rather, it is indicative about what is so important about the requirements of justice. Plato's Republic is not something easily achieved, nor is Rousseau's ideal political community, but that is not to say that the prescriptions and requirements laid out by both philosophers have no practicality. We use their frameworks as ideals, so that we might continue to evolve and reform current practices with the ideal in sight. This is exactly what Kant advises us to do as well. We must continually work towards establishing the conditions of justice in the real world, for we are morally bound to try to improve our condition and uphold the rights of others. Establishing an R2PI is not as onerous (or perhaps dangerous) as forming Plato's city, and so we can at least say that achieving those dictates are more than a mere possibility.

Kantian justice is trichotomous; it is constituted by commutative, distributive and protective elements. Without all three in place, we lack a condition of public right. With respect to R2P, we lack the distributive and protective features. There is no judicial body to provide peremptory resolutions to claims of R2P violations, and there is no public coercive enforcement mechanism to enforce (the nonexistent) judicial decisions. We might grant that the doctrine of R2P provides us with a minimal commutative element, grounding the principles to determine rights (against genocide, ethnic cleansing, crimes against humanity and war crimes), but the rest of the international system lacks any mechanisms to realize and settle rights disputes.

Making a duty of R2P peremptory may not be nearly as quick as the norm's adoption. Nevertheless, if we are to move past the charges of selectivity, of wondering who ought to do what and when, and when we might know if "enough" has been done, we must establish the institutions necessary to answer those questions, and we must continue to reform these institutions once established. In a sense, this continual reform, this unachievable idea of perfect justice, is why Kant's view of "Perpetual Peace" is only recognized in the sign above the Dutch innkeeper's doorway: a graveyard. Only in death are we free from the obligations to continually work towards justice, to ameliorate justice and enjoy our rights. The human condition, with all its wars and atrocities, is also full of hope, optimism and beauty, but it is not one of rest and ease. Humanity is, after all, a "crooked timber," warped by our self-serving inclinations and our very ability to reason. Humanity is also the most beautiful quality we have, for it presupposes that we are free beings. This freedom demands to be respected and protected; it demands that we fulfill our obligations of justice to others.

The arguments I have made here are conceptual in nature. Much work on the finer practical points remains. Our work in practice, however, ought to be guided by the theoretical underpinnings identified here. For the problem of establishing justice amongst individuals remains always tied to the problem of establishing "law-governed external relations among nations and cannot be solved until the latter is."[63]

Notes

Introduction

1 Kant, Immanuel. "Doctrine of Right" (1797) in Mary Gregor, trans. and ed.: *The Metaphysics of Morals*, Cambridge: Cambridge University Press, 1996: 6:311. Hereafter *DR*.
2 *DR*, 6:306.
3 *DR*, 6:306, 6:314.
4 Kant, Immanuel. "Theory and Practice" in H.S. Reiss (ed.) *Kant: Political Writings*, Cambridge: Cambridge University Press, 2003: p. 63.
5 Ibid., p. 63.
6 Brown, Garrett Wallace. *Grounding Cosmopolitanism: From Kant to the Idea of a Cosmopolitan Constitution*, Edinburgh: Edinburgh University Press, 2010.
7 *DR*, 6:350.
8 Bagnoli, Carla. "Humanitarian Intervention as a Perfect Duty" in Terry Nardin and Melissa Williams (eds.) *Nomos XLVII: Humanitarian Intervention*, New York: New York University Press, 2006: pp. 117–140. Tan, Kok-Chor. "The Duty to Protect" in Terry Nardin and Melissa Williams (eds.) *Nomos XLVII: Humanitarian Intervention*, New York: New York University Press, 2006: 84–116.
9 For a consequentialist approach to the problem of intervention, see Pattison, James. *Humanitarian Intervention and the Responsibility to Protect: Who Should Intervene?*, Oxford: Oxford University Press, 2010. While I applaud Pattison's attempts to formulate a theory of who should ought to intervene and when, I disagree with his consequentialist framework. The motivating force behind interventions is to stop massive human rights violations, and so the motivating factor is about the right—not the good. Cf. Roff, H.M. "Response to Pattison: Whose Responsibility to Protect?" *Journal of Military Ethics*, 8:1, 2009: pp. 79–85.
10 Cavallar, Georg. *Kant and the Theory and Practice of International Right*, Cardiff: University of Wales Press, 1999: p. 57. Cf. Tesón, Fernando. *Humanitarian Intervention: An Inquiry into Law and Morality*, New York: Transnational Publishers, 1988; Brunkhorst, Hauke. "Paradigmenwechsel im Völkerrecht? Lehren aus Bosnien", in Matthias Lutz-Bachmann and James Bohman (eds.) *Frieden durch Recht: Kants Friedensidee und das Problem einer neuen Weltordnung*, Frankfurt am Main: Suhrkamp, 1996; Bernstein, Alyssa. "Kant on Rights and Coercion in International Law: Implications for Humanitarian Military Intervention" *Jahrbuch für Recht und Ethik*, 16, 2008: pp. 57–100. Williams, Howard. *Kant and the End of War: A Critique of Just War Theory*, New York: Palgrave Macmillan, 2012.
11 Cavallar, op. cit., pp. 89–93. Cavallar cites Brunkhorst, Van der Linden, Lillich, Tesón, Taylor and Mulholland as proponents of this view.
12 Ibid., p. 57.
13 Ibid., p. 55.

14 *DR*, 6:351.
15 Byrd, Sharon and Joachim Hruschka. "From the State of Nature to the Juridical State of States." *Law and Philosophy*, 27, 2008: pp. 599–641.
16 Covell, Charles. *Kant and the Law of Peace*, New York: St. Martin's Press, 1998: p. 105.
17 Ibid., 96.
18 Flikschuh, Katrin. "Kant's Sovereignty Dilemma: A Contemporary Analysis" *Journal of Political Philosophy*, 18:3, 2010: p. 15.
19 Ibid., 15.
20 Ibid., 15.
21 Ibid., 19.
22 Ibid., 21. Flikschuh's arguments are not persuasive. While she rightly views Kant's theory of justice as a system, claiming that there are different notions of right at each level makes little sense. Right entails the authorization to use coercion, and so if there is to be international and cosmopolitan Right, then even these "different" types of right must be coercive. She does not want to grant this point, but not granting it means that we have left behind Kant's theory of justice. Furthermore, she does not explain why only "exceptional" circumstances would permit intervention, as all interventions are by their nature exceptional.
23 Flikschuh is an example of one of these critics. See Flikschuh, op. cit., p. 23.
24 Höffe, Otfried. *Kant's Cosmopolitan Theory of Law and Peace*, Cambridge: Cambridge University Press, 2006: p. 16.
25 Flikschuh, op. cit., p. 3.
26 I address this issue in depth in Chapter 4.
27 Fearon, James D. and David D. Laitin. "Ethnicity, Insurgency, and Civil War" *American Political Science Review*, 97: 1, 2003: pp. 75–90.
28 Kant, Immanuel. "On the Proverb: That May be True in Theory, But Is of No Practical Use" in *Perpetual Peace and Other Essays*, trans. Ted Humphrey, Indianapolis: Hackett Publishing Company, 1985 (hereafter *TP*), 8:313.

1 Kantian provisional duties

1 Hohfeld, Wesley Newcomb. *Fundamental Legal Conception as Applied in Judicial Reasoning*, New Jersey: The LawBook Exchange, Ltd. 2010. Hohfeld views the possibilities as rights as either claims, powers, liberties or immunities, with their jural opposites as: no rights, disabilities, duties, and liabilities respectively. Their correlatives are: duties, liabilities, no rights, disabilities, respectively.
2 These are the only situations, as listed in the 2005 World Summit Outcome Document paragraph 139, that trigger the international community's responsibility to protect. This list is broader than the original 2001 ICISS report, which listed only genocide and ethnic cleansing. International Commission on State Sovereignty. *The Responsibility to Protect: A Report of the International Commission on State Sovereignty*, Ottawa: International Development Research Centre Books, 2002.
3 Marcus Willaschek claims that because juridical laws can be obeyed for heterogeneous reasons, juridical laws cannot be derived from a categorical imperative that demands obedience for the sake of the law and nothing else. Willaschek, Marcus. "Why the Doctrine of Right does not belong in the Metaphysics of Morals" *Annual Review for Law and Ethics*, 5, 1997: p. 208.
4 See Potter, Nelson. "Applying the Categorical Imperative in Kant's Rechtslehre" *Annual Review of Law and Ethics*, 11, 2003: pp. 37–51. Höffe, Otfried. *Categorical Principles of Law*, Mark Migotti (trans.), University Park: Penn State Press, 2002. Katrin Flikschuh attempts to explain the relationship as separate yet complementary. See Flikschuh, Katrin. "Justice without Virtue," in Lara Denis (ed.), *Kant's Metaphysics of Morals: A Critical Guide*, Cambridge: Cambridge University Press, 2010:

pp. 51–70. Flikschuh argues that one can be just without being virtuous, and that Willaschek's worry that heteronomous, and therefore nonautonomous, lawgiving robs justice of is moral status is unfounded because justice does not depend so much on individual subjective, traditionally autonomous, willing as it does on a public objective unified will.

5 The contemporary German also notes the concept of *Recht* as: right, rights, being "in the right," equal rights and responsibilities, being under law (civil, common, and canon), claims, titles (to something), what is due, privilege, being or what is justified and justice. Available at: http://dict.tu-chemnitz.de/dings.cgi?lang=en&service=deen&opterrors=0&optpro=0&query=recht&iservice=&comment=&email= (accessed on December 26, 2012).

6 Kant, Immanuel. "Doctrine of Right" (1797) in Mary Gregor, (trans. and ed.). *The Metaphysics of Morals*, Cambridge: Cambridge University Press, 1996: pp. 29–31. When citing this translation, I hereafter refer to the *Metaphysics of Morals*, the "Doctrine of Right" or the "Doctrine of Virtue" with the use of the abbreviations "*MM*," "*DR*" or "*DV*," respectively. When referring to Kant's essays: "Idea for a Universal History with a Cosmopolitan Purpose" (1784), "An Answer to the Question: What is Enlightenment" (1784), "On the Proverb: That May be True in Theory, But is of No Practical Use" (1793) and "Towards Perpetual Peace" (1795), unless otherwise noted, I use Ted Humphrey (trans.), *Perpetual Peace and Other Writings*, Indianapolis: Hackett Publishing Co., Inc., 1983/1985. I will use the abbreviations, "*UH*," "*WE*," "*TP*" and "*TPP*," respectively. For Kant's *The Conflict of the Faculties*, I will abbreviate as "*CF*." Mary Gregor (trans.), Lincoln/London: University of Nebraska Press, 1992. Furthermore, for all Kant's works cited here, unless otherwise noted, I will follow with the Gesammelte Schriften, ed. Preussische Akademie der Wissenschaften citation format.

7 *DV*, 6:394.

8 Internal freedom is manifested by an agent acting autonomously, where she chooses to act in accordance with the moral law. Hence "autonomy is the ground of the dignity of human nature and of every rational nature," and dignity for Kant is "unconditional and incomparable worth [i.e., respect]" that is attributed to legislation, "which [itself] determines all worth." More clearly, autonomy is self-legislation, and the manner in which one legislates; thus an act receives more or less worth depending upon how one wills it. Kant, Immanuel. *Grounding for the Metaphysics of Morals* (1785), James Ellington (trans.), Indianapolis: Hackett Publishing Co, Inc., 1993: p. 41. Hereafter, I will abbreviate the *Grounding* as "*G*" and follow Kant's Gesammelte Schriften, ed. Preussische Akademie der Wissenschaften citation format.

9 *DR*, 6:220; 6:383.

10 I disagree with Flikschuh here, that "Right is not 'prior to' Virtue, nor is Virtue 'prior to' Right, [and that] Right is not a condition of Virtue" (Flikschuh, op. cit.). Kant's works on the progress of humanity and the necessity of the state as a fundamental vehicle for all of man's progress incline me to believe that right is prior to virtue—at least if both are to be universal. I take right and virtue to be symbiotic: one needs the other, but for the entire human race to progress towards moralization, then the state is necessary first.

11 "[A]ll lawgiving can therefore be distinguished with respect to the incentive…." *DR*, 6:218–6:219.

12 Kant states that "mere conformity or nonconformity of an action with law … is called its *legality* (lawfulness); but that conformity [what law requires] in which the idea of duty arising from the law is also the incentive to the action is called its *morality*." *DR*, 6:219 (italics in original).

13 *DV*, 6:382. Kant identifies the first of these as in accordance with the *DR*, and the second with the *DV*.

14 *DV*, 6:386–6:388.

15 *DV*, 6:382.

16 *DV*, 6:382.
17 *DV*, 6:383 (italics in original).
18 *DR*, 6:231.
19 *G*, 4:394.
20 Heyd. David "Moral and Legal Luck: Kant's Reconciliation with Practical Contingency," *Annual Review of Law and Ethics*, 5, 1997: p. 36.
21 *G*, 4:439.
22 Heyd, op. cit., p. 14.
23 *DV*, 6:379 (italics in original).
24 *DR*, 6:231.
25 *DV*, 6:383.
26 Heyd, op. cit., p. 32.
27 *DR*, 6:230.
28 The first five distinctions between Kantian perfect and imperfect duties are noted by Pippin, Robert. *Idealism as Modernism: Hegelian Variations*, Cambridge: Cambridge University Press, 1997: pp. 56–91; the next three by Nardin, Terry "Introduction," in Terry Nardin and Melissa S. Williams (eds.), *Humanitarian Intervention: NOMOS XLVII*, New York: New York University Press, 2005: pp. 1–28; and the remaining two by Murphy, Jeffrie. *Kant and the Philosophy of Right*, Macon: Mercer University Press, 1994: pp. 34–37.
29 *DR*, 6:264 and *CF*, p. 165.
30 *DR*, 6:325–326.
31 *DV*, 6:390.
32 *DV*, 6:390.
33 *DR*, 6:240.
34 *DV*, 6:422.
35 *DV*, 6:424–425.
36 *DV*, 6:427.
37 *DV*, 6:429–430. It is not immediately clear that lying to others is a perfect duty to oneself. For a good discussion of this see Korsgaard, Kristine. "The Right to Lie: on Dealing with Evil," *Philosophy and Public Affairs*, 15, 1986: pp. 325–349.
38 *DV*, 6:432–433.
39 *DV*, 6:434–436.
40 *DV*, 6:450.
41 *DV*, 6:432.
42 *DV*, 6:463.
43 *DV*, 6:464.
44 *DV*, 6:465.
45 *DV*, 6:466.
46 *DV*, 6:467.
47 *DR*, 6:240.
48 Willaschek, op. cit., p. 208.
49 Willaschek's perspective, though, is mistaken. His argument is that the entire *DR* does not belong in the *MM*, as *Recht* cannot be derived from the categorical imperative. He claims that

> Kant nowhere really says that the principle of right can be derived from, or is based on, the categorical imperative. The moral law and the categorical imperative are not even mentioned in §§ A–E of the "Introduction to the Doctrine of Right", where Kant introduces the principles of right.
>
> (Willaschek, op. cit., p. 220).

In response, I want to make several points. First, the "Introduction" is hardly the entirety of the *DR*. Second, Kant does claim in § B that without the moral law, i.e., something to guide "sources of judgment in reason alone", an empirical doctrine of right is empty—like "Phaedrus' head." Third, Kant specifically mentions the categorical imperative in three places in the *DR*. In the first instance Kant is referring to the possibility of "intelligible" possession—i.e., the ability to own a piece of property without having to have physical control over it. He says that possession of property is necessary for freedom, and that freedom "can only be inferred from the practical law of reason (the categorical imperative) as a fact of reason" (*DR*, 6:252). In the second instance, Kant is attempting to square unjust or dishonorable punishments and honor with a civil constitution. He states

> The knot [of violating the CI and maintaining the CI] can be undone in the following way: the categorical imperative of penal justice remains (unlawful killing of another must be punished by death); but the legislation itself (and consequently also the civil constitution), as long as it remains barbarous and undeveloped, is responsible for the discrepancy between the incentives of honor in the people (subjectively) and the measures that are (objectively) suitable for its purpose.
>
> (*DR*, 6:337)

Third, Kant states "the law of punishment is a categorical imperative" (*DR*, 6:331). Thus, I refute Willaschek, Q.E.D.

50 This is not the same "natural right" of Natural Law Theory. The innate right to freedom, for Kant, is a moral right, and so is required by reason. Humans by nature have reason, and thus it is a "natural right."

51 *DR*, 6:312.

52 Mulholland, Leslie Arthur. "The Difference Between Private and Public Law," *Annual Review of Law and Ethics*, 1, 1993: p. 131. Kant's understanding is similar to, but distinct from, Locke's. Law in the state of nature, i.e., natural law, is that law we can know through our reason, and what we use our private judgment to determine. Natural law here is not "God's law," as it is for Locke.

53 Ibid., 140.

54 I am employing the common usage of "objective" and "subjective" when it comes to individual judgment in relation to a principle or law. Kant, on the other hand, typically uses these terms differently, namely he uses "subjective" to refer to what a court decides is "right," and "objective" for what an individual with his reason decides is "right" (*DR*, 6:297). I thank B. Sharon Byrd for this point.

55 Mulholland, op. cit., p. 134.

56 Ibid., 134.

57 Ibid., 136.

58 Ibid., 137.

59 Ibid., 139.

60 *DR*, 6:345. I deviate from Gregor's translation here. The original German reads "*das die Verbindung doch keine souveräne Gewalt (wie in einer bürgerlichen Verfassung), sondern nur eine Genossenschaft (Föderalität) enthalten müsse; eine Verbündung, die zu aller Zeit aufgekündigt werden kann, mithin von Zeit zu Zeit erneuert werden muß.*" Gregor translates the first declination of *müssen* as "must" and not "need not," which Kant was known to commonly use. Moreover, she smuggles in a "must not" in the second clause about a sovereign authority that is not present in the original. I thank B. Sharon Byrd for pointing this out.

61 *DR*, 6:224.

62 Kant acknowledges this mistake by claiming,

> It is a common fault (*vitium subreptionis*) of experts on right to *misrepresent*, as if it were also the objective principle of what is right in itself, that rightful principle which a court is authorized and indeed bound to adopt for its own use ... in order to pronounce and judge what belongs to each as his right, although the latter is very different from the former.—It is therefore of no slight importance to recognize this

> specific distinction and to draw attention to it.... So the question here is not merely what is *right in itself*, that is how every human being has to judge about it on his own, but what is right before a court, that is what is laid down as right.
>
> (*DR* 6:297, italics in original)

Thus "right in itself" is different than cases of juridical right, even though "right" must take both the former and the latter into account.

63 *DR*, 6:234.

64 *DR*, 6:246. Gregor translates *vermögen* as capacity. However, I translate it as ability. *Vermögen* can mean ability, power, capability, faculty, to be in a position to do something, or to have assets (to do something with). Thus I translate *vermögen* as a can-do, learned or otherwise, and not as something innate or only generated by something psychological. Moreover, Kant discusses *vermögen* as more of a physical concept (the ability to use or control something) further in: *DR* 6:237; 6:246; 6:257; 6:258; 6:265; 6:267; 6:269; 6:271; 6:274; 6:356–357. The *DV* supports this translation at 6:383 and 6:404.

65 *DR*, 6:257 (italics in original).

66 *DR*, 6:234.

67 *DR*, 6:235. Kant also claims "ambiguity really arises from the fact that there are cases in which a right is in question but for which no judge can be appointed to render a decision" (*DR*, 6:234). There can be cases of equity in civil society, but the courts cannot resolve them in accordance with Right because of certain contractual stipulations.

68

> I am therefore not under obligation to leave external objects belonging to others untouched unless everyone else provides me with assurance that he will behave in accordance with the same principle with regard to what is mine.... *[I]t is only a will putting everyone under obligation, hence only a collective general (common) and powerful will, that can provide everyone this assurance.... So only in a civil condition can something external be mine or yours.*

Anything but a general will would "infringe upon freedom in accordance with universal laws" (*DR*, 6:256 italics added).

69 This quote is drawn from Kant's later discussion of international society, but it shows two things of importance. First, Kant believed that the international society is one ruled by provisional right. Second, the terminology "absolutely rightful condition" alludes to conditions that are not "absolutely" rightful but may have elements or gradations of *Recht* (*DR*, 6:341 italics added).

70 Kant discusses the acquisition of private property in a state of nature at *DR* 6:267; and institution of civil society at *DR* 6:312–313. The argument for autocrats acting as republicans appears in the *Conflict of the Faculties* (*CF*), p. 122. *TPP's* preliminary article 2 states that "no independent nation, be it large or small, may be acquired by another nation by inheritance, exchange, purchase, or gift; preliminary article 3 states "standing armies (*miles perpetuus*) shall be gradually abolished," and preliminary article 4 states "no national debt shall be contracted in connection with the foreign affairs of the nation" (*TPP*, 8:344–346). Kant notes that there is a permission to delay in implementing such articles "depending on circumstances" (*TPP*, 8:347).

71 *G*, 4:422 footnote 12.

72 It also could be argued that because Kant explicitly claims in footnote 12 that he "reserve[s] the division of duties for a future *Metaphysics of Morals*. The division presented here stands as merely an arbitrary one (in order to arrange my examples)" (*G*, 4:422). He had not yet employed the sharper linguistic distinction of "narrow" and "wide" as he does in his later *MM*.

73 Kant also discusses the same examples in the *DV*; however, the examples are much clearer and succinct in the *G*.

74 I disagree with MacIntyre that some animals are rational. While some animals do have the capacity to communicate with one another, it is not what we would call language, nor do these animals set out life plans to improve their abilities. See MacIntyre, Alasdair. *Dependent Rational Animals*, Peru: Carus Publishing Company, 1999/2001.

75 Kant is well aware that human beings are animalistic, but we have a "predisposition to humanity" where through self-realization and interaction with other human beings we can become moral. He discusses this at length in *Religion within the Boundaries of Mere Reason*, especially 6:26–6:53. Kant, Immanuel. *Religion within the Boundaries of Mere Reason* (1793), in Allen Wood/George di Giovanni (eds.), *Religion and the Boundaries of Mere Reason and Other Writings*, Cambridge: Cambridge University Press, 1998. Hereafter abbreviated as "*R*." Kant also has a clear and succinct discussion in his lectures on pedagogy. See Kant, Immanuel. *On Education* (1803) in Annette Churton (trans.), *Kant on Education*, Boston: D.C. Heath & Co. Publishers, 1906: p. 108. I will hereafter refer to this as "*OE*."

76 This does not take place only on an individual level for Kant. As he claims in *UH*, man's "unsocial sociability" moves him to form civil societies and these civil societies are ultimately forced to form a cosmopolitan state (*UH*, 8:20).

77 Kant also acknowledges elsewhere that one's ability plays a role in the determination of a duty. He writes "to be beneficent *where one can* is a duty;" again, he acknowledges capacity but with the intent to show moral worth (*G*, 4:398). I am not going to go too deeply into the question of when rational capacity is limited by the natural development of our mental capacities, but consider Kant's remarks about what it takes to will as well as his remarks about education in the following paragraph. The absence of these conditions may make it difficult to act on our duty, and even when we can act, there is a further question about whether our action will prove futile and whether this kind of futility excuses us from even having a duty of justice.

78 Indeed, a child is an agent with limited capacities, but *OE* is not directed at children, it is a guide for adults to follow in the education of children. The child has no discretion, choice or even ability to choose her way of life, duties or projects.

79 *OE*, pp. 1–8; 47–48; 58–59; 66–70; 83–94.

80 *OE*, pp. 12–13 (italics added).

81 A civil condition, for Kant, is one characterized by "a system of laws ... under a will uniting them [the people], [under] a constitution." (*DR*, 6:311).

82 Kate Moran argues that not only is Kant concerned with "public" education systems, but that ultimately Kant's theory of education is more than

> an individual question for moral perfection, [as] agents on this account have a duty to work individually and collectively to bring about the ethical community [the kingdom of ends]. These individuals will be concerned, for example, with what kinds of institutions can help realize this goal.

Education is thus tied to civic structures and institutions. Moran, Kate. "Can Kant Have an Account of Moral Education," *Journal of Philosophy of Education Society of Great Britain* Vol. 43, no. 4, 2009: pp. 471–484.

83 *UH*, 8:20.

84 *TPP*, 8:354, 8:360–368; *TP*, 8:307–313; *WE*, 8:39–40; *UH*, 8:24.

85 *UH*, 8:21. (This particular quote is from H.B. Nisbet's translation in H.S. Reiss, (ed.), *Kant Political Writings*, Cambridge: Cambridge University Press, 1970/1991: p. 45. When the Reiss edition is used, I will note "Reiss edition."

86 *DR*, 6:306.

87 *DR*, 6:312.

88 Vigilantius, Johann Friedrich. "Lectures on Kant's Metaphysics of Morals" (1793), in J.B. Schneewind (ed.) and Peter Heath (trans.), *Lectures on Ethics*, Cambridge:

Cambridge University Press, 2001: p. 278. When using this compilation of lecture notes, I will hereafter refer to the Student's Name, followed by "*LoE*" and the Akademie Ausgabe pagination.

89 *DR*, 6:263–266.
90 *DR*, 6:267 (italics in original).
91 *CF*, p. 165 (italics added).
92 See *DR* 6:320 and 6:372.
93 Ellis, Elisabeth. *Kant's Politics: A Provisional Theory for an Uncertain World*, New Haven: Yale University Press, 2006: p. 114.
94 Ibid., pp. 176–177.
95 Ellis agrees with me that this point of her argument is too strong. Private correspondence with Elisabeth Ellis (2010).
96 Kant uses the term *provisorisch* in the *DR*, though in *CF* he changes his usage to *vorläufig*. Both terms are comparable, yet *vorläufig* carries with it a more temporal connotation.
97 Ellis, op. cit., p. 114.
98 *DV*, 6:456; 6:457; 6:468.
99 This is opposite to the view of Kersting, who posits that "the postulate of public right (*öffentliches Recht*) is under the premises of their justification theory only a hypothetical imperative of prudence." Kersting, Wolfgang. "Kant's Concept of the State," in Howard Lloyd Williams (ed.), *Essays on Kant's Political Philosophy*, Chicago: Chicago University Press, 1992: p. 145.
100 Louden, Robert. *Kant's Impure Ethics*, New York/Oxford: Oxford University Press, 2000: pp. 20–21.
101 Kant, Immanuel. *On Education* as cited in Robert Louden, *Kant's Impure Ethics*, New York/Oxford: Oxford University Press, 2000: p. 21. I also follow Louden's conclusion that even if man has all of these things he is not guaranteed to be a moral person. Therefore we should say that these material factors are necessary but not sufficient conditions for justice and morality.
102 Kant, Immanuel. *Critique of Practical Reason*, T.K. Abbott (trans.), Amherst: Promethus Books, 1996: p. 54 (italics added). I hereafter refer to this as the "*CPrR*."
103 This is Kant's "fact of reason," which allows human beings to know the moral law. The fact of reason though, is not a guarantee that human beings will be moral.
104 *G*, 4:442.
105 Kant, Immanuel, as cited in Louden, op. cit., p. 8 (italics added).
106 *MM*, 6:213. The German here is *vermögen*, meaning power, ability, capability or faculty (italics added).
107 For Kant, "choice" consists of one having: (i.) the faculty of desire; (ii) consciousness of one's ability to act; (iii) actually trying to act. (*MM*, 6:213).
108 Indeed B. Sharon Byrd and Joachim Hruschka claim as well that an agent's choice, and thus the ability to freely follow the moral law, is concerned with ability. They claim that Kant's *DR* is explicit in that "an object of choice is something one has the *physical* capacity to use." Byrd, B. Sharon and Joachim Hruschka, "Kant on "Why Must I Keep My Promise?," *Chicago-Kent Law Review*, 81, 2006: p. 57.
109 Jens Timmerman. "Your Article: 'Sollen und Können'" Email. (23 August 2009).
110 Martin, Wayne. "Ought but Cannot," *Proceedings of the Aristotelian Society*, 109, 2009: pp. 102–128.
111 *DR*, 6:229–230.

2 Provisional protection: the Responsibility to Protect as a provisional duty

1 The right to intervene in this instance would be like a Hohfeldian liberty-right. That is, states are free to intervene in another's affairs given that certain thresholds for

intervention are met. Since the right is a liberty-right, this means that states are free to exercise it whenever they see fit, and that not exercising the right cannot be deemed a moral failure.

2 Grotius, Hugo. *De Jure Belli ac Pacis* (1646), Whitefish: Kessinger Publishing, 2009), Book II, ch. 20, sec. 40, vol. II.

3 Contemporary scholars such as Wheeler and Tesón argue for a redeployment of just war doctrine to establish criteria for humanitarian interventions, such as the principles of just cause, proper authority, right intention, proportionality and last resort. For a good exposition of early debates of humanitarian intervention see Chesterman, Simon. *Just War or Just Peace*, Oxford: Oxford University Press, 2001.

4 Chesterman, op. cit., pp. 36–38.

5 Article 39 states that "The Security Council shall determine the existence of any threat to the peace, breach of the peace, or act of aggression and shall make recommendations, or decide what measures shall be taken in accordance with Articles 41 and 42, to maintain or restore international peace and security." Moreover, Article 51 states that "Nothing in the present Charter shall impair the inherent right of individual or collective self-defense if an armed attack occurs against a Member of the United Nations, until the Security Council has taken measures necessary to maintain international peace and security. Measures taken by Members in the exercise of this right of self-defense shall be immediately reported to the Security Council and shall not in any way affect the authority and responsibility of the Security Council under the present Charter to take at any time such action as it deems necessary in order to maintain or restore international peace and security." United Nations, *Charter of the United Nations*, 24 October 1945 available at: www.un.org/en/documents/charter/chapter7.shtml (accessed March 15, 2013).

6 Wheeler observes that India made use of the term "refugee aggression" to justify its actions against Pakistan, and Vietnam invoked a "two-wars justification" which argued that Vietnam was fighting against Cambodian aggression and that simultaneous internal war led by the National Salvation Front is what ousted Pol Pot. Further, Tanzania argued that Uganda's invasion of Kagera Salient justified its retaliatory attack. Cf. Wheeler, Nicolas. *Saving Strangers: Humanitarian Intervention in International Society*, Oxford: University Press, 2000: pp. 60–71; 85–100; 117–132.

7 See SC/Res/688 available at: http://daccess-dds-ny.un.org/doc/RESOLUTION/GEN/NR0/596/24/IMG/NR059624.pdf?OpenElement (accessed August 8, 2010).

8 Wheeler, op. cit., p. 146.

9 Ibid., 154.

10 Hurd, Douglas, as cited in Jim Whitman, "A Cautionary Note on Humanitarian Intervention," *The Journal of Humanitarian Assistance* (1994) (italics added). Available at: http://sites.tufts.edu/jha/archives/62 (accessed March 28, 2013).

11 The 1992 intervention in Somalia (under the guidance of Resolution 794/814/837) also seemed to be strengthening this trend, until the 1993 deaths of 18 US Rangers, and the crash of two Blackhawk helicopters and capture of one pilot. Additionally, in 1992, the UN passed Resolution 770, which authorized member states to use force to deliver aid to Bosnia. After that, Resolutions 819 and 824 created safe havens within Bosnia, and Resolution 836 mandated UN soldiers to "deter attacks against the safe havens" (Wheeler, op. cit., pp. 253–254). In 1994–1995 NATO bombing helped to protect these safe areas, though they did little to save the 7,414 men who were rounded up and killed. Even though the 1995 Dayton Accords "settled" the dispute, it was evident four years later that this was not the case, and the Kosovo Albanians were now being systematically targeted and killed. This gave rise to the 1999 Kosovo intervention, led by NATO without UN approval.

12 Politicians too began to use this language as early as the 1991 Iraqi intervention. France used the language of a "duty" to intervene, but it was met with much criticism. Cf. Wheeler, op. cit., p. 142.

13 International Commission on State Sovereignty. *The Responsibility to Protect: A Report of the International Commission on State Sovereignty*, Ottawa: International Development Research Centre Books, 2002: section 1.7. Hereafter referred to as "ICISS".
14 Ibid., 1.35.
15 Ibid., 2.14.
16 Walsh, Jennifer. " 'Implementing the Responsibility to Protect': Where Expectations Meet Reality" *Ethics and International Affairs*, 24: 4, 2010: pp. 418–419.
17 Annan, Kofi. "Two Concepts of Sovereignty," *The Economist*, 352, September, 1999: pp. 49–50.
18 Ambassador to Netherlands, S/PV.4011, June 10, 1999 12–13 (cited in Wheeler, op. cit., p. 297.
19 Independent International Commission on Kosovo. *The Kosovo Report: Conflict, International Response, Lessons Learned*, Oxford: Oxford University Press, 2000. Available at: http://reliefweb.int/sites/reliefweb.int/files/resources/6D26FF88119644CFC1256989005CD392-thekosovoreport.pdf (accessed December 1, 2012).
20 ICISS, op. cit., 1.39–1.141.
21 Ibid., 1.40.
22 Weiss notes that after the 2003 invasion of Iraq this view has been significantly bolstered. Weiss, Thomas. *Humanitarian Intervention: Ideas in Action*, Cambridge: Polity Press, 2007: p. 124. Nardin also criticizes Tesón's account of the 2003 Iraq war as "humanitarian imperialism." See Tesón, Fernando R. "Ending Tyranny in Iraq" and Nardin, Terry. "Humanitarian Imperialism: Response to "Ending Tyranny in Iraq" *Ethics and International Affairs*, 19:2, 2005: pp. 1–26.
23 ICISS, op. cit., xi.
24 Ibid., 4.6–4.9.
25 Ibid., xi.
26 The ICISS report does stipulate that the Permanent Five (P-5) on the UN Security Council (SC) ought to refrain from using their veto powers in R2P situations. Furthermore, the SC ought to respond in a 'timely' manner. In the event that the SC does use its veto, or is not responding in a timely manner, the ICISS suggests that the General Assembly hold an emergency session under the "Uniting for Peace" procedure to vote on taking action in an R2P crisis. The ICISS report also suggests that if all of these options fail, regional or subregional organizations might undertake collective security actions under Chapter VIII of the Charter and then seek *ex post* approval from the SC.
27 ICISS, op. cit., 4.16.
28 Just war theory is traditionally divided into the two logically distinct parts of *jus ad bellum* and *jus en bello. Jus ad bellum*, or justice before war, determines when a state may legitimately undertake military action against another state. The ICISS's criteria are classically *jus ad bellum* principles. *Jus en bello*, or justice in war, provides principles to guide the proper conduct of fighting in war. These include only proportionality and discrimination. For an excellent treatment of the just war tradition see: Walzer, Michael. *Just and Unjust Wars: A Moral Argument with Historical Illustrations* 4th Ed., New York: Basic Books, 2006.
29 ICISS, op. cit., 4.19.
30 The International Law Association drafted a set of criteria in the early 1970s for judging the legality of unilateral HI. Numbers 3 and 9, of the 12-point document, require a state to *meet* with the Security Council to inform it and seek guidance (and implicitly approval) for an intervention. Third Interim Report of the Subcommittee on the International Protection of Human Rights by General International Law, ILA Report of the Fifty-Sixth Conference 217, New Delhi, 1974. Quoted in Wheeler op. cit., p. 43, and noted in Weiss, op. cit., p. 107.

31 Evans, Gareth. "In Defense of R2P" *New York Times*, March 11, 2012. Available at: www.nytimes.com/2012/03/12/opinion/12iht-edletmon12.html? (accessed March 11, 2012).

32 A/60/150, otherwise known as the "Outcome Document," paragraphs 138–139 (italics added). Hereafter "Outcome Document" or "OD." Since then, the UN has reaffirmed its commitment to these principles. See, for example, UN Resolution 1674 (April 2006): the international community bears a "responsibility to protect populations from genocide, war crimes, ethnic cleansing, and crimes against humanity." Since the passing of Resolution 1674, the Security Council has had four more open debates that have resulted in a reaffirmation of the responsibility to protect (italics in original).

33 Weiss, op. cit., pp. 124–129.

34 Ibid., 125.

35 The members are the United States, China and Russia. Bellamy, Alex. "Whither the Responsibility to Protect? HI and the 2005 World Summit" *Ethics and International Affairs*, 20:2, 2006: p. 165.

36 This is clearly seen in Russia, China, India, Brazil and South Africa's abstention from voting on the SC resolution to impose coercive measures on Libya in 2011 and these same member states opposing any resolution against Syria in the February 2012 vote. S/RES/1973 Available at: www.un.org/News/Press/docs/2011/sc10200.doc.htm#Resolution (accessed April 3, 2012).

37 For instance, Ban's 2009 report claims that each Pillar is of "equal length" and that institutionalizing a set of mechanisms that follows one to the other would be dangerous because any flexibility to respond to crises would be lost. Yet in November of 2011 and March of 2012, Brazil has put forward the opposite suggestion in a letter to the Secretary General. Brazil's recommendation is to institutionalize the Three Pillars to "follow a strict line of political subordination and chronological sequencing." A/66/551.

38 A/64/864, p. 7.

39 Ibid., p. 7.

40 It is odd that Ban notes that individuals bear a responsibility to protect. R2P is a statist doctrine, and while it is true that gross crimes against humanity are committed through individuals, it is not at all clear how R2P can be conceptually applied to individual persons, unless those persons are charged with crimes listed under the Rome Statutes and tried in the International Criminal Court (ICC). Yet, even in these instances, the persons charged will not be indicted on their failure to fulfill their responsibility to protect, but in committing particular crimes in particular situations. Thus Ban's rhetorical flourish does little to clarify what a duty of R2P requires. A/59/744, p. 5.

41 Ibid., p. 3.

42 There is no agreed-upon definition of ethnic cleansing in international law. I am following the ICISS's definition where it states: "large scale 'ethnic cleansing,' actual or apprehended, whether carried out by killing, forced expulsion, acts of terror or rape." ICISS, op. cit., 4.19.

43 World Federalist Movement–Institute for Global Policy, *Civil Society Perspectives on the Responsibility to Protect: Final Report*, New York: World Federalist Movement, April, 2003.

44 There is of course another legal debate over whether the Security Council has implicit powers under the Charter to authorize humanitarian interventions. The SC has always justified the use of force, for humanitarian purposes or otherwise, under Chapter VII. Nevertheless, assuming that a legal case can be made for the SC's powers to authorize an intervention for R2P, my point remains that the SC as it currently stands is dysfunctional.

45 Bellamy, op. cit., p. 164 (italics in original).

46 E.g., Tesón, Fernando. *Humanitarian Intervention*, Ardsley: Transnational Publishers Inc., 1988; Pattison, James. "Whose Responsibility to Protect? The Duties of Humanitarian Intervention," *Journal of Military Ethics*, 7: 4, 2008: pp. 262–283; Pattison, James. "Legitimacy and Humanitarian Intervention: Who Should Intervene" *The International Journal of Human Rights*, 12:3, 2008: pp. 395–413.; Evans, Gareth. *The Responsibility to Protect: Ending Mass Atrocity Crimes Once and For All*, Washington D.C.: Brookings Institute Press, 2008; Wheeler, Nicholas. *Saving Strangers: Humanitarian Intervention in International Society*, Oxford: Oxford University Press, 2000. Even Ban Ki-Moon in his 2009 report on "Implementing the Responsibility to Protect" endorses the view that the General Assembly could consider action under the "Uniting for Peace" procedure. A/63/677, paragraphs 57 and 63.

47 Bellamy, op. cit., p. 157.

48 Ibid., 158.

49 The identified regional agencies are the European Union (EU), African Union (AU), North Atlantic Treaty Organization (NATO), Organization for Security and Cooperation in Europe (OSCE), League of Arab States (LAS), Organization of American States (OAS), Commonwealth of Independent States (CIS), Association of Southeast Asian Nations (ASEAN), ASEAN Regional Forum (ARF), South Asian Association for Regional Cooperation (SAARC), Shanghai Cooperation Organization (SCO) and Economic Community of West African States (ECOWAS).

50 Evans, op. cit., p. 53 (italics in original).

51 "Outcome Document", op. cit., paragraph 138–139.

52 *TP*, 8:277.

53 Injurious offence (italics in original).

54 Vigilantius, *LoE*, 27:688.

55 Tan, Kok-Chor. "The Duty to Protect" in Terry Nardin and Melissa Williams (eds.), *Nomos XLVII: Humanitarian Intervention*, New York: New York University Press, 2006: p. 104.

56 Ibid., p. 97.

57 Ibid., p. 97.

58 Ibid., p. 100.

59 Ibid., p. 100.

60 Note here that his discussion of "institutionalization" is rather vague.

61 Tan, op. cit., p. 103 (italics added).

62 Ibid., p. 95.

63 Ibid., p. 95.

64 Nardin, Terry. "Introduction" in Terry Nardin and Melissa Williams (eds.), *Nomos XLVII: Humanitarian Intervention*, New York: New York University Press, 2006: p. 15.

65 *DV*, 6:386–6:394. Moral perfection is also considered an imperfect duty because human beings are faced with a wide array of situations, life experiences, education practices, etc. All of these differences require us to use our practical judgment in different ways.

66

> [U]nless the obligation to provide food to each claimant is actually allocated to specified agents and agencies, this "right" will provide meager pickings. The hungry know that they have a problem. What would change their prospects would be to know that it was others' problem too, and that specified others have an obligation to provide them with food. Unless obligations to feed the hungry are a matter of allocated justice rather than indeterminate beneficence, a so-called "right to food", and the other "rights" of the poor, will only be "manifesto" rights.
>
> O'Neill, Onora, cited in Tan, op. cit., endnote 20

67 O'Neill, Onora. *Towards Justice and Virtue*, Cambridge: Cambridge University Press, 1996: p. 132.

68 Ibid., p. 132.
69 As I noted in Chapter 1, all duties of respect are purely negative. One must forbear from acting, and no duties of respect—in Kant's writings—are positive.
70 *DV*, 6:452.
71 One may object that a failure in any duty is a "wrong"; however, this is not the case for Kant. "Wrong" belongs strictly to the category of *Recht*. To wrong, for Kant, is to violate a right; to fail in a duty of virtue, one cannot be held "culpable" but morally deficient. *MM* 6:384 and 6:390.
72 Tan, op. cit., p. 93. Further on, Tan asserts that "I am claiming only that the neutral state cannot appeal to the principle of sovereignty to maintain its neutrality" (ibid., p. 93).
73 Ibid., p. 104.
74 Again, in another puzzling passage Tan claims "that a duty is imperfect points only to the need for coordinating efforts and the need to cooperate. It does not mean that the duty need not be taken seriously by anyone" (ibid., p. 111). This is rather disturbing because any duty, under a Kantian framework, requires an agent to act. If Tan follows Kant "in spirit," then he should at least be aware that an imperfect duty is still a necessitation to act. Agents still have to take their imperfect duties seriously, and they must still fulfill them; it is only how and when that is discretionary. Agents cannot ignore their duties.
75 Bagnoli, Carla. "Humanitarian Intervention as a Perfect Duty" in Terry Nardin and Melissa Williams (eds.), *Nomos XLVII: Humanitarian Intervention*, New York: New York University Press, 2006: p. 119.
76 Ibid., p. 120.
77 Ibid., p. 124.
78 Ibid., p. 125.
79 Ibid., p. 133.
80 Ibid., p. 133.
81 Ibid., p. 129 (italics in original). Claiming that the right to coerce is a permission is full of problems. First, it is not a permission, as a "permission" carries with it the connotation that one is allowed to do something one is otherwise not allowed to do. The reciprocal right to coerce is rather the negating of a wrong. Coercion in the face of a wrong is a "hindrance to a hindrance" of freedom and is therefore "right" by the law of contradiction. There is a question of permitting the coercion of others when they have not already wronged, but that is not what Bagnoli is discussing here.
82 "A duty [of HI] applies to all rational agents." Thus I take her to mean that the ability to coerce also applies to all rational agents.
83 This juridical permission could be Kant's "permissive law", which I discuss in the next chapter. However, Bagnoli does not identify this, and so I am merely guessing at what she means here.
84 *DR*, 6:230.
85 *DR*, 6:256.
86 *DR*, 6:311.
87 *DR*, 6:312.
88 Bagnoli, op. cit., p. 131.
89 That is not to say that institutions cannot create authority, new duties etc. But in this particular case, we cannot claim this type of power. A duty of HI exists before the creation of the institution and not vice versa.
90 Bagnoli, op. cit., p. 119.
91 Ibid., p. 119. This is also a misunderstanding of Kant's very important distinction between worth and value. For Kant, objects or "things" have value, whereas moral agents have worth. Humanity is thus an aspect of worth, not value.
92 Honig, Bonnie. *Political Theory and the Displacement of Politics*, Ithaca: Cornell University Press, 1993: p. 27.

93 Ibid., p. 27.
94 Ibid., p. 27.
95 Ibid., p. 29.
96 Ibid., p. 29.
97 Ibid., p. 29.
98 Ibid., p. 32.
99 Ibid., p. 32.
100 Ibid., p. 35.
101 Ibid., p. 35.
102 Ibid., p. 35.
103 *DV*, 6:393 (italics added).
104 *DV*, 6:393.
105 Tan and O'Neill also use this framework to argue not for the identification of a recipient but for an agent. Williams claims "thus there is no direct legal duty for states or their citizens to offer special help when subjects of other states run into severe difficulties with their own rulers" (pp. 136–137). Further, he asserts that "where our own freedoms and rights are not endangered the duties of humanitarian intervention are ethical only and not legal" (p. 138). Williams, Howard. *Kant and the End of War: A Critique of Just War Theory*, Basingstoke: Palgrave Macmillan, 2012.
106 A duty to intervene can also exist if nonstate actors or groups within the state, over which the government has little or no control, commit these crimes. The government in these situations also fails in its duties of justice towards its people.
107 Ripstein, Arthur. "Authority and Coercion"," *Philosophy and Public Affairs*, 32:1, 2004: p. 8.
108 Ibid., p. 8.
109 Ibid., p. 11.
110 Kant's understanding of property in one's person is different than, say, Locke's. Ripstein has a very clear explication of the rights to security in one's person "prior to rights in property" for Kant. The gist of Ripstein's discussion is that there are two arguments at work in Kant: a right to humanity in our own person and acquired rights. Individuals have an innate right of humanity, which forbids certain acts such as slavery, suicide etc. Individuals can also acquire further rights through the state, rights to "external" things. However, Ripstein's discussion is problematic because of things like forced conscription and some acts of consent. Ibid., footnote 18, pp. 13–14.
111 Ibid., p. 12 (italics added).
112 *DR*, 6:230 (italics in original).
113 *DR*, 6:231.
114 *DR*, 6:231 (italics in original).
115 Ripstein, op. cit., p. 11.
116 *DR*, 6:256, 6:259, 6:260.
117 UN General Assembly, *Rome Statute of the International Criminal Court*, July 17 1998. Available at: http://untreaty.un.org/cod/icc/statute/romefra.htm (accessed March 28, 2013).
118 Byrd, Sharon. Private Correspondence.
119 I follow Bernstein's interpretation of Kant's unjust enemy but extend it to portions of populations within states because humanitarian intervention is primarily about states committing crimes against their own people and thus becoming unjust enemies to their populations. Kant claims that in a state of nature an

> enemy whose publicly expressed will (whether by word or deed) reveals a maxim by which, if it were made a universal rule, any condition of peace among nations would be impossible and, instead, a state of nature would be perpetuated.
>
> (*DR*, 6:349; Bernstein, p. 90)

Bernstein claims that

> to speak of an unjust enemy *in a state of nature* is to refer not only to the fact that the circumstances do not allow the settlement of the conflict by a lawsuit, but also to the fact that a *state* has violated another state's rights, as well as the fact that the rights-violator's maxim, if made a universal rule, would perpetuate the state of nature.
>
> Bernstein, Alyssa R. "Kant on Rights and Coercion in International Law: Implications for Humanitarian Military Intervention" *Annual Review for Law and Ethics*, 16, 2008: p. 91, footnote 200

120 The "State Fragility Index" compiled from the Polity IV data concludes that out of 162 countries, eight states are considered "extreme," 18 are "high," and 21 are "serious." These terms note the level of fragility and the likelihood of state breakdown. The Polity IV data measure the institutional strengths of countries in terms of governance. This index measures effectiveness and legitimacy by using indicators: security, governance, economic, and social dimensions of state performance. Marshall, Monty, G. and Keith Jaggers. *Polity IV Project: Political Regime Characteristics and Transitions, 1800–2010*. Available at: www.systemicpeace.org/polity/polity4.htm (accessed January 1, 2013).

121 *DR*, 6:312–6:314.

122 *DR*, 6:306 as cited and translated by Byrd, Sharon and Joachim Hruschka. "From the State of Nature to the Juridical State of States." *Law and Philosophy*, 27, 2008: p. 606.

123 Ibid., p. 606.

124 *DR*, 6:350. Sharon Byrd and Joachim Hruschka also come to this conclusion when they note that "[s]tates, and not merely individual persons, are required to enter a juridical state among states. Byrd and Hruschka, op. cit., p. 624.

125 Interestingly, Kant claims one can have no duties of justice to oneself. Duties of justice are all "external," but he does not elaborate or even venture into the discussion of duties of a government towards its citizens. If a state is, as he says, a "moral person," then duties of justice towards the citizens of the state would be like having duties of justice to oneself, as the citizens are components of the state.

126 I will spend considerable time on the "state of states" argument in chapters 4 and 5.

127 *TPP*, in Reiss p. 96.

128 Höffe, Otfried. "Foreword" in *Terror, Peace and Universalism: Essays on the Philosophy of Immanuel Kant*, Oxford: Oxford University Press, 2007: ix–x.

129 Kavka, Gregory S. "Hobbes's War of All against All" in Christopher W. Morris (ed.), *Critical Essays on Hobbes, Locke, and Rousseau*, Oxford: Rowman & Littlefield Publishers, Inc., 1999.

130 Some, like Noel Malcomb, argue that Hobbes does offer such a middle ground in his theory, and that actors can make pacts or agreements in a state of nature, "if one of them shows his good will by performing his side of the bargain first," or there is "a Power to make him performe [his contract]" because there is a "moral term" that is universal and helps to mediate between the state of nature and civil society (p. 438). Malcomb attempts to support his argument for the "moral term" by invoking Hobbes' laws of nature, where these laws oblige actors to perform (or abstain from) certain acts and intentions (e.g., drinking to excess or not being cruel). I applaud Malcomb's attempts here; however, I disagree with him. Ultimately, Hobbes' framework denies free will and endorses what Malcomb calls "pre-moral psychological terms", that is, terms that assign "good" and "bad" to objects subjectively (p. 436). I cannot go into much detail here, but if one first denies an agent's capacity to be determined by objects of sense and desire, and then one claims that the "pre-moral" (I take him to mean temporally "pre") terms of good and bad are subjective, I cannot see how a universal "moral" term can result. Furthermore, even if Hobbes' laws of

nature obligate certain acts, they do so as addendums to the Right of Nature (self-preservation), which, ultimately turns "moral" rules into "rules of prudence" and collapses the distinction between the moral and prudential. Thus, the argument that one can contract in a state of nature still faces the problem of the first person to contract; in other words, the first move is irrational. Even if one attempts a contract, that contract is still, in a sense, irrational because long-term cooperation, according to Hobbes, is likely to be impossible, so such contracts are perceived to be suckers' bets. Malcomb, Noel. *Aspects of Hobbes*, Oxford: Clarendon Press, 2002.

131 *DR*, 6:257.
132 *DR*, 6:341.
133 The international courts do not have full jurisdiction, as the court functions on treaty; states have to i) agree to jurisdiction and ii) agree to be tried by it. Cf. International Criminal Court, available at: www.icc-cpi.int/en_menus/icc/about%20the%20court/Pages/about%20the%20court.aspx (accessed March 15, 2013); and the International Court of Justice, available at: www.icj-cij.org/court/index.php (accessed March 15, 2013).
134 Williams, op. cit., p. 139.
135 Williams, op. cit., pp. 130–140.
136 *TPP*, 8:360.
137 *DR*, 6:347.
138 Williams, op. cit., p. 136.
139 *MM*, 6:209.
140 Wheeler, among others, objects that to take the intervening state as the "referent object for analysis" places too much emphasis on the agent and not enough on the recipient (the victim). Wheeler, op. cit., p. 38.
141 Tan, op. cit., p. 96.
142 Ibid., 96.
143 Pattison, op. cit., p. 264.
144 Ibid., pp. 266–267.
145 Pattison, op. cit., p. 267 and p. 401.
146 Pattison, op. cit., p. 266; citing O'Hanlon, M. *Expanding Global Military Capacity for Humanitarian Intervention*, Washington D.C., Brookings Institution Press, 2003.
147 Roff, H.M. "Response to Pattison: Whose Responsibility to Protect" *Journal of Military Ethics*, 8: 1, 2009: pp. 79–85.
148 *TPP*, 8:352.
149 Hobbes, Thomas. *Leviathan*, Richard Tuck, ed., Cambridge: Cambridge University Press, 1992: Chapter 4, paragraph 13.
150 Ripstein, Arthur. "Three Duties to Rescue," *Law and Philosophy*, 19: 6, 2000: p. 775.

3 Kant's permissive laws

1 Vigilantius, *LoE*, 27:516.
2 Lacey, A.R. *Dictionary of Philosophy*, New York: Barnes & Noble Books, 1996: p. 63.
3 Some may suggest that Kant's permissive law may be essential to his nonideal political and ethical theory, and this is why he spends so little time on it, as he was concerned primarily with working out a theory under the assumption of strict compliance to principles. However, as I will argue later, the nonideal world can present situations whereby compliance with such principles would undermine reason, and thus morality, itself.
4 Gregor, Mary. *Laws of Freedom*, Oxford: Basil Blackwell Publishing, 1963: p. 57 note 26.
5 Ibid., pp. 57–58.

6 Ibid., p. 142.
7 Tierney, Brian. "Kant on Property: The Problem of the Permissive Law," *Journal of the History of Ideas*, 62: 2, 2001: p. 309.
8 Tierney Brian, "Permissive Natural Law and Property: Gratian to Kant," *Journal of the History of Ideas*, Vol. 62: 3, 2001: p. 398.
9 Tierney, "Kant on Property," p. 311.
10 The postulate, as we will see, asserts that people may unilaterally acquire external objects of choice. *DR*, 6:246.
11 Tierney, "Permissive Natural Law and Property," p. 398.
12 See Tierney, Brian. "Natural Law and Natural Rights: Old Problems and Recent Approaches" *Review of Politics*, 64: 3, 2002; "Historical Roots of Modern Rights: Before Locke and After" *Ave Maria Law Review*, 3:1, 2005: pp. 23–43.
13 Hruschka, Joachim. "The Permissive Law of Practical Reason in Kant's Metaphysics of Morals," *Law and Philosophy*, 23, 2004: pp. 45–72.
14 See Tierney, "Permissive Natural Law and Property," p. 395; Kaufmann, Mattias. "Was erlaubt das Erlaubnisgesetz—und wozu braucht es Kant? *Annual Review of Law and Ethics*, 13, 2005: pp. 195–220.
15 See Szymkowiak, Aaron. "Kant's Permissive Law: Critical Rights, Sceptical Politics," *British Journal of the History of Philosophy* 17: 3, 2009: pp. 567–600. I say "moral" here because morality is made up of both right and virtue.
16 Brandt, Reinhard. "Das Erlaubnisgesetzt, oder: Vernunft and Geschichte in Kant's Rechtslehre," in Reinhard Brandt (ed.), *Rechtsphilosophie der Aufklarung*, Berlin: Walter de Gruyter & Company, 1982: pp. 233–285.
17 Flikschuh, Katrin. *Kant and Modern Political Philosophy*, Cambridge: Cambridge University Press, 2000: pp. 123–124.
18 *DR*, 6:254.
19 Again, Gregor's and Flikschuh's interpretation of the universal principle of right states that "any act is right if it can coexist with everyone's freedom in accordance with a universal law" (*DR*, 6:230). I, however, prefer to keep the principle in the original "*Allgemeines Prinzip des Rechts*" (Universal Principle of Right, hereafter "UPR") as *allgemein* has several meanings, such as "general," "common," "universal" and "public."
20 *DR*, 6:255 (italics in original). While Kant believes the emphasis is on the notion of possibility of "possession," it makes more sense to emphasize the word "have" in the thesis and antithesis. Depending upon what I mean by "having," and the attendant assumptions about "having", that definition will inform the different kinds of possession.
21 In this example, the "wresting" would violate my bodily integrity, but not the "right" to possession.
22 Flikschuh, op. cit., p. 122.
23 Flikschuh focuses mainly on Kant's use of the "permissive law" in § 6 and 7 in the *Rechtslehre* (*DR*), though she does discuss Kant's long footnote in "Perpetual Peace" on permissive laws, and has one reference to the *Doctrine of Virtue*. Her primary concern is to understand the permissive law's use in politics, namely the acquisition of property and how this acquisition is tied to political obligation, reflective judgment, and ultimately Kant's cosmopolitanism.
24 Flikschuh, op. cit., p. 140. Furthermore, recall that the general principle of right (UPR) states that "any action is right if it can coexist with everyone's freedom in accordance with a general law." *DR*, 6:230.
25 Flikschuh follows Bernd Ludwig's revised edition of the *Doctrine of Right* (*DR*), where he philologically rearranges § 2 of Section I, Chapter I to § 6 of Section I, Chapter I. Ludwig follows Buchda and Tenbruck's work on reorganizing some sections of the *DR* due to the belief that "illicitly included preliminary notes and provisional drafts" occur in the published text. The purpose of reconstructing these

specific paragraphs is to gain clarity in understanding the "postulate of practical reason with regard to right" (p. 114). See Buchda, Gerd. "Das Privatrecht Immanuel Kants'; Tenbruck, Friedrich. "Uber eine notwendige Textkorrektur in Kants 'Metaphysik der Sitten';" Ludwig, Bernd. "Der Platz des rechtlichen Postulats der praktischen Vernunft innerhalb der Paragraphen 1–6 der Kantischen Rechtslehre," as cited in Flikschuh, op. cit. Flikschuh notes that "Buchda and Tenbruk established independently of each other the illicit inclusion of some of Kant's preliminary notes in sections 4–8 of § 6, Section I" (ibid., footnote. p. 114). This same ordering also appears in the Gregor translation.

26 Flikschuh, op. cit., p. 25.
27 *DR* 6:246; 6:247.
28 Flikschuh, op. cit., p. 117.
29 Ibid., p. 136.
30 Ibid., p. 136.
31 Ibid., p. 139. There is little discussion of what "political agency" means. Moreover, I take her to be saying that the judgment to acquire property and impose an obligation on others to refrain from it is a tentative political judgment. That is, a judgment that is political in nature before the institution of a civil society.
32 One might object to Kant's arguments that they require something like the Lockean proviso or a principle of distributive justice to ensure that simple taking does not result in subsequent unfair or unjust distributions of property. While this may be true, Kant does not address the subject. The most he has to say about redistributions of property occurs once agents enter the civil condition. Once the civil condition is established, citizens may be taxed to support the poor. See *DR*, 6:326–327.
33 Flikschuh, op. cit., p. 141.
34 Ibid., pp. 141–142.
35 Ibid., p. 143.
36 Ibid., p. 139.
37 Hruschka, op. cit., p. 59.
38 Ibid., p. 66.
39 Ibid., pp. 48–49.
40 Ibid., p. 49 (italics in original).
41 Ibid., p. 49.
42 Ibid., pp. 53–54.
43 Ibid., p. 54.
44 Hruschka notes Walch's article on "'*Zulassung*' (license), [where] the Latin translation of '*Zulassung*' is '*permissio*,' which Kant translates as '*Erlaubnis*.'" Walch states that "'license' ('*permissio*') can mean the 'introduction of a right through a law' such as 'when, e.g., parental power, citizens' property, etc. are licensed by the law.'" Johann Georg Walch as cited in Hruschka, op. cit., p. 55 and note 26 (italics in original).
45 Gottfried Achenwall as cited in Hruschka, op. cit., p. 56 and notes 1 and 30 (italics in original).
46 Ibid., p. 58 (italics in original).
47 Ibid., p. 58 (italics in original). For Kant, "*facultas moralis*" is an authorization. This authorization is freedom in the negative sense, as Kant claims "that action is permitted (*licitum*) which is not contrary obligation; and this freedom, which is not limited by any opposing imperative, is called an authorization (*faculas moralis*)." *DR*, 6:222.
48 Hruschka, op. cit., p. 59. One might object to Hruschka's example of condominium buying as not appropriate to the discussion of power-conferring norms, as his example seems to suggest a permission right to buy and sell (bundled with claim rights against certain kinds of interference). Hruschka seems to be saying that the permissive law as power-conferring norm is rather a "power" in the proper legal (or

at least Hohfeldian) sense; that is, a right to create new rights and obligations. I believe that Hruschka intends this latter sense, but his example of condominiums is inapposite. Creating a legal institution—especially an entire legal or civil condition—is creating something that introduces new rights and obligations, and not granting the permission to do X or Y. We must first have the institution before we can have a permission to act within it. I thank David Mapel for this point.

49 Hruschka, op. cit., p. 47.
50 Ibid., p. 51.
51 Ibid., p. 51.
52 Ibid., p. 52.
53 According to Werner Stark, the Collins notes may be an earlier text, perhaps as early as 1774 or 1775. Stark, Werner. *Vorlesung zur Moralphilosophie*, Berlin: Walter de Gruyter, 2004: pp. 403–404. I thank Robert Louden for pointing this out.
54 *G*, 4:396.
55 Vigilantius, *LoE*, 27:505.
56 Vigilantius, *LoE*, 27:504.
57 Vigilantius, *LoE*, 27:502.
58 In the *Grounding* Kant thinks that the Kingdom of Ends is "a systematic union of different rational beings through common laws," and such a place he calls "certainly only an ideal". *G*, 4:433.
59 Vigilantius, *LoE*, 27:514. See also *Critique of Practical Reason*, 5:67–5:70; *Critique of Pure Reason*, J.M.D. Meiklejohn (trans.), Amherst: Prometheus Books, 1990: p. 72.
60

> Die Verbots/gesetze sind aber theils universals, die allgemein gelten, wobei also eine Ausnahme unmöglich ist; hier ist also ein Erlaubnißgesetz gar nicht denkbar: theils generales, d.i. wo das Verbot in den mehresten Fällen (im Allgemeinen) gilt. Hier lassen sich Ausnahmen denken …
>
> *LoE*, 27:514

61 Beilefeldt, Heiner. "Autonomy and Republicanism," *Political Theory*, 25: 4, 1997: p. 544. Beilefeldt's discussion of the confusion arising from Gregor's translation of "*allgemein*" as "universal" in the *Rechtslehre* is well worth noting. Beilefeldt makes an impressive case that "*allgemeine Gesetze* must be applied to an empirical society of humans whose 'actions, as facts, can have (direct or indirect) influence on each other, as Kant points out' " (p. 544).
62 Kant, in "Theory and Practice," states that "all rights consist solely in the restriction of the freedom of others, with the qualification that their freedom can coexist with my freedom within the terms of a general (*allgemeinen*) law; and public right in a commonwealth is simply a state of affairs regulated by real (*wirklichen*) legislation which conforms to this principle." Reiss translates "*allgemeinen*" as "general", whereas Humphrey has "universal" (*TP*, 8:292). Kant, Immanuel, "Theory in Practice" in H.S. Reiss (ed.) *Kant Political Writings*, Cambridge: Cambridge University Press, 1991; Kant, Immanuel, "Theory and Practice" in *Perpetual Peace and Other Essays*, Ted Humphrey (trans.), Indianapolis: Hackett Publishing Company, 1983.
63 *TP*, Reiss translation, p. 79.
64 Ibid., pp. 75–76 (italics added.) I am not here denying the universal principle of right, but I want to draw a distinction between right *as such*, and real-world instantiations of right. This quote comes from Kant's essay "Theory and Practice" where I believe him to be drawing that distinction. Metaphysically, right is universal. However, laws that come about in the real world are general.
65 Collins, *LoE*, 27: 388; *DR*, 6:277–280. I am not going to address the issue that as a contract, marriage is already an acquired right, which thus requires the use of *lex permissiva* to establish a civil condition that engenders such acquired rights. The

example is to illustrate how *lex permissiva* and general laws work together. I thank Tim Waligore for pointing this out.

66 *DR*, 6:277.

67 Kant, Immanuel. (1797). "Vorarbeiten der Metaphysic der Sitten" in *Kants Gesammelte Schriften*, Band 23, ed. Gerhard Lehmann, Akademie Ausgabe Edition, 1955. Available at: www.korpora.org/kant/aa23 (hereafter *VMdS*), 23:385.

68 For an excellent discussion of this see Donagan, Alan. "Consistency in Rationalist Systems." *Journal of Philosophy*, 81: 6, 1984: pp. 291–309. One may object that Kant is not a rationalist in the strict sense of the word (like Leibniz or Wolff); however, I would say that Kant is enough of a rationalist to not allow a conflict of duties into his system.

69 *DR*, 6:224.

70 *DR*, 6:224; Collins, *LoE*, 27:280; Vigilantius, *LoE*, 27:493; 27:501; 27:508; 27:537.

71 *DR*, 6:224.

72 Vigilantius, *LoE*, 27:508.

73 Where there is strict moral indifference, there is no need for a law, and so no need of "governance," thus the moral and permissive laws are exclusively disjunctive.

74 *DR*, 6:223.

75 Indeed, this is where I think Hruschka's distinction between "allowed" and "merely allowed" may come into play. All morally indifferent actions are allowed, that is morally permitted (*erlaubt*), but only some of these permitted actions (*bloß erlaubt*) require a law. These "merely permitted" actions on my reading are not morally indifferent in relation to Kant's teleology. They are permitted but morally important, and so have need of a law authorizing their allowance.

76 Vigilantius, *LoE*, 27:514.

77 Kant discusses *lex permissiva* in six texts: *Lectures on Ethics*, "Vorarbeiten zu die Metaphysik der Sitten" (*VdMdS*), "Towards Perpetual Peace," the "Introduction" to the *Metaphysics of Morals*, the *Doctrine of Right* and the *Doctrine of Virtue*. Moreover, in English translations of Kant's *Lectures on Ethics*, three of the four students (Collins, Mrongovius and Vigilantius) remark on permissive laws. It is also important to note that the student lecture notes are not all available in English. Of the 23 known student lecture notes, five are published in English and nine are lost. Explicit references in *LoE* to *leges permissivae*, *lex permissiva* and permissive laws (*Erlaubnisgestezt*) are at: 27:274; 29:620; 27:512; 27:514; 27:515; 27:524; 27:562.

78 Flikschuh mentions the *Doctrine of Virtue* (*DV*) but only in passing (Flikschuh, op. cit., p. 137). Her point in mentioning the *DV* is to bracket it off from her main argument for the permissive law to be a provisional solution to the antinomy of right, and, oddly, she does not cite the explicit references to *lex permissiva* in the *DV* (6:426 and 6:453). Tierney and Szymkowiak also do not look to the entire *LoE*. Tierney and Szymkowiak restrict their discussion to Vigilantius (although Szymkowiak bizarrely includes a section from Collins that has nothing to do with *lex permissiva*.)

79 The Collins notes date from 1784, though there is debate that they are from 10 years earlier.

80 Collins, *LoE*, 27:274.

81 Mrongovius dates from 1785. Mrongovious, *LoE*, 29:620.

82 Vigilantius, *LoE*, 27:514 (italics added).

83 Vigilantius, *LoE*, 27:515 (italics added).

84 *VMdS*, 23:385. ("Lex permissiva *ist das Gesetz wodurch etwas nach Naturgesetzen erlaubt ist was nach civilgesetzen verboten ist z.B. sein eigener Richter in Beleidigungen zu seyn oder Vielweiberey wenn nur ein Mann da ist oder Raub wenn Gefahr zu verhungern eintritt* …") There is a bit in the original text as well that attempts to discuss the securing of private property, but it is an incomplete sentence. It is important to note, though, that Kant did at least bring the property discussion back in here, albeit the notes do so in a fragmentary and incomplete way.

85 *DV*, 6:453.
86 *DV*, 6:426 (italics added). Nature's end is procreation, while reason's end is moralization. If a wife (or husband) is sterile or incapable for some reason of bearing children, nature's end is automatically frustrated. Reason, however, holds that sex is actually a good. Kant is a bit unclear on this point, but in his discussion of marriage (*DR*, 6:277–279), and his discussion of defiling oneself by lust (*DV*, 6:424–426), I infer that there must be some good to the "mutual enjoyment" in the act of sex that is separate from mere procreation. This, I believe, is why Kant toys with the casuistical question above.
87 It is by definition an SME; however, as I have made clear before in my distinction between formal and material definitions, this situation may not be an SME materially.
88 *DV*, 6:426.
89 *TPP*, 8:348 and 8:374. The second footnote at 374 does not really add anything further to the understanding of *lex permissiva*. The only thing it underscores is the importance of time.
90 *TPP*, 8:348.
91 *TPP*, 8:348.
92 *TPP*, 8:348.
93 This minimum condition is that of being "honest" (*TPP*, 8:348). Here I believe Kant means the principle of *honeste vive*, or live honorably. For Kant, *honeste vive* implies the maxim "Act so that you are worthy of honor in your own eyes" (*LoE*, 29:632). The relation of *honeste vive* in this example to the assertion that the act of taking possession was "honest" is important because Kant is referring to possession of external objects (namely state's territory) in a state of nature. In a state of nature, as I have previously argued, there is no full instantiation of Right, only private right, where each is judge in his own case. If I take a piece of land, with the "correct" intention, I am my own judge, and so I can say that my possession is honest, especially when this intention "rests ultimately on our own judgement of the action" (Vigilantius, *LoE*, 27:527).
94 *TPP*, 8:347.
95 Preliminary Article No. 2 in *TPP* at 8:344.
96 *TPP*, 8:348. The italics in the last sentence occur in Humphrey's translation; however, they do not occur in the original text. I have added italics to the middle portion, which seems to be the crux of what Kant is discussing.
97 Vigilantius, *LoE*: 27:514.
98 Vigilantius, *LoE*, 27:514.
99 The text reads:

> Although the laws set out above are objectively, i.e., from the perspective of those in power, merely prohibitive laws (*leges prohibitivae*), some of them are of that strict kind—that is, of that class of laws that holds regardless of circumstances (*leges strictae*)—that demands immediate implementation (viz., Nos. 1,5, and 6). However, others (viz., Nos. 2,3,4), while not exceptions to the rule of law, do permit, depending upon circumstances, some subjective leeway in their implementation (*leges latae*) as long as one does not lose sight of their end.... Delay is permitted only to prevent such premature implementation as might injure the intention of the article.
>
> (*TPP*, 8:347).

100 Vigilantius, *LoE*, 27:514–515.
101 The case would have to satisfy the legally relevant facts that allow a permission. For a very insightful discussion of legally relevant facts, the relevance of facts, mistake of law and mistake of fact, see Byrd, Sharon B. and Joachim Hruschka. "The Natural

Law Duty to Recognize Private Property Ownership: Kant's Theory of Property in His Doctrine of Right" *University of Toronto Law Journal* 56, 2006: pp. 217–282, especially footnote 44.

102 *TPP*, 8:348.

103 *TPP*, 8:348.

104 To "accompany" something assumes a separation from the thing it is accompanying. To "accompany" is "to go somewhere with" or "be present or occur at the same time as" or "provide or serve as a compliment to," according to the *Oxford English Dictionary*. All definitions assume a distinction between two objects. Catherine Soanes and Angus Stevenson (eds.), *Concise Oxford English Dictionary*, 11th edn, Oxford: Oxford University Press, 2004.

105 See *Blacks Law Dictionary*, Abridged 5th Edn, St. Paul: West Publishing Company, 1983 (italics added).

106 Vigilantius, *LoE*; 27: 512.

107 *DR*, 6:223. The italics on "permitted" in the first sentence occur in Gregor's translation; however, they are not shown in the original text. I reproduce them here, though I think the translator could have left them out and the reading would not be affected. Hruschka would argue that if there is emphasis, it ought to be placed on "merely" (*bloß*) rather than "permitted" (*erlaubt*). I have added italics to the first portion of the last sentence.

108 *DR*, 6:246.

109 *DR*, 6:247.

110 Rightful possession is different than mere possession, or "holding." Rightful possession means that anyone's use of something that belongs to me, whether I am in physical possession of it or not, wrongs me. Wrong does not have to be a physical harm. For a very good discussion of this see Ripstein, Arthur. *Force and Freedom: Kant's Legal and Political Philosophy*, Cambridge, MA: Harvard University Press, 2009: pp. 81–85.

111 *DR*, 6:246 (italics in original).

112 Flikschuh's impressive exposition of Kant's idea of property right is worth noting here. Kant does not believe, like Locke, that one can acquire rights *against* or *to* an object. One can only acquire rights against or to persons. What this means is that Kant's understanding of property is a three-way relationship between rights holder, duty bearer and object. For example, I have a right R to object O, and Jane has a duty D to refrain from using O. On the Lockean understanding, it is a two-way relationship between possessor and object (in our example R and O), but as Flikschuh rightly interprets Kant to be saying, only persons and not objects can have rights to or against something.

113 *DR*, 6: 246 (italics in original).

114 *DR*, 6:267.

115 *DR*, 6:276.

116 Wood, Allen W. *Kant's Ethical Thought*, Cambridge: Cambridge University Press, 1999: p. 56.

117 Vigilantius, *LoE*, 27:524.

118 Hruschka, op. cit., p. 70.

119 *DR*, 6:256.

120 Hruschka, op. cit., p. 56.

4 Permissible coercion

1 Krashnishi, Mehmet. Quoted in William J. Buckley (ed.), *Kosovo: Contending Voices on Balkan Interventions*, Grand Rapids: William. B. Eerdmans Publishing Company, 2000: p. 60.

2 Beardsley, Brent. Quoted in Samantha Powers, *The Problem From Hell*, New York: HarperCollins Publisher, 2002: p. 349.
3 Powers, op. cit., p. 350.
4 Walzer, Michael. *Just and Unjust Wars: A Moral Argument with Historical Illustrations Fourth Edition*, New York: Basic Books, 2006: p. 253.
5 Churchill, Winston. Quoted in Walzer, op. cit., p. 245.
6 Plato, *Republic*, G.M.A. Grube (trans.) revised by C.D.C. Reeve, Indianapolis: Hackett Publishing Company, 1992: p. 148 (line 473d).
7 Kant, Immanuel. *The Critique of Pure Reason*, J.M.D. Meiklejohn (trans.), Amherst: Prometheus Books, Inc., 1990: p. 199.
8 See Vigilantius, *LoE* 27:514. Vs. *TPP* 8:355.
9 *On Education* (*OE*), *Religion within the Bounds of Mere Reason* (*R*).
10 *DR*, 6:307.
11 *TPP*, 8:355.
12 *DR*, 6:307.
13 Vigilantius, *LoE*, 27:514.
14 *DR*: 6:344; 6:346; 6:350.
15 *DR*, 6:306.
16 *DR*, 6:209.
17 Byrd and Hruschka define a presumption as a normative proposition, "which require[s] that certain facts or circumstances generally be assumed as given." Byrd, B. Sharon and Joachim Hruschka. "From the State of Nature to the Juridical State of States" *Law and Philosophy*, 27, 2008: p. 616. Presumptions on the whole can take many forms. The use of presumptions in law, and also in philosophy can span: presumptions of law, presumptions of fact, rebuttable presumptions, irrebuttable presumptions or conclusive presumptions. Ullman-Margalit argues that, in everyday experience, presumptions are assumptions made in advance to help aid in practical deliberation and decision-making. Hers is a particular philosophy of action orientation. Ullman-Margalit, Edna. "On Presumption" *Journal of Philosophy*, 80: 3, 1983: pp. 143–163. I follow Byrd and Hruschka's understanding of presumption and conjecture, which is located in Kant's period.
18 Byrd and Hruschka, op. cit., p. 620.
19 Ibid., p. 619.
20 Ibid.
21 *TPP*, 8:355–356.
22 Interestingly, in her article "The State as a Moral Person," Byrd notes the role of corporate moral agency in Kant's conception of the state as a moral person, but refuses to recognize that a corporation as a moral agent is distinct from the individuals that comprise it (Private Correspondence). Byrd, B. Sharon. "The State as a Moral Person" *Proceedings of the Eighth International Kant Congress*, H. Robinson (ed.), Milwaukee: Marquette University Press: 1995, Vol. I.1: pp. 171–189.
23 *TPP*, 8:355.
24 *TP*, 8:312.
25 *TPP*, 8:354.
26 *DR*: 6:227; 6:274; 6:297, 6:316; 6:343; 6:347; 6:348. In *CF*, p. 133. In *TPP*, 8:344. In *TP*, 8:291. In the Vigilantius *LoE*, 27:510; 27:573.
27 *DR*, 6:223.
28 See French, Peter. "The Corporation as a Moral Person" *American Philosophical Quarterly*, 16:3, 1979: pp. 207–215.
29 Kant explicitly notes that "a state (*civitas*) has its autonomy, that is, by which it forms and preserves itself in accordance with laws of freedom" (*DR*, 6:318).
30 *DR*, 6:343. The rights of states are the rights to go to war, their rights in war and their rights after war.

31 For the view that states can have corporate moral responsibility see Erskine, Toni. "Making Sense of 'Responsibility' in International Relations: Key Questions and Concepts" in Toni Erskine (ed.) *Can Institutions Have Responsibilities? Collective Moral Agency and International Relations, Global Issues Series*, Basingstoke: Palgrave Macmillan, 2003: pp. 1–18; Erskine, Toni. "Assigning Responsibility to Institutional Moral Agents: The Case of States and 'Quasi-States'" in Toni Erskine (ed.) *Can Institutions Have Responsibilities? Collective Moral Agency and International Relations, Global Issues Series*, Basingstoke: Palgrave Macmillan, 2003: pp. 19–40; Harbor, Frances V. "Collective Moral Agency and the Political Process" in Toni Erskine (ed.) *Can Institutions Have Responsibilities? Collective Moral Agency and International Relations, Global Issues Series*, Basingstoke: Palgrave Macmillan, 2003: pp. 69–83; Arnold, Denis G. "Corporate Moral Agency" *Midwest Studies in Philosophy*, 30, 2006: pp. 279–291. For an informative account of the paradoxical nature of responsibility and states, see: Runciman, David. "Moral Responsibility and the Problem of Representing the State" in Toni Erskine (ed.) *Can Institutions Have Responsibilities? Collective Moral Agency and International Relations, Global Issues Series*, Basingstoke: Palgrave Macmillan, 2003: pp. 41–50. Eckert, Amy. "Peoples and Persons: Moral Standing, Power and the Equality of States" *International Studies Quarterly*, 50, 2006: pp. 841–859. For individualist accounts of moral responsibility see: Miller, Seumas. "Collective Moral Responsibility: An Individualist Account" *Midwest Studies in Philosophy*, 30, 2006: pp. 176–193. Miller, Seumas. *The Moral Foundations of Social Institutions: A Philosophical Study*, Cambridge: Cambridge University Press, 2010. For arguments about Kant's state as a moral person, see: Byrd, Sharon B., op. cit., pp. 171–189.

32 *DR*: 6:227; 6:274; 6:297, 6:316; 6:343; 6:347; 6:348.

33 Dubbink, Wim. "Conceptualizing Corporate Moral Responsibility: A Neo-Kantian Approach," *Annual Meeting of the Society of Business Ethics*, Honolulu, August 2005, as cited in Denis G. Arnold "Corporate Moral Agency" *Midwest Studies in Philosophy*, 30, 2006: footnote 9.

34 One might still object that a robot is an artificial moral agent and can be programmed to be evil, thereby being inherently evil. However, this objection misses the mark. If an agent has to be "programmed" it is not autonomous. It is acting within the constraints of how the system runs and cannot be said to be acting freely.

35 Erskine writes: "a collectivity is more than the sum of the identities of its constitutive parts and, therefore, does not rely on a determinate membership; a decision-making structure; an identity over time; and a conception of itself as a unit" (Erskine, "Assigning Responsibility to Institutional Moral Agents," p. 24). The last requirement for Erskine, that of identifying itself as a unit, is not a requirement of Kant's; as I previously noted, psychological personality is not necessary or the same as moral personality.

36 Byrd and Hruschka, op. cit., pp. 615–616.

37 *DR*, 6:346 (italics added).

38 *DR*, 6:346 and 6:349.

39 Kant states that states can be threatened by "another state being the first to undertake preparations … or the menacing increase in another state's power (by acquisition of territory)." *DR*, 6:346.

40 *DR*, 6:346.

41 *DR*, 6:343. The very act of making a threat is more than sufficient, but my claim is that even actions that are directed towards securing oneself, i.e., self-preservation, are sufficient for another state to judge itself in danger. One need not explicitly threaten.

42 *DR*, 6:344; 6:350–351; 6:353; *TPP*, 8:346; 8:354; 8:357.

43 The textual evidence is roughly as follows: In *TPP* and the *DR* the threat to states within the international system is to come from the outside (other states) and

individuals within states are protected *enough* because domestic states have "a lawful internal constitution, and have thus outgrown the coercive right of others to subject them to a wider legal constitution in accordance with their conception of right" (*TPP*, Reiss, p. 104). Such internal juridical arrangements of states give them the status of "moral persons;" agents who have rights against others (*DR*, 6:343). Kant states that the rights of nations include the right to go to war, the right in war, and the right after war. Much of this turns on the idea that states have a certain degree of external freedom and therefore have a right against intervention by other states. This moral personhood carries with it, in particular, the right of noninterference, and many scholars maintain that Kant holds a strict nonintervention principle. These scholars cite the Fifth Preliminary Article in *TPP* that "no state shall forcibly interfere with the constitution and government of another" (*TPP*, 8:346). Furthermore, they often cite Kant's insistence that only a "free federation of states," a federation without a constitution and sovereign rights, is permitted at the international level. *TPP*, 8:354–57; *DR*, 6:344; 6:351. Georg Cavallar makes this distinction, against someone like Fernando Tesón.

44 The presumption is moot in the sense of rendering a matter irrelevant or of no practical significance. The presumption is not completely abolished, but on Kant's reasoning, once the civil condition is in place the need to preemptively coerce others is no longer required. The presumption only authorizes coercion when the rule of law is absent, and when, or if, a state fails the presumption could once again authorize such coercion.

45 *TPP*, 8:355.

46 *TP*, Reiss, p. 84.

47 *TP*, Reiss, p. 84.

48 Cf. *TP*, 8:304, *DR*, 6:319, 6:372.

49 J.J. Messner (ed.) "The Failed State Index 2012: The Book," *The Fund for Peace Conflict Early Warning and Assessment* (June 18, 2012). Available at: www.fundforpeace.org/global/?q=cfsir1210 (accessed January 1, 2013).

50 The term "failure" in the Failed State Index has several attributes.

> One of the most common is the loss of physical control of its territory or a monopoly on the legitimate use of force. Other attributes of state failure include the erosion of legitimate authority to make collective decisions, an inability to provide reasonable public services, and the inability to interact with other states as a full member of the international community. The 12 indicators cover a wide range of elements of the risk of state failure, such as extensive corruption and criminal behavior, inability to collect taxes or otherwise draw on citizen support, large-scale involuntary dislocation of the population, sharp economic decline, group-based inequality, institutionalized persecution or discrimination, severe demographic pressures, brain drain, and environmental decay. States can fail at varying rates through explosion, implosion, erosion, or invasion over different time periods.

As to the definitions of "alert," "very high warning" or "high warning," these correspond to the rank order of the states based on the total scores of the 12 indicators. For each indicator, the ratings are placed on a scale of 0 to 10, with 0 being the lowest intensity (most stable) and 10 being the highest intensity (least stable). The total score is the sum of the 12 indicators and is on a scale of 0 to 120. For full methodological details, see: "The Failed State Index 2012: The Book," op. cit.

51 The indicators I use here are "REF," "GG," "HF" and "HR" for all respective states in the Index. "REF" refers to pressures related to refugees and internally displaced persons. "GG" refers to pressures related to group grievances and the eruption of violence due to those grievances. "HF" refers to human flight, migration and the "brain drain" problem of educated persons emigrating. "HR" refers to pressures

related to human rights violations and the rule of law. The total score possible is therefore 40; the higher the score the more pressure to fail. I set the cut-offs in similar methodological fashion to the Index: 40–30 is at "alert"; 30–20 is at a "warning"; 20–10 is considered "stable" and 10–0 is "sustainable."

52 The indicators I use here are "SL," "PS," "SEC" and "EXT" for all respective states in the Index. "SL" refers to pressures related to state legitimacy, such as corruption and lack of representatives in government. "PS" refers to pressures related the provision (or lack thereof) of public services such as police and basic infrastructure. "SEC" refers to the security apparatus of the state. "EXT" refers to external intervention, such as the presence of peacekeepers, foreign military interventions, sanctions or foreign assistance. The total score possible is therefore 40; the higher the score the more pressure to fail. I set the cut-offs in similar methodological fashion to the Index: 40–30 is at "alert"; 30–20 is at a "warning"; 20–10 is considered "stable" and 10–0 is "sustainable." I choose not to include the variable on factionalized elites (FE) as there is evidence that with sufficient payouts, the factionalization of elites is overcome. See Bueno de Mesquita, Bruce, James D. Morrow, Randolph M. Siverson and Alastair Smith. "Policy Failure and Political Survival: The Contribution of Political Institutions" *The Journal of Conflict Resolution*, 43:2, 1999: pp. 147–161. That there is an indicator for intervention is an issue of endogeneity, and I readily note this. However, for our purposes, the basic statistics prove the point.

53 For further empirical evidence of this, see Bueno de Mequita, Bruce, Alastair Smith, Randolph M. Siverson, James D. Morrow. "The Hobbes Index" in *The Logic of Political Survival*, (Boston: MIT Press, 2003). For an interactive map of the Hobbes Index see: http://freedom.indiemaps.com (accessed December 31, 2012).

54 As of 2011, there were roughly 42.5 million forcibly displaced persons (15.2 million refugees, 876,100 asylum seekers, 26.4 million internally displaced persons (IDPs)). The United Nations High Commissioner for Refugees (UNHCR) identified 12 million stateless people, and the data did not include the 895,000 individuals whose asylum applications were not complete. Thus, this picture is not even close to complete. For instance, the data show 3.5 million stateless persons, but the UNHCR believes there to be more like 12 million globally (Global Trends, p. 29). See UNHCR's 2011 report, "Global Trends" available at: www.unhcr.org/cgi-bin/texis/vtx/home/opendocPDFViewer.html?docid=4fd6f87f9&query=global%20trends%20 2011 (accessed December 31, 2012).

55 Fearon and Laitin find 25 interstate wars during this period, while there are 127 civil wars. 25 states were involved in interstate conflict, while 73 states were involved in intrastate conflict. The number of dead is staggering: 3.33 million deaths as a result of interstate conflict, while 16.2 were killed in civil wars. There study does not incorporate the number of refugees or internally displaced persons as a result of these wars, but with the sheer volume, I am sure the numbers are equally overwhelming. See Fearon, James D. and David D. Laitin. "Ethnicity, Insurgency, and Civil War" *American Political Science Review*, 97: 1, 2003: pp. 75–90.

56 The other conflicts consist of two extrastate wars and two interstate wars, both of which involve the interstate wars of Afghanistan in 2001 and Iraq in 2003. The extrastate wars are now these ongoing insurgent conflicts in these countries. The data on the battle deaths of these conflicts are not available because the conflicts are still considered ongoing. See Ghosn, Faten, Glenn Palmer, and Stuart Bremer. 2004. "The MID3 Data Set, 1993–2001: Procedures, Coding Rules, and Description." *Conflict Management and Peace Science* 21:133–154. Available at: www.correlatesofwar.org (accessed December 31, 2012).

57 Kant's views of the French Revolution are puzzling. In the *MM* and in other several essays, Kant rejects the permissibility of revolution because it destroys a condition of public right. Yet he appreciates with a "disinterested sympathy" bordering "closely on enthusiasm" the overthrow of the *ancien régime* (*OQ*, 7:85). The French

Revolution provided Kant with an opportunity to test his hypothesis that the human race is morally progressing (*OQ*, 7:88–89). The possibility of founding a republican constitution reified his prior theoretical prescriptions for this type of government.

58 *OQ*, 7:91.

59 Ibid.

60 *UH*, 8:24 (italics added).

61 A rough estimate of the major wars fought between 1648 and 1804, roughly from the emergence of the Westphalian system to Kant's death, shows that external threats of war were higher than internal threats. There were roughly 27 major wars during this period, spanning wars of succession, colonization and conquest. There were also roughly 17 revolts during this period, and four revolutions. While the total number of battle deaths is not available, there are rough estimates, and these put deaths from external conflicts above those of internal revolts or revolutions. See Black, Jeremy. *The Origins of War in Early Modern Europe*, Edinburgh: John Donald Publishers, 1987, and Bercé, Yves-Marie. *Revolt and Revolution in Early Modern Europe*, New York: St. Martin's Press, 1987.

62 *DR*, 6:351.

63 Self-interest, which is very much related to man's evil, is what Kant poetically calls "the god of this world." *R*, 6:161.

64 See *OE*, *R*.

65 I cannot here examine the question of state building. However, suffice it to say that state building is very important to the Kantian enterprise, and is indeed its first step. Some might also want to link state building to the capacity building in the R2P framework, though these are different tasks. The problem, however, is that most states violate the rights of their peoples, and what is required to end such violations is external coercion by capable agents, i.e., more powerful states.

66 Walzer, op. cit., p. 58. Recall also that Kant states:

> Since a state of nature among nations, like a state of nature among individual human beings is a condition that one ought to leave in order to enter into a lawful condition, before this happens any rights of nations, and anything external that is mine or yours which states can acquire or retain by war, are merely provisional. Only a universal association of states (analogous to that by which a people becomes a state) can rights come to hold conclusively and a true condition of peace come about.
>
> (*DR*, 6:350)

67 *DR*, 6: 343.

68 I am not here referring to popular sovereignty, but the Westphalian conception of sovereignty as control. Popular sovereignty is more sacrosanct, though in cases of gross human rights violations, genocide, etc., there was no popular sovereignty in the first place. If popular sovereignty existed, then these crimes most likely would not have been perpetrated on such a grand scale.

69 *DR*, 6:306. Kant states: "For in a state of nature, too, there can be societies compatible with rights (e.g., conjugal, paternal, domestic societies in general, as well as many others); but no law …."

70 I do not want to engage fully the question of "what is law," but I do want to engage what Kant would take as necessary for public right. *DR*: 6:312.

71 *DR*. 6:311 (italics added).

72 *DR*. 6:313.

73 Goldsmith, Jack and Eric Posner. *The Limits of International Law*, Oxford: Oxford University Press, 2005: p. 23.

74 See Hathaway, Oona. "Between Power and Principles: An Integrated Theory of International Law" *University of Chicago Law Review*, 72, 2005: pp. 469–536. For arguments on the interest based model see: Goldsmith, Jack and Eric Posner, op. cit.,

and Posner, Eric. *The Perils of Global Legalism*, Chicago: University of Chicago Press, 2000. Krasner, Stephen. "Structural Causes and Regime Consequences: Regimes as Intervening Variables" in Stephen D. Krasner (ed.), *International Regimes 1, 2*, Ithaca: Cornell University Press, 1983. For arguments on the liberal-ideational side see: Koh, Harold. "Why Do Nations Obey International Law?" *Yale Law Journal*, 106, 1997: p. 2599. Moravcsik, Andrew. "Taking Preferences Seriously: A Liberal theory of International Politics" *International Organization*, 51, 1997: p. 513.

75 Hathaway, op. cit., p. 481.

76 Without explicitly arguing or acknowledging it, Hathaway is describing (or arguing for) a theory of international law based on strategic interaction taking place on the domestic and international levels. The interaction on the domestic level is between the government and different political actors, and the interaction on the international level is between states. The hallmark of a strategic interaction is that an agent conditions his choice on the expected reaction of another agent. Hathaway's invocation of the idea of "collateral consequences" that "arise when domestic and transnational actors premise their actions toward a state on the state's decision to accept or reject international legal rules" is, therefore, a strategic interaction (Hathaway, op. cit., p. 502).

77 *DR*, 6:316.

78 *DR*, 6:317.

79 I do not here deal with any of the regional courts, such as the Inter-American Court on Human Rights, the European Court of Human Rights, the European Court of Justice or specific treaty adjudication bodies such as GATT and the WTO. Regional or topical courts do not satisfy the universal or transnational requirement necessary for Kant, and so they are not necessary for my argument.

80 The ICJ's jurisdiction is limited to three areas: all parties to a dispute make a special agreement to bring their dispute to the ICJ; states include a "jurisdiction clause" in a treaty, where one party to the treaty can bring suit against the other(s); where states have explicitly recognized the jurisdiction of the ICJ and can then bring claims against only those other states who have also expressly declared they also recognize the ICJ (otherwise known as reciprocal declaration jurisdiction). International Court of Justice: www.icj-cij.org/court/index.php?p1=1&p2=6 (accessed December 31, 2012).

81 *Request for the Interpretation of the Judgment of 31 March 2004 in the Case concerning Avena and Other Mexican Nationals* (*Mexico v. United States of America*), Judgment, ICJ Reports 2009, p. 3. Available at: http://www.icc-cpi.int/en_menus/icc/situations%20and%20cases/Pages/situations%20and%20cases.aspx (accessed March 28, 2013).

82 International Criminal Court: http://www.icc-cpi.int/en_menus/icc/about%20the%20court/icc%20at%20a%20glance/Pages/jurisdiction%20and%20admissibility.aspx (accessed March 28, 2013).

83 The three areas of jurisdiction include

> the accused is a national of a State Party or a State otherwise accepting the jurisdiction of the Court; the crime took place on the territory of a State Party or a State otherwise accepting the jurisdiction of the Court; [or] the United Nations Security Council has referred the situation to the Prosecutor; irrespective of nationality of the accused or the location of the crime.

International Criminal Court: Jurisdiction and Admissibility: www.icc-cpi.int/Menus/ICC/About+the+Court/ICC+at+a+glance/Jurisdiction+and+Admissibility.htm (accessed November 11, 2010).

84 For a list of US BIA agreements, see: www.amicc.org/usicc/bialist (accessed December 31, 2012).

85 There are a total of 102 countries and "nonstate parties" listed as having a BIA with the US. I count only those countries that are listed as having a confirmed agreement in place. Moreover, some of the countries referred to above include the notoriously poor human rights record holders of Angola, Afghanistan, the Democratic Republic of Congo, the Republic of Congo, Cambodia, Burundi, Bosnia and Herzegovina, Sierra Leone, Rwanda, Liberia, East-Timor (Timor-Leste), Pakistan and Yemen.

86 Posner, op. cit., p. 89.

87 Ibid., p. 120. Posner cites Benvenisti, Eyal. "Reclaiming Democracy: The Strategic Uses of Foreign and International Law by National Courts" 102 *Amer. J. Int'l Law* 241, 2008.

88 Posner, op. cit., p. 121.

89 *DR*, 6:297.

90 *DR*, 6:297.

91 *DR*, 6:317.

92 The terminology of "coincidence of interest" is Posner's. He claims that states solve coordination problems not because they are pursuing a joint purpose (or what Nardin would call a purposive association), but because there is a coincidence of individual interests, not a commitment to something like a scheme of rules, coming together, and so states form organizations to help them better pursue their individual interests (or what Nardin would call a practical association). Nardin, Terry. *Law, Morality, and Relations of States*, Princeton: Princeton University Press, 1983.

93 *DR*: 6:256; 6:259–260.

94 Posner, op. cit., p. 174.

95 Ibid. (italics in original).

96 The German word "*Recht*" would also fall under this usage of "law." For the question here is not merely about a law (*Gesezt*) but the rule of law (*Recht*).

97 D'Amato, Anthony. "Is International Law Really 'Law'" *Northwestern University Law Review*, 79, 1985: pp. 1303–1304.

98 Ibid., p. 1304.

99 *DR*, 6:237. Kant states that Right can be divided into two: "natural right, which rests only on a priori principles, and positive (statutory) right, which proceeds from the will of the legislator."

100 See Goldsmith and Posner, op. cit., and Posner, op. cit., especially Part 2 Chapter 3.

101 Hobbes, Thomas. *Leviathan*, Richard Tuck (ed.), Cambridge: Cambridge University Press, 1992: Chapter XVII.

102 Wendt, Alexander. "Anarchy is What States Make of It" *International Organization*, 46:2, 1992: pp. 391–425.

103 One could claim that the older "Western" states do not violate rights in this manner, and that it is merely the proliferation of new states that empirically biases this argument. Data objections aside, the fact is that, however one divides the earth's territory into old and new states, a majority of it is on shaky juridical ground.

5 Provisional to peremptory: institutionalizing a duty to protect

1 Jackson, Robert H., Chief US Prosecutor to the Nuremberg Trials, Opening Statement to the Tribunal, November 21, 1945. Available at: www.law.umkc.edu/faculty/projects/ftrials/nuremberg/jackson.html (accessed January 1, 2013).

2 This is the period when the Nuremberg Trials took place, the United Nations was created, and the Universal Declaration on Human Rights and the Genocide Convention were formulated and signed.

3 Indeed, the formation of the International Criminal Court is a great step, but, as I will address in this chapter, there are significant problems that must be addressed if it is to become an institution that has the capacity to secure rights.

4 Jackson, op. cit.

5 Bellamy, Alex. "The Responsibility to Protect: Five Years On" *Ethics and International Affairs*, 24: 2, 2010: p. 155.
6 Alex Bellamy argues that the application of R2P to cases that fall outside of its scope (namely the 2008 unilateral military intervention in Georgia and the 2008 cyclone disaster in Myanmar) help to more clearly demarcate the lines of the principle. Unfortunately, while some may argue that Russia's or France's attempts to invoke R2P are not justified, states still attempt to legitimize their action within its terms. That the actions were not seen as legitimate under this principle does not mean that states will not attempt to use it. Bellamy, op. cit., p. 152.
7 A/63/677, A/64/864, www.responsibilitytoprotect.org/index.php/edward-luck-special-adviser-with-a-focus-on-the-responsibility-to-protect (accessed March 18, 2013). In a private discussion with the UN Special Rapporteur on the Freedom of Religion, he admitted that, unofficially, all UN Special Rapporteurs have been given directives to begin viewing their work through an R2P "lens." Moreover, his opinion was that any sort of institutionalization that could happen would, and must, go through a process of what he called "soft institutionalization" whereby the norm would become part of UN language and precedent.
8 For example, after member states deliberated on the post of Special Adviser for R2P, they refused to fund the post, citing that it was not necessary. Dr. Luck worked in this post without funding from the UN. On August 9, 2010 the GA held an "interactive dialogue" on the Secretary General's recent report on early warning assessment. While this may seem like progress, only 42 member states attended (out of 192), and amongst those 42 there were still detractors. Moreover the "interactive dialogue" merely "reaffirmed" its commitment to R2P and nothing else. See: http://responsibilitytoprotect.org/index.php/component/content/article/35-R2Pcs-topics/2914-general-assembly-debate-on-early-warning-assessment-and-the-responsibility-to-protect (accessed January 1, 2013)
9 Bellamy op. cit., p. 158.
10 Since R2P is such a broad concept, involving prevention, capacity building and reaction, multiple policy approaches are required. Capacity building can be undertaken by existing UN programs. What is required for R2P to be truly institutionalized is implementation of a monitoring system (the early warning capacity for which Ban Ki-moon is currently vying), and public rules governing the practice of coercive intervention methods. An R2PI would govern the monitoring and early warning as well as reaction portions of R2P.
11 I am using the word "law" here to signify current international rules. As I have noted in Chapter 4, the rules fall short of the Kantian requirements for "law," but they are still social rules that, for the most part, constrain states. Thus, I am not suggesting that one must break "law" to make law, like Allen Buchanan. I think one can stretch some of the existing rules or practices to enhance what is already there. Cf. Buchanan, Allen. "Reforming the International Law of Humanitarian Intervention" in J.L. Holzgrefe and Robert O. Keohane (eds.) *Humanitarian Intervention: Ethical, Legal and Political Dilemmas*, Cambridge: Cambridge University Press, 2003: pp. 130–174.
12 In the Second Appendix to *TPP*, Kant claims that "all maxims that require publicity (in order not to fail of their end) agree with both politics and morality." Notice the "in order not to fail" clause. Earlier in the Appendix Kant also claims that if one did publicize his maxim, and that undermined his purpose, it would be "wrong." Efficacy and right therefore are linked. *TPP*, 8:384, 8:386.
13 Cf. note 7 above.
14 Cohen, Jean. "A Global State of Emergency or the Further Institutionalization of International Law: A Pluralist Approach" *Constellations*, 15: 4, 2008: pp. 456–484.
15 Ibid., p. 461. Cohen's solution is to reform the UN Charter system to be more equal amongst its members. Moreover, she argues for what she calls "dualistic sovereignty" where states would alienate only particular rights to the UN, retaining all others.

Unfortunately, I do not see how this notion of dualistic sovereignty is different than what is already enumerated in the Charter. The problem is not dueling sovereignties; the problem is that states, while signing on to the Charter and in principle alienating certain rights (such as the right to the use of force), have not in fact alienated such rights. They are still judges in their own causes.

16 Cf. Chapter XVII, Article 108. Available at: www.un.org/en/documents/charter/chapter18.shtml (accessed January 1, 2013)

17 Cohen, op. cit., pp. 460–464.

18 S/RES/1373 especially cites precedence in former SC resolutions, GA declarations and its Chapter VII powers. S/RES/1540 does not draw as heavily on precedent, but does attempt to legitimize its prescriptions by calling attention to previous meetings, treaties and agreements on arms control and demilitarization.

19 In S/RES/1735, the SC states: "*Stressing* that terrorism *can only be defeated by a sustained and comprehensive approach involving the active participation and collaboration of all States*, and international and regional organizations to impede, impair, isolate, and incapacitate the terrorist threat" (italics added).

20 In the Vigilantius *LoE*, Kant states that all political constitutions were originated by coercion, and only later supplanted by law. He uses the examples of King Romulus to symbolize coercion, and Numa to symbolize the rule of law. While the analogy is not perfect, it still works. The SC is using its power to coerce other states into an agreement that they would otherwise have not have made for the sake of protecting rights. Vigilantius, *LoE*, 27:514.

21 Smith, Anne. "The Unique Position of National Human Rights Institutions: A Mixed Blessing?" *Human Rights Quarterly*, 26: 4, 2006: pp. 904–946.

22 There are also other nonhuman rights institutions that have existed with similar structures; these are typically referred to as "shadow states."

23 Smith, op. cit., p. 913. The 1993 Paris Principles and the Office of the United Nations High Commissioner for Refugees (OHCR) Handbook mandate these guidelines.

24 Hoffmann, Florian and Frédéric Mégret. "Fostering Human Rights Accountability: An Ombudsperson for the United Nations?" *Global Governance*, 11, 2005: pp. 43–63.

25 Madison, James. "Federalist Paper 57" in Clinton Rossiter (ed.), *Hamilton, Madison and Jay: The Federalist Papers*, New York: Signet Classic, 2003: pp. 348–353. One could argue that policy advisors and NGOs play key roles as well.

26 Ibid., 348–353. Kant also has the same requirements; if a legislator attempts to pass a law that an entire people could not agree to, then this law is considered unjust (*TP*, 8:299).

27 This is similar to what the ICISS Commission sought to do by including experts from every region of the earth, and to provide rules and advice for "what is politically achievable in the world as we know it today." International Commission on State Sovereignty. *The Responsibility to Protect: A Report of the International Commission on State Sovereignty*, Ottawa: International Development Research Centre Books, 2002: viii (hereafter ICISS).

28 The 2005 World Summit Outcome Document adopts a broader just cause threshold than the ICISS report. The Outcome Document follows the Rome Statutes in requiring that states act to prevent and stop genocide, war crimes, ethnic cleansing and crimes against humanity (A/60/150, paragraph 138). However, the Outcome Document does not provide any suggestions for rules governing R2P, where the ICISS report does.

29 The GA has a two-tier voting system. On matters pertaining to budget and the admission of new members, it requires a two-thirds majority vote. All other issues need only a simple majority. As Fasulo maintains, "if, as often happens, the leadership can establish a consensus on a given matter, a formal vote may not even be required." Fasulo, Linda. *An Insider's Guide to the UN*, New Haven: Yale University Press, 2009: pp. 63–64.

30 Orford, Anne. *International Authority and the Responsibility to Protect*, Cambridge: Cambridge University Press, 2011: p. 103.
31 Ibid., 108.
32 Ibid., 199.
33 Kelsen, Hans. *Peace Through Law* (1944), as cited in Archibugi, Daniele. "The Reform of the UN and Cosmopolitan Democracy: A Critical Review" *Journal of Peace Research*, 30: 3, 1993: p. 309.
34 For an extensive bibliography of this literature, see Archibugi, op. cit. For literature on the ICC, see: *Governance, Order and the International Criminal Court: Between Realpolitik and a Cosmopolitan Court*, ed. Steven C. Roach, Oxford: Oxford University Press, 2009.
35 If one were to require reforms, then universal and compulsory jurisdiction would be first amongst them. The way in which the Court could dovetail with the function of an R2PI would be the similar to that of the ICC, as a post-conflict judicial body to hold states accountable, via referrals from member states or the Security Council.
36 Article 17 states:

> Having regard to paragraph 10 of the Preamble and article 1, the Court shall determine that a case is inadmissible where: (a) The case is being investigated or prosecuted by a State which has jurisdiction over it, unless the State is unwilling or unable genuinely to carry out the investigation or prosecution; (b) The case has been investigated by a State which has jurisdiction over it and the State has decided not to prosecute the person concerned, unless the decision resulted from the unwillingness or inability of the State genuinely to prosecute; (c) The person concerned has already been tried for conduct which is the subject of the complaint, and a trial by the Court is not permitted under article 20, paragraph 3; (d) The case is not of sufficient gravity to justify further action by the Court. 2. In order to determine unwillingness in a particular case, the Court shall consider, having regard to the principles of due process recognized by international law, whether one or more of the following exist, as applicable: (a) The proceedings were or are being undertaken or the national decision was made for the purpose of shielding the person concerned from criminal responsibility for crimes within the jurisdiction of the Court referred to in article 5; (b) There has been an unjustified delay in the proceedings which in the circumstances is inconsistent with an intent to bring the person concerned to justice; (c) The proceedings were not or are not being conducted independently or impartially, and they were or are being conducted in a manner which, in the circumstances, is inconsistent with an intent to bring the person concerned to justice. 3. In order to determine inability in a particular case, the Court shall consider whether, due to a total or substantial collapse or unavailability of its national judicial system, the State is unable to obtain the accused or the necessary evidence and testimony or otherwise unable to carry out its proceedings.

United Nations General Assembly, Rome Statute of the International Criminal Court 17 July 1998, Available at: www.preventgenocide.org/law/icc/statute/part-a.htm#2 (accessed January 1, 2013).
37 Branch, Adam. "Uganda's Civil War and the Politics of Intervention" *Ethics and International Affairs*, 21: 2. 2007: p. 187.
38 Robinson, Darryl. "The Mysterious Mysteriousness of Complemenarity" *Criminal Law Forum*, 21, 2010: pp. 67–102.
39 For a very informative piece on the problems associated with the Ugandan situation, see: Greenawalt, Alexander K., "Complementarity in Crisis: Uganda, Alternative Justice, and the International Criminal Court" *Virginia Journal of International Law*, 50: 1, 2009: pp. 108–162.
40 Hayden, Patrick. "Political Evil, Cosmopolitan Realism, and the Normative Ambivalence of the International Criminal Court" in Steven C. Roach (ed.), *Governance,*

Order and the International Criminal Court: Between Realpolitik and a Cosmopolitan Court, Oxford: Oxford University Press, 2009: p. 171. Hayden cites Branch (2007) as belonging to the former group and Allen (2005) and the Refugee Law Project (2005) as belonging to the latter.

41 Rome Statute, Article 52(2)(c): "If, upon investigation, the Prosecutor concludes that there is not a sufficient basis for a prosecution because … prosecution is not in the interests of justice, taking into account all the circumstances, including gravity of the crime, the interests of victims and the age or infirmity of the alleged perpetrator, and his or her role in the alleged crime." Rome Statute, op. cit.

42 Robinson, Darryl, cited in Greenawalt, op. cit., p. 134.

43 For discussion on how Uganda used the ICC as a political tool, see Branch, op. cit. Member states may refer a situation to the ICC under Rome Statute Articles 13 and 14.

44 The case with Sudan is slightly different. While Sudan is not a member state of the ICC, the UN Security Council recommended the case to the ICC in 2005 and because of this Sudan is legally obliged to comply with ICC investigations, proceedings etc. (S/Res/1593). The prosecutor formally opened an investigation into the situation in Darfur in June 2005.

45 In July 2010 President al-Bashir travelled from Sudan to Chad. Chad is a signatory state to the Rome Statutes, and so is obliged to arrest al-Bashir. Unfortunately, Chad has taken no action to do so. "Sudan's President Bashir Defies Arrest Warrant in Chad" *BBC News*. Available at: www.bbc.co.uk/news/world-africa-10718399 (accessed July 21, 2010).

46 Moreno-Ocampo, Luis. "Now End This Darfur Denial" *Guardian*. Available at: www.guardian.co.uk/commentisfree/libertycentral/2010/jul/15/world-cannot-ignore-darfur (accessed July 15, 2010).

47 Eckert, Amy. "The Cosmopolitan Test: Universal Morality and the Challenge of the Darfur Genocide" in Steven C. Roach (ed.), *Governance, Order and the International Criminal Court: Between Realpolitik and a Cosmopolitan Court*, Oxford: Oxford University Press, 2009: p. 219.

48 Caney, Simon. *Justice Beyond Borders*, Oxford: Oxford University Press, 2005; Conetta, Carl and Charles Knight. *Vital Force: A Proposal for the Overhaul of the UN Peace Operations System and for the Creation of a UN Legion*, Cambridge: Commonwealth Institute, 1995; Held, David. *Democracy and the Global Order: From the Modern State to Cosmopolitan Governance*, Cambridge: Polity Press, 1995; Held, David. "Democracy and Globalization" in D. Archibugi, D. Held and M. Köhler (eds.), *Re-imagining Political Community: Studies in Cosmopolitan Democracy*, Cambridge: Polity Press, 1998: 11–17; Kaysen Carl and George Rathjens. *Peace Operations by the United Nations: The Case for a Volunteer UN Military Force*, Cambridge: American Academy of Arts and Sciences, 1996; Kinloch-Pichat, Stephen. *A UN "Legion": Between Utopia and Reality* London: Frank Cass, 2004; Langille, H.P. "Preventing Genocide: Time for a UN 911" *Globe and Mail*, (October 19, 2004); Pattison, James. "Humanitarian Intervention and a Cosmopolitan UN Force" *Journal of International Political Theory*, 4:1, 2008: pp. 126–145; Pattison, James. *Humanitarian Intervention and the Responsibility to Protect: Who Should Intervene?* Oxford: Oxford University Press, 2010; Smith, M. "Humanitarian Intervention: An Overview of the Ethical Issues" *Ethics and International Affairs*, 12, 1998: pp. 63–79; Urquhart, Brian. "For a UN Volunteer Military Force", *New York Review of Books* (June 10, 1993); Woodhouse, T. and O. Ramsbotham. "Cosmopolitan Peacekeeping and the Globalisation of Security" *International Peacekeeping*, 12: 2, 2005: pp. 139–156.

49 The arguments differ on whether it should be one year, several months etc. The RRF, though, is supposed to be seen as a temporary force and not a permanent peacekeeping force.

50 Kinloch-Pichat, op. cit.
51 *DR*, 6:306 (italics in original).
52 *DR*, 6:256.
53 *DR*, 6:256.
54 *TP*, 8:305.
55 *TP*, 8:290.
56 *UH*, 8:22.
57 Kant notes that an individual's civil personality is based, a priori on three principles: "the freedom of every member of society as a human being"; "the equality of each member with every other as a subject"; and "the independence of every member of the commonwealth as a citizen" (*TP*, 8:290). He also states this again in the *DR* at 6:314.
58 ICISS, op. cit., p. 48 and p. 53.
59 This may also help to guard against one of the P-5 abusing its citizens without fear of intervention.
60 "General Assembly Demands Syria Halt Violence Without Delay" *United Nations News.* Available at: www.un.org/apps/news/story.asp?NewsID=41265 (accessed February 16, 2012).
61 *TPP*, 8:356.
62 *DR*, 6:306 (italics in original).
63 Byrd, B. Sharon and Joachim Hruschka. *Kant's Doctrine of Right: A Commentary* Cambridge: Cambridge University Press, 2010: p. 33.
64 Ibid., p. 33.
65 Ibid., p. 36.
66 *DR*, 6:284. For a very good discussion about Kant's theory of property, and how it is fundamentally different than Locke's theory (where one can have a right to things) see: Flikschuh, Katrin. *Kant and Modern Political Philosophy*, Cambridge: Cambridge University Press, 2000, pp. 117–121.
67 Byrd and Hruschka, op. cit, pp. 37–38.
68 The reason why the executive authority corresponds to commutative justice is fully explained in Byrd and Hruschka op. cit., Chapter 7, section 3.
69 United Nations Charter, Chapter 15, Article 99 and 101. Available at: www.un.org/en/documents/charter/chapter15.shtml (accessed January 1, 2013).
70 Weiss, Thomas G. *What's Wrong with the United Nations and How to Fix It*, Cambridge: Polity Press, 2008: p. 114.
71 *DR*, 6:313.
72 Hoffman and Mégret argue that the United Nations requires an ombudsperson to oversee accusations made against UN troops. Such accusations for rape, murder or any other crimes are presently addressed by the member state whose troops are "on loan" to the UN. Unfortunately, Hoffmann and Mégret's solution would not do much to change existing practices, as ombudsmen "are not full-blown judicial bodies, their remedial powers are usually recommendatory rather than binding, and their ability to effect compliance rests primarily on the publicity of their reports rather than on formal prosecutorial competences" (Hoffman and Mégret, op. cit., p. 54).
73 Byrd and Hruschka, op. cit., Chapter 9.
74 Ibid., p. 203.
75 *TPP*, 8:356.
76 *TPP*, 8:356.
77 Kant, recall, calls acquisition provisional in a condition of provisional right. "Conclusive" acquisition is where external objects of my choice are secured through public laws, arbitrated by a neutral judge, and backed by a public and authoritative coercive force. Conclusive, therefore, corresponds to a rightful condition, where duties of right are peremptory (and therefore perfect). *DR*, 6:256–257.
78 *DR*, 6:256 (italics added).

79 *DR*, 6:256.
80 *DR*, 6:256.
81 *DR*, 6:307.
82 Fuller, Lon. L. *The Morality of Law*, New Haven: Yale University Press, 1964: p. 157.
83 *DR*, 6:231.
84 *TPP*, 8:357 (italics in original).

6 Conclusion: The Responsibility to Protect and the real world—Libya and Syria

1 In political science parlance, it is a way of approaching case study through "most similar systems design." The cases are for all intents and purposes similar in set-up (i.e., independent variables), but in their results (i.e., dependent variables) they are different. My use of the cases is to show that despite their similarities, the main reason for the variance in outcome is systemic and not one independent variable.
2 "Libya Protests: Defiant Gaddafi Reuses to Quit" *BBC News*, February 22, 2011.
3 Ibid.
4 Hooper, John and Ian Black. "Libya Defectors: Pilots Told to Bomb Protesters Flee to Malta" *The Guardian*, February 21, 2011.
5 African Union. Communiqué of the 261st Meeting of the Peace and Security Council, PSC/PR/COMM (CCXLI), February 23, 2011. Available at: http://auc.au.int/en/dp/ps/content/communiqué-261st-meeting-peace-and-security-council-situation-libya?q=content/communiqué-261st-meeting-peace-and-security-council-situation-libya (accessed January 1, 2013).
6 S/Res/1970 2011.
7 Ibid.
8 Greenblatt, Alan. "Leaders of the Libyan Opposition Emerge" *NPR News*, March 14, 2011.
9 Garcia-Navarro, Lourdes. "Provisional Government Forming in Eastern Libya" *NPR News*, February 23, 2011. Available at: www.npr.org/2011/02/23/134003954/New-Government-Forms-In-Eastern-Libya (accessed February 23, 2011). "Libyan Rebels Form 'Interim Government'" *Al Jazeera News*, March 24, 2011. Available at: www.aljazeera.com/news/africa/2011/03/2011322193944862310.html (accessed March 24, 2011); "Founding Statement of the Interim Transitional National Council," March 5, 2011. Available at: http://ntclibya.org/english/founding-statement-of-the-interim-transitional-national-council (accessed March 24, 2011).
10 "Clinton Meets Libyan Opposition Figure" *NPR News*, March 14, 2011. Available at: www.npr.org/2011/03/14/134527902/gadhafi-warplanes-strike-rebel-held-libya-city (accessed March 14, 2011).
11 Cooper, Helene and Steven Lee Myers. "Obama Takes Hard Line with Libya after Shift by Clinton" *New York Times*, March 18, 2011.
12 S/Res/1973 2011.
13 Ibid.
14 S/PV.6498.
15 Ibid.
16 Ibid.
17 "Operation Odyssey Dawn: U.S. Launches Military Strikes in Libya" *Huffington Post*, March 3, 2011. Available at: www.huffingtonpost.com/2011/03/19/operation-odyssey-dawn-us_n_838009.html (accessed March 5, 2011).
18 Parrish, Karen. "Gates Outlines U.S. Role as NATO Takes Libyan Mission" *American Forces Press Service*, March 31, 2011. Available at: www.defense.gov/news/newsarticle.aspx?id=63378 (accessed April 2, 2011).

19 "NATO and Libya", available at www.nato.int/cps/en/natolive/topics_71652.htm (accessed December 15, 2012).
20 Adams, Simon. "R2P and the Libya Mission: When Does 'Responsibility to Protect' Grant Countries the Right to Intervene?" *Los Angeles Times*, September 28, 2011.
21 "Syrian Police Seal Off City of Daraa After Security Forces Kill Five Protesters" *The Guardian*, March 19, 2011. Available at: www.guardian.co.uk/world/2011/mar/19/syria-police-seal-off-daraa-after-five-protesters-killed (accessed March 19, 2011).
22 Chulov, Martin. "Syrian President Sacks Cabinet in Effort to Quell Protests" *Guardian*, March 29, 2011.
23 Marsh, Katherine. "Syrian Crackdown: Hundreds Resign from Ba'ath Party" *Guardian*, April 28, 2011.
24 Traynor, Ian. "EU Slaps Arms Embargo on Syria but Spares President Bashar al-Assad" *Guardian*, May 9, 2011.
25 "U.N. Security Council Issues Statement Condemning Violence in Syria" *CNN*, August 3, 2011. Available at: www.cnn.com/2011/WORLD/meast/08/03/syria.unrest/index.html (accessed August 3, 2011).
26 Holliday, Joseph. "Syria's Armed Opposition" *Middle East Security Report 3*, March 2012. Available at: www.understandingwar.org/sites/default/files/Syrias_Armed_Opposition.pdf (accessed December 15, 2012).
27 Sly, Liz. "Arab League Announces Peace Plan for Syria" *Washington Post*, 2 November 2011.
28 SC/10536. "Security Council Fails to Adopt Draft Resolution on Syria as Russian Federation, China Veto Text Supporting Arab League's Proposed Peace Plan" *United Nations Department of Public Information*, February 4, 2012. Available at: www.un.org/News/Press/docs/2012/sc10536.doc.htm (accessed March 1, 2012).
29 "Syria Unrest: Who are the Shabiha?" *BBC News*, 29 May 2012. Available at: www.bbc.co.uk/news/world-middle-east-14482968 (accessed December 1, 2012).
30 Ibid.
31 MacFarquhar, Neil and Hwaida Saad. "Dozens of Children Die in Brutal Attack on Syrian Town" *New York Times*, May 26, 2012.
32 Annan, Kofi. "My Departing Advice on How to Save Syria" *Financial Times*, August 2, 2012.
33 Roff, Heather. "The Politics of Intervention" *Huffington Post*, October 29, 2012. Available at: www.huffingtonpost.com/heather-roff/syria-intervention_b_2025305.html (accessed October 29, 2012).
34 Barnard, Anne. "Syrians Killed in Gas Line; U.N. Raises War's Casualty Figures" *New York Times*, January 2, 2013.
35 Ali, Nour. "Syrian City's Attorney General Resigns in Protest at Government Crackdown" *Guardian*, September 1, 2011. For information on Syrian torture centers, see Human Rights Watch Interactive Map available at: www.hrw.org/interactive-map-syria-torture-centers (accessed December 12, 2012); Keane, Fergal. "Syria Ex-Detainees Allege Ordeals of Rape and Sex Abuse" *BBC News*, 25 September 2012.
36 Keane, op. cit.
37 "Syria Displaced Number 2.5m, Says Red Crescent" *BBC News*, November 13, 2012. Available at: www.bbc.co.uk/news/world-middle-east-20311194 (accessed November 15, 2012).
38 Amos, Deborah. "'It's a Disaster': Life Inside a Syrian Refugee Camp" *NPR News*, December 6, 2012. Available at: http://m.npr.org/news/World/166615692 (accessed December 6, 2012).
39 Barnard, Anne. "Turkey Fires Back at Syria a Fourth Day in a Row", *New York Times*, October 6, 2012.
40 Watson, Ivan and Saad Abedine. "Security Council Condemns Syria's Attack on Turkey" *CNN*, October 4, 2012. Available at: www.cnn.com/2012/10/04/world/meast/syria-civil-war/index.html (accessed October 15, 2012).

41 Sterling, Joe. "NATO Oks Patriots and Delivers Warning: 'Don't Even Think About Attacking Turkey'" *CNN*, December 5, 2012. Available at: www.cnn.com/2012/12/04/world/meast/syria-civil-war/index.html (accessed December 5, 2012).
42 "Syria Chemical Weapons: Obama Says World is Watching" *BBC News*, July 23, 2012. Available at: www.bbc.co.uk/news/world-middle-east-18963720 (accessed December 8, 2012).
43 "UK's Hague Confirms 'Evidence' of Syria Chemical Arms Plan" *BBC News*, December 8, 2012. Available at: www.bbc.co.uk/news/world-middle-east-20650582 (accessed December 8, 2012).
44 Gordon, Michael and Eric Schmitt. "Syria Fires More Scud Missiles at Rebels, U.S. Says" *New York Times*, December 20, 2012. Chivers, C.J. "Syria Unleashes Cluster Bombs on Town, Punishing Civilians" *New York Times*, December 20, 2012.
45 "U.N. Nations Condemn Syria; Russia, China Seen Isolated" *Reuters*, August 3, 2012. Available at: www.reuters.com/article/2012/08/03/us-syria-crisis-un-idUSBRE8720ZN20120803 (accessed August 3, 2012).
46 Klapper, Bradley. "Clinton Says US, Russia Agree on Mediation in Syria, But Stresses Anew that Assad Must Go" *The Associated Press*, December 7, 2012. Available at: www.vancouversun.com/news/Clinton+says+Russia+agree+back+mediation+Syria+Assad+must+step/7666320/story.html (accessed December 12, 2012).
47 Associated Press, "New Talks on Syria Involving Russia, US" *Time*, December 9, 2012. Available at: http://world.time.com/2012/12/09/new-talks-on-syria-involving-russia-u-s/ (accessed December 10, 2012).
48 MacFarquhar, Neil. "Syrian Group Fights Effort to Unify Foes of Government" *New York Times*, November 10, 2012.
49 "National Coordination Committee for Democratic Change," *Carnegie Middle East Center*, January 15, 2012. Available at: http://carnegie-mec.org/publications/?fa=48369 (accessed March 18, 2013).
50 MacFarquhar, Neil and Michael R. Gordon. "As Fighting Rages, Clinton Seeks New Syrian Opposition," *New York Times*, October 31, 2012.
51 MacFarquhar, Neil and Hala Droubi, "With Eye on Aid, Syria Opposition Signs Unity Deal," *New York Times*, November 11, 2012. Available at: www.nytimes.com/2012/11/12/world/middleeast/syrian-opposition-groups-sign-unity-deal.html (accessed December 15, 2012).
52 Barnard, Anne, Michael R. Gordon and Christine Hauser. "Pressure Builds on Syrian Opposition Coalition; Fears of Chemical Weapons Rise" *New York Times*, December 5, 2012.
53 Arango, Tim. "European Union Backs Syrian Opposition Coalition" *New York Times*, November 19, 2012.
54 Dougherty, Jill. "Obama Recognizes Syrian Opposition Coalition" *CNN*, December 12, 2012. Available at: www.cnn.com/2012/12/11/world/us-syria-opposition/index.html (accessed December 12, 2012).
55 Sterling, Joe, Saad Abedine and Holly Yan. "As Syria Suffering Spirals, Envoy Hopes for Political Transition" *CNN*, December 28, 2012. Available at: http://edition.cnn.com/2012/12/27/world/meast/syria-civil-war/index.html (accessed December 29, 2012).
56 Bellamy, Alex. "Libya and the Responsibility to Protect: The Exception and the Norm" *Ethics and International Affairs*, 25:3, 2011: pp. 263–269.
57 Roff, Heather and Bessma Momani. "The Tactics of Intervention" *The Globe and Mail*, October 25, 2011.
58 Alsharif, Asma. "Organisation of Islamic Cooperation Suspends Syria" *Reuters*, August 15, 2012. Available at: www.reuters.com/article/2012/08/15/us-syria-crisis-islamic-summit-idUSBRE87E19F20120815 (accessed September 1, 2012).

59 Blair, David and Bruno Waterfield. “Syria: Gulf Cooperation Council Denounces Assad for ‘Mass Slaughter’” *The Telegraph*, February 7, 2012.
60 Bellamy, Alex and Paul D. Williams “Principles, Politics, and Prudence: Libya and the Responsibility to Protect, and the Use of Military Force” *Global Governance*, 18, 2012: p. 281.
61 Feaver, Peter and Christopher Gelpi, *Choosing Your Battles* ,Princeton: Princeton University Press, 2005.
62 Feinberg, Joel. “Collective Responsibility” *The Journal of Philosophy*, 65:21, 1968: pp. 683–684.
63 *UH*, 8:24.

Bibliography

Adams, Simon. "R2P and the Libya Mission: When Does 'Responsibility to Protect' Grant Countries the Right to Intervene?" *Los Angeles Times*, September 28, 2011.

African Union. Communiqué of the 261st Meeting of the Peace and Security Council, PSC/PR/COMM (CCXLI), February 23, 2011. Available at: http://auc.au.int/en/dp/ps/content/communiqué-261st-meeting-peace-and-security-council-situation-libya?q=content/communiqué-261st-meeting-peace-and-security-council-situation-libya (accessed January 1, 2013).

Ali, Nour. "Syrian City's Attorney General Resigns in Protest at Government Crack-down" *The Guardian*, September 1, 2012.

Al Jazeera News. "Libyan Rebels Form 'Interim Government'," March 24, 2011. Available at: www.aljazeera.com/news/africa/2011/03/2011322193944862310.html (accessed March 24, 2011).

Alsharif, Asma. "Organisation of Islamic Cooperation Suspends Syria" *Reuters*, August 15, 2012. Available at: www.reuters.com/article/2012/08/15/us-syria-crisis-islamic-summit-idUSBRE87E19F20120815 (accessed September 1, 2012).

Amos, Deborah. "'It's a Disaster': Life Inside a Syrian Refugee Camp" *NPR News*, December 6, 2012. Available at: http://m.npr.org/news/World/166615692 (accessed December 6, 2012).

Annan, Kofi. "Two Concepts of Sovereignty" *The Economist* 352 (September 1999): pp. 49–50.

Annan, Kofi. "My Departing Advice on How to Save Syria" *Financial Times*, August 2, 2012.

Arango, Tim. "European Union Backs Syrian Opposition Coalition" *New York Times*, November 19, 2012.

Archibugi, Daniele. "The Reform of the UN and Cosmopolitan Democracy: A Critical Review" *Journal of Peace Research*, vol. 30, no. 3 (1993): pp. 301–315.

Arendt, Hannah. *Lectures on Kant's Political Philosophy*, Chicago: University Of Chicago Press, 1989.

Arnold, Denis G. "Corporate Moral Agency" *Midwest Studies in Philosophy*, vol. 30 (2006): 279–291.

Associated Press, "New Talks on Syria Involving Russia, US" *Time*, December 9, 2012. Available at: http://world.time.com/2012/12/09/new-talks-on-syria-involving-russia-u-s/ (accessed December 10, 2012).

Bagnoli, Carla. "Humanitarian Intervention as a Perfect Duty: A Kantian Argument" in Terry Nardin and Melissa Williams (eds.), *Nomos XLVII: Humanitarian Intervention*, New York: New York University Press, 2006: pp. 117–140.

Barnard, Anne. "Turkey Fires Back at Syria a Fourth Day in a Row" *New York Times*, October 6, 2012.

Barnard, Anne. "Syrians Killed in Gas Line; U.N. Raises War's Casualty Figures" *New York Times*, January 2, 2013.

Barnard, Anne, Michael R. Gordon and Christine Hauser. "Pressure Builds on Syrian Opposition Coalition; Fears of Chemical Weapons Rise" *New York Times*, December 5, 2012.

Barry, Christian and Thomas Pogge. *Global Institutions and Responsibilities: Achieving Global Justice*, Oxford: Wiley-Blackwell, 2006.

BBC News. "Sudan's President Bashir Defies Arrest Warrant in Chad," July 21, 2010.

BBC News. "Libya Protests: Defiant Gaddafi Reuses to Quit," February 22, 2011.

BBC News. "Syria Unrest: Who are the Shabiha?," May 29, 2012.

BBC News. "Syria Chemical Weapons: Obama Says World is Watching," July 23, 2012.

BBC News. "Syria Displaced Number 2.5m, Says Red Crescent," November 13, 2012.

BBC News. "UK's Hague Confirms 'Evidence' of Syria Chemical Arms Plan," December 8, 2012.

Beilefeldt, Heiner. "Autonomy and Republicanism: Immanuel Kant's Philosophy of Freedom" *Political Theory*, vol. 25, no. 4 (1997): pp. 524–558.

Bellamy, Alex. "Whither the Responsibility to Protect? HI and the 2005 World Summit" *Ethics and International Affairs*, vol. 20, no. 2 (2006): pp. 143–169.

Bellamy, Alex. "The Responsibility to Protect—Five Years On" *Ethics and International Affairs*, vol. 24, no. 2 (2006): pp. 143–169.

Bellamy, Alex. *The Responsibility to Protect: The Global Effort to End Mass Atrocities*, Cambridge: Polity Press, 2009.

Bellamy, Alex. "Libya and the Responsibility to Protect: The Exception and the Norm" *Ethics and International Affairs*, vol. 25, no. 3 (2011): pp. 263–269.

Bellamy, Alex and Paul D. Williams "Principles, Politics, and Prudence: Libya and the Responsibility to Protect, and the Use of Military Force" *Global Governance*, vol. 18, 2012: 273–297.

Bercé, Yves-Marie. *Revolt and Revolution in Early Modern Europe*, New York: St. Martin's Press, 1987.

Bergen, Doris L. *War and Genocide: A Concise History of the Holocaust*, Oxford: Rowman & Littlefield Publishers, Inc., 2003.

Bernstein, Alyssa. "Kant on Rights and Coercion in International Law: Implications for Humanitarian Military Intervention" *Annual Review for Law and Ethics*, vol. 16 (2008): pp. 57–100.

Black, Jeremy. *The Origins of War in Early Modern Europe*, Edinburgh: John Donald Publishers, 1987.

Black, Henry Campbell. *Black's Law Dictionary*, abridged 5th edn., St. Paul: West Publishing Co., 1983.

Blair, David and Bruno Waterfield. "Syria: Gulf Cooperation Council Denounces Assad for 'Mass Slaughter'" *The Telegraph*, February 7, 2012.

Bohman, James, and Matthias Lutz-Bachmann. *Perpetual Peace: Essays on Kant's Cosmopolitan Ideal*, Boston: MIT Press, 1997.

Branch, Adam. "American Morality over International Law: Origins in UN Military Interventions, 1991–1995" *Constellations: An International Journal of Critical and Democratic Theory*, vol. 12, no. 1 (March, 2005): pp. 103–127.

Branch, Adam. "Uganda's Civil War and the Politics of Intervention" *Ethics and International Affairs*, vol. 21, no. 2 (2007): pp. 179–198.

Brandt, Reinhard. "Das Erlaubnisgesetz, oder: Vernunft und Geschichte ins Kants Rechtslehre" in Reinhard Brandt (ed.), *Rechtsphilosophie der Aufklärung*, Berlin: Walter de Gruyter Press, 1982: pp. 233–285.

Brekke, Torkel. *The Ethics of War in Asian Civilizations: A Comparative Perspective*, Oxford: Routledge, 2005.

Brown, Garrett Wallace. *Grounding Cosmopolitanism: From Kant to the Idea of a Cosmopolitan Constitution*, Edinburgh: Edinburgh University Press, 2010.

Brunkhorst, Hauke. "Paradigmenwechsel im Völkerrecht? Lehren aus Bosnien" in Matthias Lutz-Bachmann and James Bohman (eds.), *Frieden durch Recht: Kants Friedensidee und das Problem einer neuen Weltordnung*, Frankfurt am Main: Suhrkamp, 1996: pp. 251–271.

Buchanan, Allen. "Reforming the International Law of Humanitarian Intervention" in J.L. Holzgrefe and Robert O. Keohane (eds.), *Humanitarian Intervention: Ethical, Legal and Political Dilemmas*, Cambridge: Cambridge University Press, 2003: pp. 130–174.

Buchanan, Allen. *Justice, Legitimacy, and Self-Determination: Moral Foundations for International Law*, Oxford: Oxford University Press, 2006.

Buckley, William J. *Kosovo: Contending Voices on Balkan Interventions*, Grand Rapids: Wm. B. Eerdmans Publishing Company, 2000.

Bueno de Mequita, Bruce, Alastair Smith, Randolph M. Siverson and James D. Morrow. "The Hobbes Index" in *The Logic of Political Survival*, Boston: MIT Press, 2003.

Butler, Michael J. "U.S. Military Intervention in Crisis, 1945–1994: An Empirical Inquiry of Just War Theory" *The Journal of Conflict Resolution*, vol. 47, no. 2, (April 2003): pp. 226–248.

Byrd, B. Sharon. "The State as a Moral Person" *Proceedings of the Eighth International Kant Congress*, vol. I.1, H. Robinson (ed.), Milwaukee: Marquette University Press: 1995: pp. 171–189.

Byrd, B. Sharon and Joachim Hruschka. "Kant on "Why Must I Keep My Promise?" *Chicago-Kent Law Review* vol. 81 (2006): pp. 47–74.

Byrd, B. Sharon and Joachim Hruschka. "The Natural Law Duty to Recognize Private Property Ownership: Kant's Theory of Property in His Doctrine of Right" *University of Toronto Law Journal*, vol. 56, no. 2 (Spring 2006): pp. 217–282.

Byrd, B. Sharon and Joachim Hruschka. "From the State of Nature to the Juridical State of States" *Law and Philosophy*, vol. 27 (2008): pp. 599–641.

Byrd, B. Sharon and Joachim Hruschka. *Kant's Doctrine of Right: A Commentary*, Cambridge: Cambridge University Press, 2010.

Caney, Simon. *Justice Beyond Borders*, Oxford: Oxford University Press, 2005.

Cavallar, Georg. *Kant and the Theory and Practice of International Right*, Cardiff: University of Wales Press, 1999.

Chan, Steve. "Mirror, Mirror on the Wall: Are Freer Countries More Pacific?" *Journal of Conflict Resolution*, vol. 28, no. 4: (1984): pp. 617–648.

Chandler, David. *From Kosovo to Kabul and Beyond: Human Rights and International Intervention*, London: Pluto Press, 2006.

Chesterman, Simon. *Just War or Just Peace: Humanitarian Intervention and International Law*, Oxford: Oxford University Press, 2002.

Chivers, C.J. "Syria Unleashes Cluster Bombs on Town, Punishing Civilians" *New York Times*, December 20, 2012.

Chulov, Martin. "Syrian President Sacks Cabinet in Effort to Quell Protests" *The Guardian*, March 29, 2011.

Clark, Jeffery. “Debacle in Somalia” *Foreign Affairs*, vol. 72, no. 1 (1993/1994): pp. 109–123.

CNN. “U.N. Security Council Issues Statement Condemning Violence in Syria” *CNN*, August 3, 2011. Available at: www.cnn.com/2011/WORLD/meast/08/03/syria.unrest/index.html (accessed August 3, 2011).

Cohen, Jean. “A Global State of Emergency or the Further Institutionalization of International Law: A Pluralist Approach” *Constellations*, vol. 15, no. 4 (2008): pp. 456–484.

Conetta, C. and Knight C. Vital *Force: A Proposal for the Overhaul of the UN Peace Operations System and for the Creation of a UN Legion*, Cambridge, MA:, Commonwealth Institute, 1995.

Cooper, Helene and Steven Lee Myers. “Obama Takes Hard Line with Libya after Shift by Clinton” *New York Times*, March 18, 2011.

Covell, Charles. *Kant and the Law of Peace*, New York: St. Martin’s Press, 1998.

D’Amato, Anthony. “Is International Law Really ‘Law’” *Northwestern University Law Review*, vol. 79 (1985): pp. 1303–1304.

Donagan, Alan. *The Theory of Morality*, Chicago: University Of Chicago Press, 1979.

Donagan, Alan. “Consistency in Rationalist Systems” *Journal of Philosophy*, vol. 81, no. 6 (1984): pp. 291–309.

Donnelly, Jack. *Universal Human Rights in Theory and Practice*, Ithaca: Cornell University Press, 2002.

Dougherty, Jill. “Obama Recognizes Syrian Opposition Coalition” *CNN*, December 12, 2012. Available at: www.cnn.com/2012/12/11/world/us-syria-opposition/index.html (accessed December 12, 2012).

Doyle, Michael W. and Nicholas Sambanis. *Making War and Building Peace: United Nations Peace Operations*, Princeton: Princeton University Press, 2006.

Eckert, Amy. “Peoples and Persons: Moral Standing, Power and the Equality of States” *International Studies Quarterly*, vol. 50 (2006): pp. 841–859.

Eckert, Amy. “The Cosmopolitan Test: Universal Morality and the Challenge of the Darfur Genocide” in Steven C. Roach (ed.), *Governance, Order and the International Criminal Court: Between Realpolitik and a Cosmopolitan Court*, Oxford: Oxford University Press, 2009: pp. 205–224.

Ellis, Elisabeth. *Kant’s Politics: A Provisional Theory for an Uncertain World*, New Haven: Yale University Press, 2006.

Ellis, Elisabeth. “Citizenship and Property Rights: A New Look at Social Contract Theory” *Journal of Politics*, vol. 68, no. 3 (2006): pp. 544–555.

Erskine, Toni. “Making Sense of ‘Responsibility’ in International Relations: Key Questions and Concepts” in Toni Erskine (ed.), *Can Institutions Have Responsibilities? Collective Moral Agency and International Relations, Global Issues Series*, Basingstoke: Palgrave Macmillan, 2003: pp. 1–18.

Erskine, Toni. “Assigning Responsibility to Institutional Moral Agents: The Case of States and ‘Quasi-States’” in Toni Erskine (ed.), *Can Institutions Have Responsibilities? Collective Moral Agency and International Relations, Global Issues Series*, Basingstoke: Palgrave Macmillan, 2003: pp. 19–40.

Evans, Gareth. *The Responsibility to Protect: Ending Mass Atrocity Crimes Once and For All*, Washington D.C.: Brookings Press, 2008.

Evans, Gareth. “In Defense of R2P” *New York Times*, March 11, 2012. Available at: www.nytimes.com/2012/03/12/opinion/12iht-edletmon12.html (accessed March 11, 2012).

Fasulo, Linda. *An Insider's Guide to the UN*, New Haven: Yale University Press, 2009.

Fearon, James D. and David D. Laitin. "Ethnicity, Insurgency, and Civil War" *American Political Science Review*, vol. 97, no. 1 (2003): pp. 75–90.

Feaver, Peter and Christopher Gelpi, *Choosing Your Battles*, Princeton: Princeton University Press, 2005.

Feinberg, Joel. "Collective Responsibility" *The Journal of Philosophy*, 65:21, 1968: pp. 683–684.

Finnemore, Martha. *The Purpose Of Intervention: Changing Beliefs About The Use Of Force*, Ithaca: Cornell University Press, 2004.

Flikschuh, Katrin. *Kant and Modern Political Philosophy*, Cambridge: Cambridge University Press, 2000.

Flikschuh, Katrin. "Kant's Sovereignty Dilemma: A Contemporary Analysis" *Journal of Political Philosophy*, vol. 18, no. 3 (2010): pp. 1–25.

Flikschuh, Katrin. "Justice without Virtue" in Lara Denis (ed.), *Kant's Metaphysics of Morals: A Critical Guide*, Cambridge: Cambridge University Press, 2010: pp. 51–70.

Follesdal, Andreas and Thomas Pogge. *Real World Justice: Grounds, Principles, Human Rights, and Social Institutions* (Studies in Global Justice), Dordrecht: Springer Press, 2005.

French, Peter. "The Corporation as a Moral Person" *American Philosophical Quarterly*, vol. 16 no. 3 (1979): pp. 207–215.

Fuller, Lon. L. *The Morality of Law*, New Haven: Yale University Press, 1964.

Garcia-Navarro, Lourdes. "Provisional Government Forming in Eastern Libya" *NPR News*, February 23, 2011. Available at: www.npr.org/2011/02/23/134003954/New-Government-Forms-In-Eastern-Libya (accessed February 23, 2011).

Ghosn, Faten, Glenn Palmer and Stuart Bremer. "The MID3 Data Set, 1993–2001: Procedures, Coding Rules, and Description." *Conflict Management and Peace Science*, vol. 21 (2004): pp. 133–154. Available at: www.correlatesofwar.org (accessed December 31, 2012).

Glover, Jonathan. *Humanity: A Moral History of the Twentieth Century*, New Haven: Yale University Press, 2001.

Goldsmith, Jack and Eric Posner. *The Limits of International Law*, Oxford: Oxford University Press, 2005.

Gordon, Michael and Eric Schmitt. "Syria Fires More Scud Missiles at Rebels, U.S. Says" *New York Times*, December 20, 2012.

Gourevitch, Philip. *We Wish to Inform You That Tomorrow We Will Be Killed With Our Families: Stories from Rwanda*, New York: Picador Press, 1999.

Gregor, Mary. *Laws of Freedom*, Oxford: Basil Blackwell Publishing, 1963.

Greenawalt, Alexander K., "Complementarity in Crisis: Uganda, Alternative Justice, and the International Criminal Court" *Virginia Journal of International Law*, vol. 50, no 1 (2009): pp. 108–162.

Greenblatt, Alan. "Leaders of the Libyan Opposition Emerge" *NPR News*, March 14, 2011.

Grotius, Hugo. *De Jure Belli ac Pacis* (1646), Whitefish: Kessinger Publishing, 2009.

Guardian. "Syrian Police Seal Off City of Daraa After Security Forces Kill Five Protesters," March 19, 2011. Available at: www.guardian.co.uk/world/2011/mar/19/syria-police-seal-off-daraa-after-five-protesters-killed (accessed March 19, 2011).

Guyer, Paul. *The Cambridge Companion to Kant*, Cambridge: Cambridge University Press, 1992.

Harbor, Frances V. "Collective Moral Agency and the Political Process" in Toni Erskine (ed.), *Can Institutions Have Responsibilities? Collective Moral Agency and International Relations, Global Issues Series*, Basingstoke: Palgrave Macmillan, 2003: pp. 69–83.

Hathaway, Oona. "Between Power and Principles: An Integrated Theory of International Law" *University of Chicago Law Review* vol. 72 (2005): pp. 469–536.

Hayden, Patrick. "Political Evil, Cosmopolitan Realism, and the Normative Ambivalence of the International Criminal Court" in Steven C. Roach (ed.) *Governance, Order and the International Criminal Court: Between Realpolitik and a Cosmopolitan Court*, Oxford: Oxford University Press, 2009: pp. 157–178.

Heinze, Eric A. "The Moral Limits of Humanitarian Intervention: Reconciling Human Respect and Utility" *Polity*, vol. 36, no. 4 (July, 2004): pp. 543–558.

Held, David. *Democracy and the Global Order: From the Modern State to Cosmopolitan Governance,* Cambridge: Polity Press, 1995.

Held, David. "Democracy and Globalization" in D. Archibugi, D. Held and M. Köhler (eds.), *Re-imagining Political Community: Studies Cosmopolitan Democracy*, Cambridge: Polity Press, 1998: pp. 11–17.

Heyd, David "Moral and Legal Luck: Kant's Reconciliation with Practical Contingency" *Annual Review of Law and Ethics*, vol. 5 (1997): pp. 27–42.

Hill, Thomas E. *Respect, Pluralism, and Justice: Kantian Perspectives*, Oxford: Oxford University Press, 2000.

Hobbes, Thomas. *Leviathan*, Richard Tuck, ed., Cambridge: Cambridge University Press, 1992.

Höffe, Otfried. *Categorical Principles of Law: A Counterpoint to Modernity*, Mark Migotti, trans., University Park: Penn State Press, 2002.

Höffe, Otfried. *Kant's Cosmopolitan Theory of Law and Peace*, Cambridge: Cambridge University Press, 2006.

Höffe, Otfried. "Foreword" in *Terror, Peace and Universalism: Essays on the Philosophy of Immanuel Kant*, Oxford: Oxford University Press, 2007: pp. ix–x.

Hoffmann, Florian and Frédéric Mégret. "Fostering Human Rights Accountability: An Ombudsperson for the United Nations?" *Global Governance*, vol. 11 (2005): pp. 43–63.

Hohfeld, Wesley Newcomb. *Fundamental Legal Conception as Applied in Judicial Reasoning*, New Jersey: The LawBook Exchange, Ltd. 2010.

Holliday, Joseph. "Syria's Armed Opposition" *Middle East Security Report 3*, March 2012. Available at: www.understandingwar.org/sites/default/files/Syrias_Armed_Opposition.pdf (accessed March 18, 2013).

Holzgrefe, J.L. The Humanitarian Intervention Debate" in J.L. Holzegrefe and Robert O. Keohane (eds.) *Humanitarian Intervention: Ethical, Legal and Political Dilemmas*, Cambridge: Cambridge University Press, 2003: pp. 15–52.

Honig, Bonnie. *Political Theory and the Displacement of Politics*, Ithaca: Cornell University Press, 1993.

Hooper, John and Ian Black. "Libya Defectors: Pilots Told to Bomb Protesters Flee to Malta" *Guardian*, February 21, 2011.

Hruschka, Joachim. "The Permissive Law of Practical Reason in Kant's Metaphysics of Morals" *Law and Philosophy*, vol. 23 (2004): pp. 45–72.

Hruschka, Joachim. "The Natural Law Duty to Recognize Private Property Ownership: Kant's Theory of Property in His Doctrine of Right" *University of Toronto Law Journal*, vol. 56 (2006): pp. 217–282.

Huffington Post. "Operation Odyssey Dawn: U.S. Launches Military Strikes in Libya," March 3, 2011. Available at: www.huffingtonpost.com/2011/03/19/operation-odyssey-dawn-us_n_838009.html (accessed March 5, 2011).

Ignatieff, Michael. *The Warrior's Honor: Ethnic War and the Modern Conscience*, London: Owl Books, 1998.

Ignatieff, Michael. *Virtual War: Kosovo and Beyond*, London: Picador Press, 2001.

Independent International Commission on Kosovo. "The Kosovo Report: Conflict, Interim Transitional National Council: Founding Statement of the Interim Transitional National Council," March 5, 2011. Available at: http://ntclibya.org/english/founding-statement-of-the-interim-transitional-national-council (accessed March 24, 2011).

Independent International Commission on Kosovo. *Conflict, International Response, Lessons Learned*, Oxford: Oxford University Press, 2000. Available at: http://reliefweb.int/sites/reliefweb.int/files/resources/6D26FF88119644CFC1256989005CD392-thekosovoreport.pdf (accessed December 1, 2012).

International Commission on State Sovereignty. *The Responsibility to Protect: A Report of the International Commission on State Sovereignty*, Ottawa: International Development Research Centre Books, 2002.

International Criminal Court. Assembly of States Parties to the Rome Statute, ICC-ASP/2/Res.3, 2003.

Jackson, Robert H., Chief U.S. Prosecutor to the Nuremberg Trials, "Opening Statement to the Tribunal, November 21, 1945." Available at www.law.umkc.edu/faculty/projects/ftrials/nuremberg/jackson.html (accessed March 18, 2013).

Jackson, Robert. *Quasi-States: Sovereignty, International Relations and the Third World*, Cambridge: Cambrdige University Press, 1993.

Kant, Immanuel. *On Education* (1803); *Kant on Education*, Annette Churton (trans.), Boston: D.C. Heath & Co. Publishers, 1906.

Kant, Immanuel. *Perpetual Peace and Other Writings*, Ted Humphry (trans.), Indianapolis: Hackett Publishing Co., Inc., 1983/1985.

Kant, Immanuel. *Critique of Pure Reason*. J.M.D. Meiklejohn (trans.), Amherst: Prometheus Books, 1990.

Kant, Immanuel. *Kant: Political Writings*, H.S. Reiss (ed.), Cambridge: Cambridge University Press, 1970/1991.

Kant, Immanuel. *The Conflict of the Faculties*, Mary Gregor (trans.), Lincoln/London: University of Nebraska Press, 1992.

Kant, Immanuel. *Grounding for the Metaphysics of Morals* (1785), James Ellington (trans.), Indianapolis: Hackett Publishing Co, Inc., 1993.

Kant, Immanuel. *The Metaphysics of Morals*. Mary Gregor (trans. and ed.), Cambridge: Cambridge University Press, 1996.

Kant, Immanuel. *Critique of Practical Reason*, T.K. Abbott (trans.), New York: Promethus Books, 1996.

Kant, Immanuel. *Religion within the Boundaries of Mere Reason* (1793) in *Religion and the Boundaries of Mere Reason and Other Writings*, Allen Wood and George di Giovanni (eds.), Cambridge: Cambridge University Press, 1998.

Kant, Immanuel. "Lectures on Kant's Metaphysics of Morals" in *Lectures on Ethics*, J.B. Schneewind (ed.) and Peter Heath (trans.), Cambridge: Cambridge University Press, 2001.

Kant, Immanuel. "An Old Question Raised Again: Is the Human Race Constantly Progressing?" in *Kant: On History*, Lewis Beck White (ed.), Upper Saddle River: Prentice Hall, 1963/2001.

Kant, Immanuel. "Vorarbeit zur Metaphysik der Sitten" in *Handschriftlicher Nachlass: Vorarbeiten und Nachträge* (Band 23), Gerhard Lehmann (ed.), Akademie Ausgabe Edition, 1955. Available at: www.korpora.org/kant/suche.html (accessed March 28, 2013).

Kaufman, Alexander. *Welfare in the Kantian State*, Oxford: Oxford University Press, 1999.

Kaufmann, Mattias. "Was erlaubt das Erlaubnisgesetz—und wozu braucht es Kant? *Annual Review of Law and Ethics*, vol. 13 (2005): pp. 195–220.

Kavka, Gregory S. "Hobbes's War of All against All" in Christopher W. Morris (ed.), *Critical Essays on Hobbes, Locke, and Rousseau*, Oxford: Rowman & Littlefield Publishers, Inc., 1999.

Kaysen, Carl and George Rathjens. *Peace Operations by the United Nations: The Case for a Volunteer UN Military Force*, Cambridge, MA: American Academy of Arts and Sciences, 1996.

Keane, Fergal. "Syria Ex-Detainees Allege Ordeals of Rape and Sex Abuse" *BBC News*, September 25, 2012.

Kersting, Wolfgang. "Kant's Concept of the State" in Howard Lloyd Williams (ed.), *Essays on Kant's Political Philosophy*, Chicago: Chicago University Press, 1992: pp. 143–165.

Kinloch-Pichat, Stephen. *A UN "Legion": Between Utopia and Reality*, London: Frank Cass, 2004.

Klapper, Bradley. "Clinton Says US, Russia Agree on Mediation in Syria, But Stresses Anew that Assad Must Go" *The Associated Press*, December 7, 2012. Available at: www.vancouversun.com/news/Clinton+says+Russia+agree+back+mediation+Syria+Assad+must+step/7666320/story.html (accessed December 12, 2012).

Knight, Mark and Alpaslan Özerdem. "Guns, Camps and Cash: Disarmament, Demobilization and the Reinsertion of Former Combatants in Transitions from War to Peace" *Journal of Peace Research*, vol. 41, no. 4 (2004): pp. 499–516.

Koh, Harold. "Why Do Nations Obey International Law?" *Yale Law Journal*, vol. 106 (1997): pp. 2599–2659.

Korsgaard, Kristine. "The Right to Lie: on Dealing with Evil" *Philosophy and Public Affairs*, vol. 15, (1986): pp. 325–349.

Korsgaard, Kristine. *The Sources of Normativity*, Cambridge: Cambridge University Press, 1996.

Korsgaard, Kristine. *Creating the Kingdom of Ends*, Cambridge: Cambridge University Press, 1996.

Krasner, Stephen. "Structural Causes and Regime Consequences: Regimes as Intervening Variables" in Stephen D. Krasner (ed.), *International Regimes*, Ithaca: Cornell University Press, 1983.

Laberge, Pierre. "Kant on Justice and the Law of Nations" in David R. Mapel and Terry Nardin (eds.), *International Society: Diverse Ethical Perspectives*, Princeton: Princeton University Press, 1998: pp. 82–102.

Lacey, A.R. *Dictionary of Philosophy*, New York: Barnes & Noble Books, 1996.

Lang, Anthony F. *Just Intervention*, Washington, D.C.: Georgetown University Press, 2003.

Langille, H.P. "Preventing Genocide: Time for a UN 911" *Globe and Mail*, October 19, 2004.

Fearon, James D. and David D. Laitin. "Ethnicity, Insurgency, and Civil War" *American Political Science Review*, vol. 97, no. 1, 2003: pp. 75–90.

Locke, John. *Second Treatise of Government*, Indianapolis: Hackett Publishing Company, 1980.

Louden, Robert. *Kant's Impure Ethics*, Oxford: Oxford University Press, 2000.

MacFarlane, S. Neil. *Human Security And the UN: A Critical History*, Bloomington: Indiana University Press, 2006.

MacFarquhar, Neil. "Syrian Group Fights Effort to Unify Foes of Government" *New York Times*, November 10, 2012.

MacFarquhar, Neil and Hala Droubi, "With Eye on Aid, Syria Opposition Signs Unity Deal," *New York Times*, November 11, 2012. Available at: www.nytimes.com/2012/11/12/world/middleeast/syrian-opposition-groups-sign-unity-deal.html (accessed December 15, 2012).

MacFarquhar, Neil and Michael R. Gordon. "As Fighting Rages, Clinton Seeks New Syrian Opposition" *New York Times*, October 31, 2012.

MacFarquhar, Neil and Hwaida Saad. "Dozens of Children Die in Brutal Attack on Syrian Town" *New York Times*, May 26, 2012.

MacIntyre, Alasdair. *Dependent Rational Animals*, Peru: Carus Publishing Company, 1999/2001.

Madison, James. "Federalist Paper 57" in Clinton Rossiter (ed.), *Hamilton, Madison and Jay: The Federalist Papers*, New York: Signet Classic, 2003: pp. 348–353.

Mahon, James Edwin. "Kant and the Perfect Duty to Others Not to Lie" *British Journal for the History of Philosophy* vol. 14, no. 4 (November 2006): pp. 653–685.

Malcomb, Noel. *Aspects of Hobbes*, Oxford: Clarendon Press, 2002.

Mapel, David R., and Terry Nardin. *International Society*, Princeton: Princeton University Press, 1999.

Marsh, Katherine. "Syrian Crackdown: Hundreds Resign from Ba'ath Party" *The Guardian*, April 28, 2011.

Marshall, Monty, G. and Keith Jaggers. *Polity IV Project: Political Regime Characteristics and Transitions, 1800–2010*. Available at: www.systemicpeace.org/polity/polity4.htm (accessed January 1, 2013).

Martin, Wayne. "Ought but Cannot" *Proceedings of the Aristotelian Society*, vol. 109 (2009): pp. 102–128.

McCoubrey, Hilaire. *International Humanitarian Law: Modern Developments in the Limitation of Warfare*, Farnham: Ashgate Publishing, 1999.

Messner, J.J. "The Failed State Index 2012: The Book" *The Fund for Peace Conflict Early Warning and Assessment*, (June 18, 2012). Available at: www.fundforpeace.org/global/?q=cfsir1210 (accessed January 1, 2013).

Miller, Seumas. "Collective Moral Responsibility: An Individualist Account" *Midwest Studies in Philosophy*, vol. 30 (2006): pp. 176–193.

Miller, Seumas. *The Moral Foundations of Social Institutions: A Philosophical Study*, Cambridge: Cambridge University Press, 2010.

Moran, Kate. "Can Kant Have an Account of Moral Education" *Journal of Philosophy of Education Society of Great Britain*, vol. 43, no. 4, (2009): pp. 471–484.

Moravcsik, Andrew. "Taking Preferences Seriously: A Liberal Theory of International Politics" *International Organization*, vol. 51, no. 4 (1997): pp. 513–553.

Moreno-Ocampo, Luis "Now End This Darfur Denial" *Guardian*, July 15, 2010. Available at: www.guardian.co.uk/commentisfree/libertycentral/2010/jul/15/world-cannot-ignore-darfur (accessed July 15, 2010).

Morris, Christopher W. *The Social Contract Theorists: Critical Essays on Hobbes, Locke, and Rousseau*, Oxford: Rowman & Littlefield Publishers, Inc., 1999.

Mulholland, Leslie Arthur. "The Difference Between Private and Public Law" *Annual Review of Law and Ethics*, vol. 1, (1993): pp. 113–158.

Murphy, Jeffrie. *Kant and the Philosophy of Right*, Macon: Mercer University Press, 1994.

Murphy, Sean D. *Humanitarian Intervention: The United Nations in an Evolving World Order*, Philadelphia: University of Pennsylvania Press, 1996.

Mychajlyszyn, Natalie and Timothy M. Shaw. *Twisting Arms And Flexing Muscles: Humanitarian Intervention And Peacebuilding In Perspective*, Farnham: Ashgate Publishing, 2005.

Nardin, Terry. *Law, Morality, and Relations of States*, Princeton: Princeton University Press, 1983.

Nardin, Terry. "Introduction" in Terry Nardin and Melissa S. Williams (eds.), *Nomos XLVII: Humanitarian Intervention*, New York: New York University Press, 2005): pp. 1–28.

Nardin, Terry. "Humanitarian Imperialism: Response to "Ending Tyranny in Iraq" *Ethics and International Affairs*, vol. 19, no. 2 (2005): pp. 21–26.

Nardin, Terry and David R. Mapel. *Traditions of International Ethics*, Cambridge: Cambridge University Press, 1993.

Negretto, Gabriel L. "Kant and the Illusion of Collective Security" *Journal of International Affairs*, vol. 46, no. 2 (Winter 1993): pp. 501–524.

Nell, Onora. *Acting on Principle: An Essay on Kantian Ethics*, New York: Columbia University Press, 1975.

"National Coordination Committee for Democratic Change," *Carnegie Middle East Center*, January 15, 2012. Available at: http://carnegie-mec.org/publications/?fa=48369 (accessed March 18, 2013).

National Public Radio News: "Clinton Meets Libyan Opposition Figure" *NPR News*, March 14, 2011. Available at: www.npr.org/2011/03/14/134527902/gadhafi-warplanes-strike-rebel-held-libya-city (accessed March 14, 2011).

O'Hanlon, M. *Expanding Global Military Capacity for Humanitarian Intervention*, Washington, D.C.: Brookings Institution Press, 2003.

O'Neill, Onora. *Constructions of Reason: Explorations of Kant's Practical Philosophy*, Cambridge: Cambridge University Press, 1990.

O'Neill, Onora. *Towards Justice and Virtue: A Constructive Account of Practical Reasoning*, Cambridge: Cambridge University Press, 1996.

O'Neill, Onora. *Bounds of Justice*, Cambridge: Cambridge University Press, 2000.

O'Neill, Onora. "Agents of Justice" *Metaphilosophy*, vol. 32, no. 1/2 (January 2001): pp. 180–195.

O'Neill, Onora. "The Dark Side of Human Rights" *International Affairs*, vol. 81, no. 2 (March 2005): pp. 427–439.

Orford, Anne. *International Authority and the Responsibility to Protect*, Cambridge: Cambridge University Press, 2011.

Orend, Brian. *War and International Justice: A Kantian Perspective*, Waterloo: Wilfrid Laurier University Press, 2000.

Paris, Roland. *At War's End: Building Peace after Civil Conflict*, Cambridge: Cambrdige University Press, 2004.

Parrish, Karen. "Gates Outlines U.S. Role as NATO Takes Libyan Mission" *American Forces Press Service*, March 31, 2011. Available at: www.defense.gov/news/newsarticle.aspx?id=63378 (accessed April 2, 2011).

Pattison, James. "Whose Responsibility to Protect? The Duties of Humanitarian Intervention" *Journal of Military Ethics*, vol. 7 no. 4 (2008): pp. 262–283.

Pattison, James. "Legitimacy and Humanitarian Intervention: Who Should Intervene" *The International Journal of Human Rights*, vol. 12, no. 3 (2008): pp. 395–413.

Pattison, James. "Humanitarian Intervention and a Cosmopolitan UN Force" *Journal of International Political Theory*, vol. 4, no. 1 (2008): pp. 126–145.

Pattison, James. *Humanitarian Intervention and the Responsibility to Protect: Who Should Intervene?* Oxford: Oxford University Press, 2010.

Pippin, Robert. *Idealism as Modernism: Hegelian Variations*, Cambridge: Cambridge University Press, 1997.

Plato, *Republic*, G.M.A. Grube (trans.), revised by C.D.C. Reeve, Indianapolis: Hackett Publishing Company, 1992.

Pogge, Thomas. "Justice Beyond Borders: A Global Political Theory" *Ethics and International Affairs*, vol. 19, no. 3 (2005): pp. 101–103.

Pogge, Thomas. "Severe Poverty as a Violation of Negative Duties" *Ethics and International Affairs*, vol. 19, no. 1 (2005): pp. 55–83.

Pogge, Thomas. "Real World Justice" *Journal of Ethics*, vol. 9, no. 1/2 (January 2005): pp. 29–53.

Pogge, Thomas. "Rawls on International Justice" *Philosophical Quarterly*, vol. 51, no. 203 (April 2001): pp. 246–253.

Pogge, Thomas. "Cosmopolitanism and Sovereignty" *Ethics*, vol. 103, no. 1 (October 1992): pp. 48–75.

Posner, Eric. *The Perils of Global Legalism*, Chicago: University of Chicago Press, 2009.

Potter, Nelson. "Applying the Categorical Imperative in Kant's Rechtslehre" *Annual Review of Law and Ethics*, vol. 11 (2003): pp. 37–51.

Power, Samantha. *The Problem From Hell*, New York: HarperCollins Publishers, 2002.

Rawls, John. *The Law of Peoples*, Cambridge, MA: Harvard University Press, 2001.

Mexico v. United States of America, Judgment, ICJ Reports 2009, p. 3. Available at: www.icj-cij.org/docket/files/139/14939.pdf?PHPSESSID=81340a17293631037a58c57156015db8 (accessed December 31, 2012).

Reuters. "U.N. Nations Condemn Syria; Russia, China Seen Isolated," August 3, 2012. Available at: www.reuters.com/article/2012/08/03/us-syria-crisis-un-idUSBRE8720ZN20120803 (accessed August 3, 2012).

Ripstein, Arthur. "Three Duties to Rescue" *Law and Philosophy*, vol. 19, no. 6 (2000): pp. 751–779.

Ripstein, Arthur. "Authority and Coercion" *Philosophy and Public Affairs*, vol. 32, no. 1 (2004): pp. 2–35.

Ripstein, Arthur. *Force and Freedom: Kant's Legal and Political Philosophy*, Cambridge, MA: Harvard University Press, 2009.

Steven C. Roach (ed). *Governance, Order and the International Criminal Court: Between Realpolitik and a Cosmopolitan Court*, Oxford: Oxford University Press, 2009.

Robinson, Darryl. "The Mysterious Mysteriousness of Complementarity" *Criminal Law Forum*, vol. 21 (2010): pp. 67–102.

Rodin, David. *War and Self-Defense*, Oxford: Oxford University Press, 2005.

Roff, Heather M. "Response to Pattison: Whose Responsibility to Protect?" *Journal of Military Ethics*, vol. 8, no. 1 (2009): pp. 79–85.

Roff, Heather M. "Kantian Provisional Duties" *Annual Review for Law and Ethics*, vol. 18 (2010): pp. 533–562.

Roff, Heather M. "A Provisional Duty to Intervene" *Global Responsibility to Protect*, vol. 3 (2011): pp. 152–171.

Roff, Heather M. "The Politics of Intervention" *Huffington Post*, October 29, 2012. Available at: www.huffingtonpost.com/heather-roff/syria-intervention_b_2025305.html (accessed October 29, 2012).

Roff, Heather and Bessma Momani. "The Tactics of Intervention" *The Globe and Mail*, October 25, 2011.

Rosen, Allen D. *Kant's Theory of Justice*., Ithaca: Cornell University Press, 1996.

Rousseau, David L., Christopher Gelpi, Dan Reiter and Paul K. Huth. "Assessing the Dyadic Nature of the Democratic Peace 1918–1988" *American Political Science Review*, vol. 90, no. 3 (2006): pp. 512–533.

Rousseau, Jean Jacques. *The Social Contract*, Maurice Cranston (trans.), New York: Penguin Books, 1968.

Runciman, David. "Moral Responsibility and the Problem of Representing the State" in Toni Erskine (ed.), *Can Institutions Have Responsibilities? Collective Moral Agency and International Relations, Global Issues Series*, Basingstoke: Palgrave Macmillan, 2003: pp. 41–50.

Sarooshi, Dan. *The United Nations and the Development of Collective Security: The Delegation by the UN Security Council of Its Chapter VII Powers*, Oxford: Oxford University Press, 2000.

Sarooshi, Dan. *International Organizations and their Exercise of Sovereign Powers*, Oxford: Oxford University Press, 2007.

Sly, Liz. "Arab League Announces Peace Plan for Syria" *The Washington Post*, November 2, 2011.

Smith, Anne. "The Unique Position of National Human Rights Institutions: A Mixed Blessing?" *Human Rights Quarterly*, vol. 26, no. 4, (2006): pp. 904–946.

Smith, Michael J. "Humanitarian Intervention: An Overview of the Ethical Issues" *Ethics and International Affairs*, vol. 12, no. 1 (1998): pp. 63–79.

Smith, Patricia. *Liberalism and Affirmative Obligation*, Oxford: Oxford University Press, 1998.

Soanes, Catherine and Angus Stevenson (eds.).*Concise Oxford English Dictionary*, 11th edn., Oxford: Oxford University Press, 2004.

Stark, Werner. *Vorlesung zur Moralphilosophie*, Berlin: Walter de Gruyter, 2004.

Sterling, Joe. "NATO Oks Patriots and Delivers Warning: 'Don't Even Think About Attacking Turkey'" *CNN*, December 5, 2012. Available at: www.cnn.com/2012/12/04/world/meast/syria-civil-war/index.html (accessed December 5, 2012).

Sterling, Joe, Saad Abedine and Holly Yan. "As Syria Suffering Spirals, Envoy Hopes for Political Transition" *CNN*, December 28, 2012. Available at: http://edition.cnn.com/2012/12/27/world/meast/syria-civil-war/?hpt=hp_t1 (accessed December 29, 2012).

Stratton-Lake, P. *Kant, Duty and Moral Worth*, Oxford: Routledge Press, 2004.

Stromseth, Jane. "Rethinking Humanitarian Intervention" in J.L. Holzgrefe and Robert Keohane (eds.), *Humanitarian Intervention: Ethical, Legal, and Political Dilemmas*, Cambridge: Cambridge University Press, 2003: pp. 232–272.

Stromseth, Jane, David Wippman and Rosa Brooks. *Can Might Make Rights?: Building the Rule of Law After Military Interventions*, Cambridge: Cambridge University Press, 2006.

Szymkowiak, Aaron. "Kant's Permissive Law: Critical Rights, Sceptical Politics" *British Journal of the History of Philosophy*, vol. 17, no. 3 (2009): pp. 567–600.

Tan, Kok-Chor. "The Duty to Protect" in Terry Nardin and Melissa Williams (eds.), *Nomos XLVII: Humanitarian Intervention*, New York: New York University Press, 2006: pp. 84–116.

Tesón, Fernando. *Humanitarian Intervention: An Inquiry into Law and Morality*, New York: Transnational Publishers, 1988.

Tesón, Fernando. "Ending Tyranny in Iraq" *Ethics and International Affairs*, vol. 19, no. 2 (2005): pp. 1–20.

Tierney, Brian. "Kant on Property: The Problem of the Permissive Law" *Journal of the History of Ideas*, vol. 62, no. 2 (2001): pp. 301–312.

Tierney, Brian. "Permissive Natural Law and Property: Gratian to Kant" *Journal of the History of Ideas*, vol. 62, no. 3 (2001): pp. 381–399.

Tierney, Brian. "Natural Law and Natural Rights: Old Problems and Recent Approaches" *Review of Politics*, vol. 64, no. 3 (2002).

Tierney, Brian. "Historical Roots of Modern Rights: Before Locke and After" *Ave Maria Law Review*, vol. 3 no. 1 (2005): pp. 23–43.

Timmerman, Jens. "Your Article: 'Sollen und Können'" Email (August 23, 2009).

Timmons, Mark. *Kant's Metaphysics of Morals: Interpretative Essays*, Oxford: Oxford University Press, 2002.

Traynor, Ian. "EU Slaps Arms Embargo on Syria but Spares President Bashar al-Assad" *Guardian*, May 9, 2011.

Turner, Scott. "The Dilemma of Double Standards in U.S. Human Rights Policy" *Peace and Change*, vol. 28, no. 4 (October 2003): pp. 524–554.

Ullman-Margalit, Edna. "On Presumption" *Journal of Philosophy*, vol. 80, no. 3 (1983): pp. 143–163.

Urquhart, Brian. "For a UN Volunteer Military Force" *New York Review of Books*, June 10, 1993.

United Nations, *Charter of the United Nations*, October 24, 1945 available at: www.un.org/en/documents/charter/index.shtml (accessed March 19, 2013).

United Nations General Assembly, Sixtieth Session, Official Records, "Provisional Agenda of the sixtieth regular session of the General Assembly", A/60/150, 2005.

United Nations General Assembly. Sixty-Third Session, Official Records, "The Responsibility to Protect," A/RES/63/308, 2009.

United Nations General Assembly. Fifty-Ninth Session, Official Records, "The Situation in Afghanistan and its Implications for International Peace and Security," A/59/744, 2005.

United Nations General Assembly. Sixty-Third Session, Official Records, "Implementing the Responsibility to Protect: Report of the Secretary General," A/63/677, 2009.

United Nations General Assembly. Sixty-Third Session, Official Records, "Early Warning, Assessment and the Responsibility to Protect: Report of the Secretary General," A/64/864, 2010.

United Nations General Assembly. Sixty-Sixth Session, Official Records, "Letter dated 9 November 2011 from the Permanent Representative of Brazil to the United Nations addressed to the Secretary General," A/66/551, 2011.

United Nations High Commissioner for Refugees. "2011: Global Trends: Refugees, Asylum-Seekers, Returnees, Internally Displaced and Stateless Persons" Available at: www.unhcr.org/cgi-bin/texis/vtx/home/opendocPDFViewer.html?docid=4fd6f87f9&query=global%20trends%202011 (accessed December 31, 2012).

United Nations News. "General Assembly Demands Syria Halt Violence Without Delay" Available at: www.un.org/apps/news/story.asp?NewsID=41265 (accessed February 16, 2012).

United Nations News. "Security Council Fails to Adopt Draft Resolution on Syria as Russian Federation, China Veto Text Supporting Arab League's Proposed Peace Plan" *United Nations Department of Public Information*, February 4, 2012. Available at: www.un.org/News/Press/docs/2012/sc10536.doc.htm (accessed March 1, 2012).

United Nations Security Council, 4385th Meeting, "Threats to International Peace and Security Caused by Terrorist Acts," S/RES/1373, 2001.

United Nations Security Council. 2983nd meeting, "Iraq," S/RES/688, 1991.

United Nations Security Council. 4956th meeting, "Nonproliferation of Weapons of Mass Destruction," S/RES/1540, 2004.

United Nations Security Council. 5158th meeting, "Reports of the Secretary General on the Sudan" S/Res/1593, 2005.

United Nations Security Council. 5430th meeting, "Protection of Civilians in Armed Conflict", S/RES/1674, 2006.

United Nations Security Council. 5609th meeting, "Threats to International Peace and Security Caused by Terrorist Acts", S/RES/1735, 2006.

United Nations Security Council. 6498th meeting, "Libya," S/RES/1970, 2011.

United Nations Security Council. 6498th meeting, "Libya," S/RES/1973, 2011.

Walsh, Jennifer. "'Implementing the Responsibility to Protect': Where Expectations Meet Reality" *Ethics and International Affairs*, vol. 24, no. 4 (2010): pp. 418–419.

Walzer, Michael. *Just and Unjust Wars*, 3rd edn., New York: Basic Books, 2000.

Walzer, Michael. *Arguing About War*, New Haven: Yale University Press, 2006.

Watson, Ivan and Saad Abedine. "Security Council Condemns Syria's Attack on Turkey" *CNN*, October 4, 2012. Available at: www.cnn.com/2012/10/04/world/meast/syria-civil-war/index.html (accessed October 15, 2012).

Weiss, Thomas. *Humanitarian Intervention: Ideas in Action*, Cambridge: Polity Press, 2007.

Weiss, Thomas. *What's Wrong with the United Nations and How to Fix It*, Cambridge: Polity Press, 2008.

Wendt, Alexander. "Anarchy is What States Make of It" *International Organization*, vol. 46, no. 2 (1992): pp. 391–425.

Wheeler, Nicolas. *Saving Strangers: Humanitarian Intervention in International Society*, Oxford: Oxford University Press, 2000.

Whitman, Jim. "A Cautionary Note on Humanitarian Intervention" *The Journal of Humanitarian Assistance* (1994). Available at: http://jha.ac/1994/10/31/a-cautionary-note-on-humanitarian-intervention-2/ (accessed September 15, 2010).

Willaschek, Marcus. "Why the Doctrine of Right does not belong in the Metaphysics of Morals" *Annual Review for Law and Ethics*, vol. 5 (1997): pp. 205–227.

Williams, Howard Lloyd. *Essays on Kant's Political Philosophy*, Chicago: University of Chicago Press, 1992.

Williams, Howard Lloyd. *Kant and the End of War: A Critique of Just War Theory*, Basingstoke: Palgrave MacMillan, 2012.

Wolch, Jennifer R. 1990. *The Shadow State: Government and Voluntary Sector in Transition*, New York: Foundation Center, 1990.

Wood, Allen W. *Kant's Ethical Thought*, Cambridge: Cambridge University Press, 1999.

Wood, Allen W. *Kantian Ethics*, Cambridge: Cambridge University Press, 2007.

Woodhouse, T. and Ramsbotham, O. "Cosmopolitan Peacekeeping and the Globalisation of Security" *International Peacekeeping*, vol. 12, no. 2 (2005): pp. 139–156.

World Federalist Movement–Institute for Global Policy, *Civil Society Perspectives on the Responsibility to Protect: Final Report*, New York: World Federalist Movement, April, 2003.

Index

Page numbers in **bold** denote figures.